Grandfather's Tales of North Carolina History

Yours truly R. B. Creecy

GRANDFATHER'S TALES

OF

NORTH CAROLINA HISTORY

BY

RICHARD BENBURY CREECY

Look abroad throughout the land and see North Carolina's sons contending
manfully for the palm of honor and distinction.   -- *Gaston.*

RALEIGH
EDWARDS & BROUGHTON, PRINTERS
1901

TO THE

YOUTH OF NORTH CAROLINA

I DEDICATE THIS VOLUME, WITH THE EARNEST HOPE

THAT THEY WILL LEARN FROM ITS PAGES

SOME LESSONS OF PATRIOTISM,

AND WILL BE

STRENGTHENED IN THEIR LOVE FOR

THEIR NATIVE STATE

THESE MEMORIALS OF THE PAST THAT I HAVE SOUGHT

TO PERPETUATE FOR THEIR BENEFIT.

THE AUTHOR.

PREFACE.

GRANDFATHER'S TALES OF NORTH CAROLINA HISTORY was an inspiration of State love, and was at first intended for the private instruction of my children and grandchildren. Its preparation was commenced ten years ago, as a labor of love, in the leisure time taken from my regular editorial work. As the work progressed we occasionally published specimen chapters of the work in order to ascertain whether it met the public approval. It seemed to do so, and some of our friends expressed their approval in gratifying terms of commendation.

Then we thought it might be a useful offering to the public and to our schools and perhaps give a new stimulus to the State love of the rising generation and cause them to know more of their illustrious progenitors, and to emulate their virtues and their patriotic deeds.

One boulder was in our pathway. It costs labor to prepare a book for publication. But we were raised to hard work and were never afraid of it. But, in addition to that, there's much expense in money in getting a book before the public, and we never had the gift of money getting and we were largely gifted with the talent for getting rid of it, which talent we honestly confess, we have never "hid in a napkin," but cultivated assiduously by constant practice—that is to say, when we had it to get rid of. However, we have never been an Elijah that the ravens had to feed. So we looked around to accomplish by our wits what our purse refused to do.

Judge Clark is the head of the "Literary and Historical Association of North Carolina," a man of literary instincts, and being a young man himself, we thought he would naturally be helpful to a young man who was knocking for admission into the guild of letters. He responded kindly and graciously, and under his direction we sent in to the next meeting of the Association specimens of our work, representing its leading features historical, biographical, legendary and poetical to be examined by the Association. They were referred to a committee of which Professor Hill, of the A. and M. College, was chairman. The committee reported favorably and "commended and recommended it" to the public and the schools. We breathed easier and the skies wore a more cerulean aspect.

We had asked our friend, Judge H. G. Connor, a member of the House of Representatives of the General Assembly of North Carolina, that in case the L. and H. Association gave "Grandfather's Tales" a favorable endorsement, would he introduce a resolution in the Legislature pledging the State to take a certain number of copies of the work when published and to endorse it for use in the public schools of North Carolina, and we, at the same time, requested Professor Hill to hand over the manuscripts to Judge Connor, after he had finished with them, which he did.

On the last day of the regular session of the Legislature Judge Connor introduced a resolution in the House, endorsing the book, recommending its use in the schools of the State and appropriating two hundred dollars ($200) to aid in its publication, and the resolution was unanimously and immediately passed, both parties uniting in its passage. Then we breathed easier, deeper, longer, broader, and every inspiration was a joy.

Thanking my friends for the kind words of encourage ment and the assistance they have given me in the prepa ration of this work, and trusting that it may meet the approval of my countrymen, I bid them an affectionate adieu.

R. B. Creecy.

Elizabeth City. N. C., Oct. 12. 1901.

TABLE OF CONTENTS.

GRANDFATHER'S TALES.

--

CAROLINA, THE MOTHER OF THE STATES.

(AN IRREGULAR HISTORICAL ODE)

At the gateway of our history,
Stands one whose fame is ours,
A gallant man and noble, our father and our son;
"A man to note right well, as one
Who shot his arrows straightway at the sun.
His was all the Norman's polish
And sobriety of grace,
All the Goth's majestic figure,
All the Roman's noble face,
And he stood the tall exemplar
Of a grand, historic race."

His fame is ours,
This foster-child of fame,
Who made his Queen and country
His brightest, noblest aim.
Who dare challenge our heritage
Of Walter Raleigh's name!
His fame is ours.
As he rides with knightly bearing
Down the corridors of time
We bow in homage to his name
And claim him as our own.
We weep at his misfortunes,
We rejoice at his renown,
And at his final ghastly doom,
We place our green forget-me-not
In sorrow on his tomb.
As I look back through the vista
Of three hundred years ago,

My heart is swelled with varying tides—
Alternate joy and woe—
I pause in thought and sadness at those immortal men
Who perished at Roanoke; but how, or where, or
    when,
Will ne'er be known while time endures to any mortal
    men,
'Till that great day when all shall see the secrets of
    the past.
But this sad thought comes to cheer us,
In this far-distant time—
If round the brow of any land
We twine the cypress leaf,
It is lovely in its sadness
With its coronet of grief.
So, cheer up, Carolinians!
The seed, watered by your tears,
Has grown to mighty greatness
In all the coming years.
But as I search again our ample store
Of vast and misty legendary lore,
And view its scenes and sights with pleasure rife,
I find the old kaleidoscope of life,
The thorns and rosebuds nestling side by side,
The bane and antidote of life allied:
As, ofttime at the fall of some sad tear,
There stands a smile to comfort and to cheer.
And so the fountain of our grand old State
Was not all bitter waters,
At that time of ancient date.
The purple grape, the perfume-laden air,
The weird music from the mockbird's note,
The willet's whistle and the gull's wild scream
Wrapped all their senses in a soothing dream
When first they anchored in old *Ocean's* stream.
After God, the Father,
Came their country and its Queen:
Then the pageant of possession,

A grand and gorgeous scene.
The shout, the drum, the cannon's roar
Resound from shore to shore,
And with the loud acclaim
Was mingled oft the virgin Queen and great Sir
  Walter's name.
They called the land Virginia,
Through its limitless domain,
From sea to sea, from North to South,
From mountain top to plain.
They builded, they planted,
They reared a sightly town:
They named it after Raleigh,
That man of high renown.
They built a fort, they worshipped,
They raised altars to our God.
All this, and more, was done
On Carolina's sod.

By the law of cause and sequence,
By the ordering of the Fates,
Carolina was the first-born
And the mother of the States.
Virginia was her first name,
Her baptismal name at birth.
But at her confirmation
And renewal of her vow,
Carolina, Carolina, became her name as now.

By the fiat of Omnipotence,
No word or action dies,
But, borne up by angels
To the chancery of the skies,
The recording angel,
In his justice-seat on high,
Records it and files it,
And with a smile or sigh,
'Till that great day and dread

When earth and sea deliver up
Their living and their dead.

No word or action dies,
'Tis filed away in heaven,
Perennial on earth,
And goes on reproducing,
From the moment of its birth.
The acorn which was planted
And produced Columbia's oak,
Was the acorn that was planted
On the island of Roanoke.
That oak, now grown to giant height,
Which shadows all our land,
Was from the acorn planted
By Sir Walter Raleigh's hand.
That oak that's now a giant,
And of all men known and spoken,
Was planted first and nourished,
On the island of *Wokoken.*
Jamestown was its first fruit,
And John Smith's fame and glory
Was but the early sequel
Of Roanoke's saddened story.
And pretty Pocahontas,
With her romance all aglow,
Is but the reproduction
Of kind old Manteo.

But why drop the name Virginia
And give it to another?
It was the sweet baptismal name
Of our dear old mother;
Her's by right of first discovery,
Her's by the loud acclaim,
Her's by the primal title,
When that battle flag unfurled
Proclaimed the land Virginia,

And challenged all the world
To dispute it, face to face,
As the rightful, just possession
Of the Anglo-Saxon race.

Why drop the name Virginia
And take another name?
'Tis the same old tender tale,
The old maternal love,
The same,
That weeps when others smile,
And pours out tears like water
At the happy bridal
Of her first-born lovely daughter.
It was in part her bridal dowry
She gave young Virginia with,
When with heart and hand united,
She married Captain Smith.
Virginia grew to greatness,
She bore her mother's name,
Who, true to all her children,
Speaks no word of blame;
But sometimes with maternal pride
She whispers, soft and tame,
Virginia has no fault,
If fault it be,
But avarice of fame.
But avarice, my daughter,
Becomes a noxious weed
When you feed on other's laurels
In your avaricious greed.

So lift up your heads, my countrymen,
And with uncovered brow,
Before the great Eternal One,
Make this your sacred vow,
"Carolina, Carolina, heaven's blessings attend her!
While we live we will cherish, protect and defend
    her."

SIR WALTER RALEIGH.

At the gateway of our history stands Walter Raleigh's name,
A gem of purest lustre in our coronet of fame

If you were asked the question, which one of the United States you loved best, you would say North Carolina. You would say so because it is the home of your parents, and of your forefathers since it was first settled, and because their graves are here.

North Carolina is sometimes called the "Old North State," because it was the first settled of the Carolinas, and when a part of it was taken off for convenience, that part was called South Carolina, and the old part was called North Carolina, or the "Old North State."

During the late unhappy war between the States it was sometimes called the "Tar-heel State," because tar was made in the State, and because in battle the soldiers of North Carolina stuck to their bloody work as if they had tar on their heels, and when General Lee said, "God bless the Tar-heel boys," they took the name.

You all know something about the State; but I know you would like to know more about it, and I will try to let you know more, if you will keep still and listen to the tales I will tell you about it.

The first public man whose name is connected with North Carolina history is Sir Walter Raleigh. He was an English nobleman, and his life is full of interest. He lived about three hundred years ago, in the most famous period of English history, and he was the foremost man of his time. As a writer, he was the companion of Shakespeare. As a soldier, he was the companion of Howard. As a statesman, he was the companion of Bacon. As an adviser, he was the nearest to Queen Elizabeth's distinguished company.

Do you know what gave Raleigh his start in the world when he was a young man? It was simply a little piece of politeness.

He was passing down a street in London dressed in a

SIR WALTER RALEIGH.

stylish scarlet cloak. The Queen, with her attendants, was walking down the same street, and when near Raleigh she stopped at a muddy place in her way. Raleigh ran up, took off his scarlet cloak and threw it over the mud for the Queen to walk on.

This act of politeness made him a great favorite with the Queen, and she bestowed many favors upon him. Among other favors, she gave him the right to make discoveries in America, and gave him the lands which he might discover which were not owned by Christian people.

Raleigh sent out persons to explore the country. The land they first discovered was Roanoke Island, and they examined the country on the waters of Albemarle and Pamplico Sounds.

The world is full of changes for the better and for the worse, and after Queen Elizabeth's death the good fortune of Raleigh changed for the worse.

James I, King of England, succeeded Elizabeth. He was weak-minded, credulous, and easily influenced. The flatterers that were around him did not like Raleigh because he had been the favorite of the late Queen, and they determined that he should not be the favorite of King James.

They brought accusations against Raleigh. They made the King believe that he was not faithful to his King and country. Raleigh had been engaged in war with Spain, and they made the King believe that he loved Spain more than England, and that he had betrayed his country.

King James believed these charges, and Sir Walter Raleigh was arrested, imprisoned for twelve years, tried for treason and condemned to be beheaded, which was done in the year 1618. The judge was a corrupt tool of the King, and used his office against Raleigh.

He died as he lived, a brave, faithful, Christian man, and his memory is dear to North Carolina and to the English people.

THE LOST COLONY.

Darkness there and nothing more
Dreaming dreams no mortal ever dared to dream before.
Let my heart be still a moment, and this mystery explore.
—Poe's Raven.

SIR WALTER RALEIGH laid out $200,000 to make a settlement on Roanoke Island. He sent out four separate expeditions. All came to the same island, and all failed to make a permanent settlement.

He first sent out Captain Philip Amadas and Captain Arthur Barlowe in two vessels. They landed at Ballast Point on Roanoke Island, remained some days, and while here examined Albemarle and Pamplico Sounds, and Roanoke, Chowan and Scuppernong rivers. They returned to England and gave Sir Walter Raleigh and the Queen of England a very favorable account of the country they had discovered.

They carried back with them on their return some products of the country and two Indians, one named Manteo and the other Wanchese.

That was in the year 1584, and was the first time that any white man of the Anglo-Saxon race, to which race you belong, ever put his foot on America.

He soon sent over another expedition of some ships loaded with settlers.

They reached Roanoke Island, and soon began to build and make preparation for a permanent settlement. They called their place of building the City of Raleigh, and the remains of it are seen at this day.

An old fort is still plainly to be seen on the lands of Walter Dough. It was probably built to afford a defence to the settlers against the attacks of hostile Indians.

They soon got into trouble with the Indians, and all except fifteen men returned home to England.

Raleigh had set his heart upon establishing a colony at Roanoke Island. After awhile he sent out another colony of one hundred and fifty men, women and children.

They were provided with farming utensils, stock, provisions and vegetable seeds, and Raleigh thought he would now certainly succeed.

This colony was under the lead of Governor White. He had with him everything that was necessary for a complete society. He was accompanied by men of learning, men of skill, men of science, and a pious clergyman of the English Church. A Christian community to whom the ordinances of our holy religion were administered.

When the colony of Governor White reached Roanoke Island, their first thought was of the fifteen men that the last colony had left there.

All that they could find of them were the bleaching bones of a white man scattered on the ground. The fort in which they lived was there. It was unoccupied, and wild deer were feeding on the deserted grounds. They had evidently been killed by the Indians.

The new colony of Governor White soon commenced the work of settlement on the island where so much trouble had overtaken the other colonies. Soon after their arrival, Virginia Dare, daughter of Eleanor Dare, and grand-daughter of Governor White, was born. She was the first child of our race born in America.

The colony found the Indians unfriendly to them, and they proposed to White to return to England and bring out more persons, in order to strengthen their power. He left for England with fifty of the men. Before leaving, it was agreed between them that if the colony should be compelled to leave the island they should go to Croatan, where the Indians were more friendly to them. And if they left, they should write on a tree in plain letters the name CROATAN and if their leaving was caused by any trouble with the Indians, they should make a plain cross mark over the word.

White returned to England, and, on account of the disturbance of the country by the war with Spain, he was not able to return to Roanoke Island in two years.

After two years he returned to the island and could

not find any of the colony that he left there. They were all gone, and he could find nothing of them at the city of Raleigh where he had left them.

Near the shore he found a tree with the letters C R O plainly cut on it, and not far off he found another tree with the letters CROATAN cut on it. There was no cross-mark on the tree. So he thought they were all safe at Croatan, and he made preparations to go there.

He went on board his vessels to make sail for Croatan, but a storm came on which prevented his leaving, and his provisions were nearly exhausted.

So he concluded he would first go to the West Indies to get a new supply of provisions and make some repairs to his vessels.

But he was compelled by stress of weather to abandon the intention of going to the West Indies, and directed his course to England.

This was the last attempt to sustain an English colony on Roanoke Island. White's colony was never heard of again, and their fate will always be a mystery.

There have been several opinions of what became of them, but all is mystery, and nothing is certain. They are merely the opinions of persons feeling in the dark for what can never be positively known.

Some are of the opinion that they went to Croatan, and, after years of hardship and despair of ever seeing their English friends and kindred again, they intermarried with the Indians and fell back into their savage mode of life.

This opinion can hardly be correct, because there were nearly an hundred men, women and children of the colony, and some of them would have kept the blood pure in their families.

Another reason to prove that they were not absorbed and mixed with the Indian race, is that North Carolina was settled by the white race on Albemarle Sound only sixty years from the time of the lost colony.

Some of them would have been found living among the Indians when the white settlers came to Albemarle Sound.

When the settlers came to Albemarle from Virginia, Virginia Dare would not have been much over sixty years old, if she had been living.

If a number of white people had been living at the lower end of Albemarle Sound, the Indians living at the other end of the Sound would have known it, and would have let the new comers of the same color know of it.

The Indian tribes were migratory, and knew each other who were distant. The Indians on Roanoke Island knew the Indians who lived on Chesapeake Bay and on James River.

It is not possible, then, that a race of men entirely different in color could have lived among the Indians of Croatan without being known to the Indians of Albemarle Sound.

Another opinion is that White's colony went to Croatan, and then moved higher up Albemarle Sound and settled among the Yeopom Indians in Perquimans County and kept themselves apart from the Indians.

This opinion is formed from this circumstance:

The names of the settlers who came to Roanoke Island with Governor White are known, and it is a little surprising that many of the same names have been well-known names among the people living in the Yeopom neighborhood of Perquimans County. The same names are known there to this day.

This is a strong circumstance. Many historical facts are traced to the names of families.

It is commonly believed that two of the brothers of Oliver Cromwell came to Halifax County, in North Carolina, after the restoration of the English monarchy, to avoid punishment in England.

They changed their names to Crowell, but their first names were the same with the Cromwells of England for many generations, and this, with other circumstances, caused them to be taken for Cromwell's brothers.

But the lost colony could not have settled in Perquimans.

When the settlements were made on Albemarle Sound

from Virginia, if there had been a colony of English people there when they came, it would have been mentioned in the records of that time relating to the Albemarle settlement.

What, then, became of the lost colony about which there has been so much unsatisfied curiosity?

My opinion is that they were murdered by the Indians. The Indian character for cruelty favors that opinion. The hostility of race favors it. The Indians of Roanoke Island were unfriendly to the whites. The Croatan Indians were supposed to be friendly to the whites. But they were only a few miles from Roanoke Island, and were in sympathy with those Indian tribes.

BEGINNING OF A NATION.

SCRAPS OF ANTIQUARIAN LORE OF SIR WALTER RALEIGH'S COLONY.

In 1865 there were discovered in the British Museum original drawings of the Indians that were seen by Sir Walter Raleigh's colony on Roanoke Island, tombs of the Indian Chiefs and a map of the country, as seen by the colonists. These drawings were made by John White, who came to Roanoke Island as an artist with the first colony and was afterwards sent out as Governor with the second colony, and who was the grandfather of Virginia Dare, the first Anglo-Saxon born in America. They are now preserved with great care in the Grenville collection of American antiquities in the British Museum, and were first given to the public, with permission of the managers of the Museum, by John Eggleston in 1882.

White appears to have been no mean artist. His sketch of the tombs of the Indian Chiefs (the Westminster Abbey of the savages) would do no discredit to art in our time. It is probable that some such sepulchre may yet be found on Roanoke Island, if proper diligence were used in the examination.

It is to be regretted that no likeness is extant, so far as we know, of old Manteo, the friend of the whites, constant through all their trials, the first Indian admitted by baptism within the pale of the Christian Church, admitted under the adopted title by baptism of "Lord of Roanoke." One so distinguished by title and by baptism surely awakened curiosity at the court of Elizabeth, to which he was carried on the return voyage of some of the colonists, and that public curiosity must have placed his face on the artist's canvas. It may yet be found. The drawings of White were unknown for nearly three hundred years.

The map executed by White has adopted the names of some localities which have come down to our time. "Roanoke" is evidently our Roanoke Island, as appears from the name and the location. "Chawanoke" is evidently intended for our Chowan, from its location on the map high up the broad waters. "Pasquotae," lower down on the map, must be intended for our corrupt spelling of Pasquotank. "Hattrask" is our Hatteras, "Wococon" would be our Wiccakon Creek, of Hertford County, but its locality in the sounds below Roanoke Island would not seem to indicate it. "Croatan" preserves its name and locality through all time. "Weapomeoe," from its locality, might be Yeopim, with some reach of the imagination. "Etarretoae" and "Nansagoe" and "Menteo" and "Paquippe" and "Ragniae," and some others, are prominent names on White's map which have faded from the memories of men.

The map of White is profusely illustrated with the finny monsters of the deep. Whales, and porpoise, and sharks, and devil-fish, and flying-fish abound.

But the most curious of the drawings of White is the mode of sepulture of the magnate savages, chiefs of the tribe and dignitaries of the land. In his own description it is:

"The tombe of ther Cheronnes or chiefe personages,

their flesh clene taken of from the bones save the skynn and heare of theire heads, which flesh is dried and enfolded in matts laid at theire feete, their bones also being made dry ar covered with deare skins not altering their formic or proportion. With theire Kywash, which is an Image of woode keeping the deade."

The descriptive drawing of the Indian mode of disposing of their dead, is altogether singular to us. After arranging the bodies as mentioned by White, they are placed under a canopy with their heads downward and their feet confined in mats and a wood idol placed beside them, as if in protection of the sacred deposit.

The conjurer, as drawn by White, an official character among the Indians of Roanoke Island, is a grotesque looking fellow, a dancing, gay, pantomimic character, altogether out of keeping with our conceptions of the gravity of one who deals with the mysterious and the supernatural. The conjurer, as drawn by White, must have placed or broken the spell of conjuration by the aid of the terpsichorean art.

The priest and the doctor, the medicine man and the minister in holy offices among the Indians of the Island, as drawn by White, is a different looking character from the lively conjurer, although their offices were kindred. His dress resembles the Roman toga, a tunic extending below the thighs. Grave, demure, serious, and solemn-looking, he evidently was fully impressed with, or affected to be impressed with, the importance of his solemn office. He was evidently a man of sorrows and acquainted with grief, and the transports of beatitude did not enter into his conceptions of the dark, mysterious unknown.

Wyngino's wife, the King of the tribe, or one of them, for polygamy was part of the Mormonatic faith of the Indians of Roanoke, as drawn by White, is attired in short tights that stop above the knee. She is a comely-looking maiden and was drawn by White, with arms folded over her shoulders, with calves crossed, with head and arms ornamented with jewels of bead work, probably obtained from the colonists, and, from appearance, is not unadapted to awaken the King's love.

The village of Secotan, which was on the Island, we believe, is also drawn by White. The houses are not the wigwams of our youthful conception, but are built in simple style, all alike, resembling somewhat the round-top, huge tobacco wagons of Granville County, some nestling in shade, some out, some located in pairs, some without reference to order or design, not laid off in streets, built irregularly. To give artistic effect, we suppose, White, in his drawing of the village Secotan, scatters Indians about, generally grouping in pairs, one with the emblematic bow and arrow, some around a camp fire. The houses are without chimneys or smoke valves, but seem to have abundant ventilation.

This was the Roanoke Island of the aborigines. Men of Roanoke, you have a goodly heritage and tread consecrated ground. You are at the fountain of a great stream that has gone on widening and deepening until it has become the master work of the great Anglo-Saxon race, a race beyond compare among the sons of men, a race without whose record the history of the world would be incomplete.

—

LEGEND OF THE WHITE DOE.

Across the twilight of the ages past
A spectral figure moves vague, undefined:
And where it goes a shade comes o'er the mind,
As 't were some picture overcast

IN the early part of the seventeenth century, that is, about the year 1615, or 1620, the Indian hunters who lived on Roanoke Island were greatly excited by seeing a milk-white doe among the herd of deer that were then commonly found on the island.

It attracted the attention of the hunters because it was

the most beautiful one of all the herd, because it was the fleetest, and because the most skilful marksmen had never been able to kill it with an arrow. Okisco, a noted hunter, who lived among the Chawanooke tribe, was sent for, and he drew his bow upon the beautiful white doe, but he never could do her harm.

She came to be well known to the Indian hunters of Roanoke Island, and was often found on the situation of the old city of Raleigh, apart from the herd of deer, with her sad face toward the east. Again and again she was hunted, but all the arrows aimed at her life fell harmless beside her. She bounded over the sand-hills with the swiftness of the winds and always turned in the direction of Croatan.

Hunting parties of Indians were made up to entrap her by stationing themselves along the tracks of her flight, which had become known to the hunters by her always taking the same course. But all their efforts were without avail. The swift white doe seemed to have a charmed life, or to be under the protection of some Divine power. Everyone now talked of the white doe, and everyone had his own opinion about her. The braves, the squaws, and the papooses talked of the milk-white doe. Some had fears of evil from the strange apparition. Some thought she was the omen of good, and some thought it was the spirit of some sad departed.

Sometimes she would be seen on the high grounds of Croatan, sometimes in the swamps of Durant's Island, sometimes upon the Cranberry bogs of East Lake, often on Roanoke Island near Raleigh City, and sometimes, though rarely, on the sands of Kill Devil Hills; sometimes alone, always sad and beautiful.

The news of the white doe spread far and wide, and old Wingina determined to call a council of chiefs to determine what to do.

'Okisco, chief of the Chawanookes; Kuskatenew and Kilkokanwan, of the Yeopems, and others, attended the council. They all came with their attendants, all armed with their war weapons, the bow and arrow. They determined to have a grand hunt in the early Indian summer time, and without delay. In November, when the leaves had fallen and the earth was carpeted with its brown and russet covering of forest leaves, all the friendly chiefs came to Roanoke Island to join the fierce Wingina in his appointed hunt for the milk-white doe, and each with his chosen weapon of the chase.

The chiefs, after their feast, prepared by the wife of Wingina, agreed that they should station themselves along the course of the white doe when pursued by the hunters, and either exhaust her in the chase, or slay her with their deadly arrows. Wingina, the most powerful of all, took his place at Raleigh City, where the doe always passed and always stopped.

Old Granganimeo, the brother of Wingina, took his stand at Croatan Sound, where she crossed to Roanoke Island.

Okisco took his stand upon the goodly land of Pomonik, in the low grounds of Durant's Island.

Kind old Manteo went up into the shaky land Wocokon, among the prairies and cranberry bogs of East Lake.

Minatonon, the fierce chief who made his home at Sequaton, took his stand at Jockey's Ridge, by the sea, in the land of the Coristooks.

Wanchese took his stand at Kill Devil, in the country of Secotan.

They had all brought with them their best bows and arrows, and also their chosen archers. But the bow of Wanchese differed from the others. When, long ago, he had gone over the sea to England, the great Queen had given him an arrow-head made of solid silver, like the stone arrow-head that Amadas carried to Sir Walter Raleigh with his other Indian curiosities. It was made by her most expert workers in silver, and she told him it would kill the bearer of a charmed life that no other arrow could wound. Wanchese carried this with his other weapons, and determined to test its power upon the swift white doe

2

Manteo started the doe in the shaky land of Wocokon. She started unharmed at the twang of the bow-string. She sped with the swiftness of the north wind's breath. Through the tangle wood of Wocokon, through the bogs and morasses of Pomonik, across the highlands of Croatan, on, on, she went, and the twang of the bowstring was the harmless music of her flying bounds. She plunged into the billows of Croatan Sound. She reached the sand hills of Roanoke, leaving the Indian hunters far behind her. As she came to the island, old Granganimeo drew his bow and sped his harmless arrow. She stood upon the top of the old fort at Raleigh City, sniffed the breeze and looked sadly over the sea. Wingina carefully and steadily drew upon her panting side the deadly arrow. All in vain. She bounded into Roanoke Sound and across to the sea. Menatonon was at Jockey's Ridge, but his arrow, too, was harmless. The panting white doe found time at the Fresh Ponds to slake her thirst, and then, turning to the sea that she seemed to love with an unnatural affection, sped onward, until she reached the steep hills of Kill Devil. There, alas! was her doom. Wanchese, taking aim with his silver arrow, aimed at her heart, let fly the fated bowstring, and the sad and beautiful milk-white doe sprang into the air with the fatal arrow in her heart, and fell to the ground.

Wanchese ran to the spot and found the victim writhing in the death agony. She lifted her dying, soft eyes to the red man and uttered her last sound, "Virginia Dare." Under her throat the words "Virginia Dare" were plainly pencilled in dark hair, and on her back was pencilled in brown hair the name "Croatan."

LEGEND OF BATZ'S GRAVE.

NEAR Drummond's Point, on the upper waters of Albemarle Sound, lies a solitary island, now uninhabited, once the home where the goat browsed and the gull built its nest and defied the storm with its discordant scream. Its name is "Batz's Grave." Within living memory no man has dwelt thereon, but, within living memory it was the roost of myriads of migratory gulls, who held undisturbed possession of their island home.

There is a legend about that desert island that furnishes food for the contemplative, a legend of love and sadness, a legend of Jesse Batz and Kickowanna, a beautiful maiden of the Chowanoke tribe of Indians.

Batz was a hunter and trapper on the upper waters of Albemarle Sound, and was one of the earliest settlers that made a home in that paradise of the Indian hunter, where the wild game alone disputed his supremacy.

Jesse Batz made his temporary home on the island that the Indians sometimes visited and called Kalola, from the innumerable flocks of sea-gulls that disturbed its solitude. Batz was friendly, and sometimes joined the Indians in their hunting parties. He was young, comely and athletic. He became familiar to the Indians in their wigwams and the chase.

There was one who was the light of the wigwam of the Chowanokes--who sometimes looked at Jesse Batz with the love-light in her eye—the pretty, nut-brown Kickowanna. Her eye was as a sloe, and her long and glossy hair was as a raven's wing. Her step was agile and graceful as the "down that rides upon the breeze." While Batz, the hunter, let fly the bowstring that brought down the antlered stag of the forest, a better archer aimed at Jesse's heart the fatal arrow, and he, too, fell, a victim of Cupid's unerring aim. The insidious poison rankled in his veins. He was a changed man in every look and tissue of his being. The chase had lost its charm. His eye would droop when Kickowanna came. She was daughter of the old King of the Chowanokes, Kilkanoo, the jewel of his eye. Kickowanna was a Peri of beauty. Famed she was throughout the land. The great Pamunky chief of the Chasamonpeak tribes to the north had sought her hand, and had offered alliance to Kilkanoo, chief of the Chowanokes, but his suit was rejected and he sought to obtain by violence what he could not by courtly supplication. War raged for a time between Pamunky and Kilkanoo. Batz fought with the Chowanokes. His valor, his strategy and his success were conspicuous. He led the Indian braves. In a hand-to-hand personal encounter with Pamunky he clove him down with his claymore, and in the fierce grapple would have brained him with his Indian club, but the prostrate Pamunky sued for mercy. Batz's ire softened, and he gave him his life. For Batz's deeds of bravery Kilkanoo adopted him as a member of the Chowanoke tribe, under the adopted name of Secotan, which, interpreted, is—"The Great White Eagle."

Batz grew in favor and influence with the Chowanokes. He was always present at their councils, at their harvest dances, their war dances, and when they smoked the calumet he was given the biggest pipe of peace. Batz became an adopted Indian of the Chowanoke tribe. He adopted the Indian dress and customs. The pretty Indian maiden, Kickowanna, whom he loved, and by whom he was loved, with winning words of love distilled into his willing ears the siren voice of ambition, and whispered low that when her father, Kilkanoo, should be beckoned up to the "happy hunting grounds," he would be his chosen successor, King of the warlike Chowanokes. Batz and Kickowanna lived and loved together. She pencilled his eyebrows with the vermillion of the cochukee root. She put golden rings in his nose and ears. She wound long strings of priceless pearls around his neck. She put the moccasin shoes and leggins around his feet and limbs. She folded his auburn locks in fantastic folds around the top of his head, and decked it with the eagle's feather, emblematic of his rank and station. And then she gave him the calumet of peace and love. And while he smoked the calumet of peace and happiness, eye met eye responsive in language known alone to love. He then looked the big Indian indeed, and the dream of love encompassed them.

While this dreamy delirium prevailed the stream of love ran on in its varying smooth and turbulent current. Batz, now a recognized power with the Chowanokes, made frequent visits to his old island home, sometimes prolonged. While there in his solitude, the waves and the sea-gulls sang a lullaby to his weird fancies. The beauteous Indian maiden sometimes came from her home at the upper broad waters, and her visits were love's own paradise. She came from the opposite shore of the mainland, paddling her light canoe. No season knew her coming. Sometimes in the silent watches of the night, sometimes in the glare of midday. Always alone. Always aglow with love. And when she came it was love's high pastime. The scream of the white gull was the chant of love. The monotone of the waves was the lullaby of love. The sighing of the winds as they swept through the pendant mosses was a sigh of love, the very solitude and silence of the forest was love's chosen temple, and every nook and recess was a shrine.

One night, alas! it was a night of destiny! the Indian maiden came, as was her wont. The angry clouds looked down, the storm raged, every scream of every sea-bird betokened danger nigh. The wind blew as 'twas its last, the lightning flashed, thunder pealed and the welkin rang with the echoes of the blast. But love defies danger, and the pretty Indian maiden pushed through the storm to the lone island with the roar of thunder for her watery funeral requiem.

Batz never left the island more. He remained there till he died, a broken-hearted man, shattered in mind and body, and he rests there in his final rest till the resurrection note calls him to meet his loved Kickowanna.

AN UNSETTLED QUESTION.

A LIFE ON THE OCEAN WAVE.

Many events in history derive their public interest from their antiquity. Some from their intrinsic importance, some from the fact that it was a matter in dispute, and men are naturally attracted to any matter of contention or conflict, from the clash of arms in battle array to a common dog fight in which Tige gnaws off the ears of Lion in a rough-and-tumble fight.

The question of where Amadas and Barlowe first landed on the coast of North Carolina, and through what inlet on our sand-barred coast they came to Roanoke Island, is now a controverted question that antiquarians have failed to satisfactorily settle. It is of no practical importance. It interests only a few old fossils as it interested a few of the old departed, like Dr. Frank Hawks, of sainted memory, and John H. Wheeler, likewise sainted. But yet it interests these old men, and the younger generation are tolerant of them, and from a spirit of charity and kindness turn from the practical athletic tilts of life to listen to these speculations, which are of as much practical importance as the mediæval angry disputes as to the difference between "tweedledum and tweedledee."

Nevertheless, we are in the fight, and we will venture a few suggestions upon the subject of the entrance of the primal discoverers into the North Carolina sounds. There are many explorers of that subject, and if Amadas and Barlowe had known the good work they were building, and had only driven down a stake in the sand and by a suitable inscription had marked the place of their entry, they would have saved enough printer's ink to run seventeen weekly country newspapers during their existence. For a hundred years and more it was considered a settled fact that the two ships of Sir Walter Raleigh's expedition to America came in at Ocracoke Inlet and sailed north for Roanoke Island, where they settled and builded the old fort on the west end of the island. This theory was undisputed for over a hundred years. But after the lapse of ages the old inlet opposite Roanoke Island, which was closed to navigation about 1800, became a commercial factor, and a handy football of the politicians, and probably from that cause was given prestige as the old inlet through which Amadas and Barlowe entered the inland sounds. This theory was generally accepted until Dr. Hawks, who was too great a genius for a historian, discovered that the historians before him were all mistaken, and that the explorers came in at New Inlet. He determined it by the measurement of leagues from Roanoke Island to New Inlet, which corresponds with the distance mentioned by the navigators. But New Inlet has not been navigable for sea vessels within living tradition or historical record. It is now nearly closed, as is Roanoke Inlet, which, according to maps of recent discovery, had through it in 1738 twenty-four feet of water.

Old Mrs. Hayman, who lived beyond one hundred years, said that a deep inlet came through the "Fresh Ponds" when she was a little girl. Some say Raleigh's navigators came through "Old Taffy's Inlet." And so it goes. Amadas and Barlowe little dreamed of the trouble they have given us.

GEORGE DURANT AND KILCOKANNAN.

A wit's a feather, a fool's a rod,
An honest man's the noblest work of God.

Did you ever hear the name "Poor Lo?" Well, I will tell you.

The race of American Indians is called Poor Lo, because they are the "poor" of all the races of men. "Lo" is an exclamation, meaning "behold!" Behold the poor Indian!

The Indians are a revengeful race, and when they are wronged, they return injury for injury, and are cruel in the treatment of their enemies.

They have suffered much from the Anglo-Saxon race, and our race has suffered much from them. They are a race of red men, and the race of white men have driven them back and back from their homes and hunting grounds. The race, in a few years more, will be utterly extinct, and, like the buffalo of the plains that they hunted, will be unknown upon the earth.

The discoverers of America thought that no men had any right to a country unless they were Christian men, and they claimed all the land that they discovered that was not inhabited by Christian people. But this was not the teaching of our holy religion.

That religion teaches that all men have rights, and that they must have what belongs to them, though they may be of different color, and the commandment applies to heathen as well as to Christian men.

But the early discoverers of America did not think the Indians had any right to the land they lived and hunted on, and so they took their lands.

But there were exceptions to this. George Durant, of North Carolina, and the Quaker, William Penn, of Pennsylvania, are honorable exceptions, and should always be honored as men who dealt justly with the Indians.

William Penn purchased of the Indians in Pennsylvania the land upon which the city of Philadelphia now stands, and paid them for it. George Durant purchased from Kilcokannan, King of the Yeopim Indians, the land now called Durant's Neck, in Perquimans County, and paid him for it. The tract of country that George Durant bought was then called Wecocomicke.

Would you like for me to tell you how he bought Wecocomicke, and how he paid for it?

George Durant had come down from Virginia and settled on Albemarle Sound, and after being in the country now called Durant's Neck about a year, he said to one of his friends: "This is a good country to make a home in: the land is rich: the forest is full of wild animals of every kind: the waters are full of fish, and the red men are friendly. If I only knew of whom to buy the land, I would purchase and settle down for life."

"Whom?" said his friend: "why Kilcokannan, King of the Yeopims, is the owner, if there is any owner; or you might take the land. Kilcokannan is a heathen, and none but Christians own these lands."

'That may be Christian law," said Durant; "but it is not the law of Christ. He did not take away from Cæsar what belonged to Cæsar, and Cæsar was a heathen, just as Kilcokannan is. Cæsar was a learned and powerful heathen, and Kilcokannan is poor and helpless. The goodly land of Wecocomicke belongs to Kilcokannan, and if I get it, I shall pay him for it: I had rather settle with Kilcokannan than hereafter with that Judge who knoweth all things and punisheth the unjust."

The friend with whom Durant had these kind words was named Pritlove, and it was agreed between them that Pritlove should offer to purchase the Wecocomicke from Kilcokannan for George Durant.

Some days after this conversation between Pritlove and George Durant, Pritlove met Kilcokannan on a bear hunt, and mentioned, by signs and language as best he could, that George Durant would like to buy of him the goodly land of Wecocomicke.

Kilcokannan was silent. He then lifted his eyes toward the sun, bowed his head to the earth, watched the direction of the wind, and, by signs and language, said: "My braves."

By this he meant that he would consult his Indian warriors about it.

The warriors assembled at Kilcokannan's request. George Durant was invited to be present. Kilcokannan had a bear's head scalp on his head, an alligator's tooth hung from his breast, and scarlet moccasins were on his legs. His warriors sat around him decked in the plumage of birds and the skins of wild animals.

George Durant sat apart from the rest, dressed in broad-brim hat and long Quaker coat. All were seated on a cloth spread out on the ground. All were silent. A large pipe was handed around, and each one smoked in silence.

Then Kilcokannan spoke to the assembled warriors for some time, but his words were not understood by Durant.

The warriors then arose from their seats and, one by one, they passed before Kilcokannan, bowing low as they passed him. They then seated themselves, and Kilcokannan, taking his pipe, smoked first and then handed it in turn to the others.

At the first smoke, the pipe was handed to Durant last. This time Durant smoked next after Kilcokannan, and after all had smoked, Kilcokannan arose, walked over to where Durant was sitting, touched him on each cheek, and again took his seat.

All this Indian ceremony meant that the Indians would sell the land to George Durant and live in peace.

THE STORY OF WILLIAM DRUMMOND.

" We stand aghast with horror,
   At the deep damnation of his taking off."
                              —*Macbeth.*

Soon after the country along Albemarle Sound was settled, William Drummond was appointed Governor. He was the first Governor of the colony that was known as North Carolina.

He was appointed by the Lords Proprietors, to whom the King of England had granted all the Albemarle country.

These Proprietors were eight English noblemen to whom the King gave the country. They had power to establish a government over the country, to make laws and appoint officers.

This was about the year 1664 that they appointed Drummond Governor.

Drummond was by birth a Scotchman, and when he was appointed Governor he was living in Virginia.

He was a good man and made a good Governor.

Like most of the Scotchmen that came to America, he was industrious, energetic and attentive to business.

The people liked him, and named Drummond's Point on Albemarle Sound after him. They also named Lake Drummond, in the Dismal Swamp, after him, and these places keep his name to this day.

He visited different parts of the country that he was appointed over. He was interested in the people living in North Carolina, and was popular with them.

While he held the office of Governor, the country was prosperous and the population grew in numbers.

He was appointed Governor for three years, but made such a good chief officer that he would probably have been reappointed to the same office.

But the ways of an overruling Providence in the things of this world are past finding out. What seems to us cruel, time proves to have been kind. What looks to us unwise, time proves it wise.

Our place and our duty is patience and waiting, submission, trust. Time, perhaps, may show us that "all things work together for good." Perhaps not. But wait.

The close of Drummond's life was an unhappy one. His death was a cruel one. He met death with a hero's courage, without a word of supplication or complaint.

He died for popular liberty. He fell in an uprising for freedom. He shed his blood against tyranny. He died an ignominious death at the hands of a tyrant.

It is an honor to North Carolina and to the Albemarle country that her first Governor died a martyr in the cause of the people. His name—the name of William Drummond, the first Governor of North Carolina—should have a warm place in the hearts of his countrymen.

Would you like to know how and why he came to die? Listen.

William Drummond was a citizen of the colony of Virginia when he was appointed Governor of North Carolina.

When he came into the Albemarle country to be Governor of the colony, I think he settled about Edenton or in Durant's Neck. I think so, because the Chowanook Indians had a considerable settlement where Edenton now stands.

Or he may have settled in Durant's Neck, where the Yeopim Indians lived, because most of the early white settlers came to Perquimans County, in Durant's Neck.

Governor Drummond was visiting his old home in Virginia, and while there he found the people of Virginia in arms against the government.

It was an armed rebellion against the authority of Governor Berkley, of Virginia.

Berkley was a harsh, rough man of ungoverned temper. He was an ignorant man himself, and wanted the people under him to be more ignorant than he was. He despised education, and in one of his public papers said he did not want a school or a printing press in Virginia. If you were not too polite and refined to use the word, you would say he was a "fool."

When Drummond went to Virginia the people were violent against Berkley.

The leader in opposition to him was a young lawyer named Nicholas Bacon.

Bacon was a good speaker and a popular man. He inflamed the passions of the people. He denounced Berkley as a corrupt despot.

He drew his own sword and called upon the people to drive Berkley from power, Many of the people took sides with him.

Drummond, with his hot Scotch blood, was fresh from a people who loved liberty, and had left Virginia for the freedom of the Albemarle country.

He naturally took sides with Bacon and the people. He knew Berkley; knew him to be a selfish tyrant, an ignorant ruler who used his power for his own benefit, and had sometimes used his authority to the injury of the Albemarle settlers.

Drummond took up arms for Bacon and the people of Virginia. He gave to the cause his wise council and his brave arm.

Might and power prevailed. The popular outbreak was put down.

Some fled. Some surrendered. Some were captured. Drummond was one of those who were captured.

He was brought before the tyrant, probably in irons, who saluted him with mock courtesy.

"Good morning, Mr. Drummond," said Berkley, making him a low bow, "you are welcome. I had rather see you than any one else. You shall be hanged in half an hour."

Then, turning to his attendants, he ordered a trial, sentenced Drummond to death, and he was executed in less time than Berkley had said.

Drummond died a martyr to popular liberty. He was the first noted rebel of North Carolina. He was the first Governor of North Carolina that took arms against a tyrant. Caswell was the second, and Ellis and Vance were later in arms against usurpation.

When King Charles of England heard of Drummond's death, he said, speaking of Berkley; "That old fool has taken more lives in that naked country without offence than I have in all England for the murder of my father."

But the King did not go far enough. He ought to have ordered him to England and had him tried and punished for tyranny and murder.

Such was the sad fate of our first Governor. It was a cruel fate. But he died a hero. No word of fear fell from his lips. Cherish his memory, sympathize with his misfortunes. Turn from the tyrant who caused his death.

Drummond has no monument of marble or brass. But his monument is in our hearts, and we keep fresh therein the inscription of his virtues.

Our good old mother State has not been generous to the memory of her dead sons. She has raised few marble monuments to their honor. It is not well. But we must love her none the less. We must make our hearts their monuments and mark their virtues there.

Loving hearts are imperishable. Marble monuments moulder into dust. Your young hearts are of wax. I want you to inscribe upon their waxen tablets the name of DRUMMOND.

OUR PARLIAMENTARY GENESIS

(The hole whence we were digged.—Is.)

NATURE's work is upward from small beginnings, as oaks from acorns and large streams from fountains. St. Peter's at Rome is the successor of the "Groves that were God's first temples." Rome from twin brothers nurtured by a wolf. England from the thick mists of its early history. Massachusetts from wandering pilgrims in search of liberty. North Carolina, the cradle of our country, started at its first attempt at settlement in an environment of sorrow that crowns it with the cypress wreath of mourning. That abortive struggle was followed by the trapper and the hunter, that by the successful quest of "bottom lands," and that by organized government in its humblest forms.

The earliest record of organized government in North Carolina is of a general assembly of the people of the colony at the house of Captain Hecklefield, which is supposed to have been located at the present site of Nixonton, in Pasquotank County, long familiarly known as "Old Town," because it was the first county-seat of government of Pasquotank County, and was succeeded by Elizabeth City, on Pasquotank River, in the year 1800.

But tradition is the parent of history, and, like all unwritten history, is typified by the sybelline leaves of classic story, written on leaves and scattered to the winds.

We have a tradition of our early Parliamentary history that has never before, as we remember, been committed to the custody of written language: and as it came to us from an authentic source in which we have great faith, we hand it down on the wings of "Grandfather's Tales."

When a lad in our formative period of life, somewhere about a dozen years, on its sunny or shady side, we were the ready boy of a large kindred family connection. We went on errands, we visited the sick; when an old member of the family visited their children or grandchildren, we were the ready boy to carry them around from place to place. It was a convenience to them, and not without profit to us, which profits we quickly invested in ginger cakes and beer, which, though not a very permanent investment, doubtless brought us as much real happiness as if invested in real estate or government bonds.

Gen. Duncan McDonald, of Edenton, was our kinsman by marriage, a good man, fond of children, indulgent and liberal with them. He was a military man by training and position, and his official business often called him to distant places in his military district. On one of these occasions he was called to Elizabeth City to review the militia of Pasquotank County. The ready boy was ready to take him, and more particularly as he was companionable with boys.

On the day appointed we equipped ourselves with a "double gig" and a nice stepping horse, and started on our day's journey. The General was kind, chatty and companionable.

Toward evening we crossed "Hall's Creek" bridge in Pasquotank County, a mile from the Hecklefield farm at Nixonton. On rising the hill at Hall's Creek, the General stopped the horse and said to us: "The first General Assembly of North Carolina met under that tree," at the same time pointing to a large oak tree on the left-hand side of the road, that towered above the oaks that surrounded it.

He then chuckled to himself, and said that one of the by-laws of the Assembly was that "the members should wear shoes, if not stockings, during the sessions of the body, and that they must not throw their chicken and other bones under the tree."

General McDonald was a man of literary culture, and particularly fond of antiquarian lore. He was greatly amused at the humble origin of our legislative history, and laughed over it with great glee. If the oak is still standing, it might be a good speculation to have it cut up into memorial walking canes to clog the pride of our dandy legislators in Prince Albert coats, with kid gloves and gold-headed canes. It would serve as a lesson of humility to remind them of the hole whence they were digged.

CULPEPPER'S REBELLION.

A land, rent with civil feuds,
Drenched, it may be, in fraternal blood.
—*Webster.*

In 1677 there was a "revolutionary time" in the Albemarle, which section then constituted the chief settlement of Carolina. There was a dual government, or rather a dual usurpation of government. Miller and Culpepper both claimed supremacy. Miller had the best show of authority, being the representative of the duly authorized Governor, by appointment of the Lords Proprietors, who lingered in the West Indies, allured by love, as it was supposed, but professing to be detained by sickness. Miller, his secretary, was sent on ahead to hold the office of Governor by a temporary tenure. He came over to Albemarle with some show of authority and administered the government in an autocratic way. The people respected his authority and obeyed the laws which he enacted for them. He imposed taxes, laid duties upon foreign imports, and ruled by his own free will.

Culpepper, seeing that Miller was usurping power, set up a claim to the Governorship for himself, and soon established a contraband trade with Boston, then a pretentious village in New England. He defied the authority of Miller. He refused to pay the import duties imposed by Miller, and continued to trade with the rich planters of Albemarle Sound and its tributary waters, and was encouraged by them. There was absolute free trade, and Culpepper's profits from the government became greater than Miller's.

3

This contraband trade was carried on mainly by one Gilliam, who commanded a "skipper" vessel, engaged in the trade with Boston. He was a shrewd fellow, and found a free trade with the farmers of the Albemarle, without the burden of impost duties, was profitable both to the rich planters and to himself. Culpepper winked at this contraband traffic. Gilliam winked back and pursued his business with great diligence.

George Durant, who lived on Little River, was a very wealthy man, and, while a good and upright man, was thrifty in business and successful in the accumulation of wealth. Finding authority disputed, with two men contending for supremacy, and not authorized or caring to solve the trouble, he took sides with that in which he found most profit and favored Culpepper. Favoring Culpepper, he favored Gilliam, and Durant's plantation became Gilliam's headquarters for his illicit trade.

Miller had the largest following, and having gone into office by peaceful methods he had the support of the more conservative classes of the population. Culpepper was a usurper, and made no claim to rightful authority. He was denounced by Miller as a lawless man, and attempts were made to arrest him for treason.

Miller heard that Gilliam was in Little River, pursuing his unlawful business, and that he intended to come round into Pasquotank River and stop at Pembrook (now Cobb's Point) for the purpose of trading. Later he heard that Culpepper was to come round with him in his "skipper." He thought his opportunity had come, and determined to go to Pembrook, board the skipper when she anchored, and arrest Culpepper as a lawless traitor. Relying upon his authority as Chief Magistrate of Carolina, he went to Pembrook and awaited the coming of Culpepper and Gilliam. He did not wait long. The skipper soon arrived and cast anchor in the stream. Miller pushed off in a boat, boarded the skipper, found Culpepper and Gilliam, and demanded their surrender in the name of the Province of Carolina.

Culpepper and Gilliam showed fight, and instead of being arrested by Miller, they overpowered and arrested him, took him ashore and imprisoned him in the jail at Pembrook.

Thus, having Carolina's questionable Governor in durance vile, Culpepper administered his usurped authority for eight years.

What became of Miller in that lawless time, history and tradition is silent, but history tells us that Culpepper was afterwards arrested by order of the Lords Proprietors and taken to England for trial upon the charge of treason.

He was defended by Lord Shaftesbury, the most distinguished jurist of the period, and acquitted upon the ground that there was no organized government in Carolina.

THE EDENTON TEA PARTY.

"Do have a cup of tea, sir."

Tea is a historic beverage. Before the dawn of civilization it was the national drink in the oldest Empire of the world. Before coffee became known in the social and festive world, it was the solace and comfort of the aged. When coffee became its rival, it never supplanted it, and to this day tea is the favorite drink of the old, refined and luxurious. Doctor Johnson, the leviathan of English literature, astonished Mrs. Thrale by quaffing a dozen cups of his favorite tea at one sitting, at her hospitable board.

It is not strange, then, that the tax on tea by the British Parliament excited so much complaint among the patriots of the Revolution, and that the wives and mothers of the Revolution felt the burden of the tax on tea, and that the ladies of Edenton felt the pressure more than elsewhere in the State, because it was the social and commercial seat of empire in North Carolina in the colonial times.

So they met in a body, the prominent society ladies of the town, at the residence of Mrs. Barco, the wife of a distinguished barrister of the town, organized by appointing Mrs. Barco to take the chair as president of the body, and adopted a set of patriotic resolutions, denouncing the tea tax of the British Parliament, and pledging themselves not to use any more tea of British manufacture after that social evening while the odious tax on their favorite beverage continued in force.

That patriotic indignation meeting was held October 25, 1774. It was doubtless the sensation of the town, and gave new fuel to the fires that soon burst into flame in the outburst of the Revolution.

This was the only Tea Party that was ever held in North Carolina or the United States that became a factor in our great Revolutionary struggle. The Boston Tea Party was an Indian Masque Party. Without intending to disparage that famous historical event of our Boston brethren, the Masque Tea Party of Boston was an inspiration of commerce rather than of patriotism. The Revolutionary Tea Party of Edenton was purely social and patriotic, and by that social and patriotic act of the Edenton dames, the "hand that rocked the cradle" nerved the arm of the heroes that fought the battles of the Revolution from Moore's Creek to Yorktown.

From that Tea Party in Edenton hangs a tale, and a tale of romance and history. Its identity is established by the local traditions of the period and by the enduring record of the painter's art.

In the early twenties of the last century, about the year 1823 or 1824, there was brought to the town of Edenton by Captain Halsey, a worthy and intelligent sea-captain who traded from Edenton up the Mediterranean Sea, a painting on glass, headed "The Edenton Tea Party." On a voyage to the Mediterranean he met with William

The Ladies of Edenton signing their Association.

T. Muse, a lieutenant in the United States Navy, a native of Pasquotank County, but long a resident of Edenton, where he had been our schoolmate at the old Edenton Academy. Bill Muse (how that loved name still makes the heart-strings of our memory tingle at the touch of the "Auld Lang Syne") gave Captain Halsey the painting above mentioned, and asked him to carry it home to Edenton and deposit it in a place of safety. Muse stated that he had found it hanging in a barber-shop in one of the islands of the Mediterranean Sea.

Captain Halsey brought it home and placed it on exhibition in old Captain Manning's tailor shop. For several days it was the sensation of the town. Everybody went to see it. Some of the oldest people remembered the Tea Party that the painting commemorated. Some recognized the faces of some of the ladies in the painting. Mrs. Dickerson, a society lady of Edenton at the time, was pointed out as a most striking likeness.

That painting on glass was broken in pieces some years after, and the broken pieces were put in place and photographed and preserved as it was when it was brought home.

JOHN HARVEY.

(THE GREAT REVOLUTIONARY LEADER.)

It is one of the unsolved problems in human life whether circumstances make great men or great men create the circumstances from which they spring, or whether they act and react upon each other. However that may be, John Harvey was the great leader of the Revolution in North Carolina. The man and the circumstances met. Of illustrious descent, his ancestor John Harvey having been Governor of the Province many years before, of large wealth, of great influence, possessing that dominant will-power of which heroes are made, and with natural gifts that were formed for command, John Harvey was born with nature's signet of authority.

He had long been the foremost man in the troublous times that preceded the Revolution, and had rode upon the storm of that ominous period that betokened the birth of the greatest event in the world's history. He was the central political figure in North Carolina. All eyes turned to him in this crisis in the history of the Province. He rode upon its whirlwind and directed the storm. He was in the confidence of royal authority. He presided in the Assemblies convened by the order of the Governor appointed by the King of Great Britain; but he was not the submissive tool of its authority. His heart was imbued with the spirit of independence that inspired a people who were "freest of the free." He was Speaker of the Assembly that Governor Martin prorogued in order that the Legislature might "cool" and be more complaisant in some controversy with the Governor. The Legislature met on the 4th of December, 1773. Meanwhile the portents of the Revolution had grown more imminent, and at a meeting of the Legislature on the 8th inst. following, a committee was appointed to obtain the "earliest intelligence of proceedings in England relating to America, and to keep up correspondence with the other colonies."

This was the germ-seed of the Revolution in North Carolina. It was a seed mainly planted by the hand of John Harvey. We will see later how that seed "fell upon good ground," and how the hand that planted it cultivated it with diligence. John Harvey was a skilled husbandman when he drove his plow in the Revolutionary furrow, and he produced fruits an hundred fold and more.

Governor Martin's eyes were wide open to the impending crisis, and he determined that North Carolina should not co-operate with the other colonies while he was the Governor of the Province. He recognized the spirit of independence that animated the people of the Province of North Carolina. He saw the swelling current of co-operation among the colonies, and he determined to thwart it by gubernatorial authority in North Carolina. He had the authority to convoke the Legislature, and he determined that it should not meet, and that, consequently, the Province should not be represented in any Congress of the Colonies, for the purpose of co-operating in hostile declarations against Great Britain, "until matters were in better shape."

Harvey was not sleeping at his post. He was informed of the designs of Governor Martin by the Governor's private secretary, probably with his approval, to intimidate Harvey. The lion-hearted hero of the Revolution held a meeting with Governor Johnston, of Edenton, and Colonel Buncombe, of Tyrrell County, at "Buncombe Hall," the hospitable seat of the Colonel, and at their interview Harvey said, as he had declared to Martin's secretary, that if Governor Martin did not convoke the Assembly, "then the people will convene one themselves."

The Governor did not convene the Assembly.

Johnston, writing of that meeting at "Buncombe Hall" to William Hooper, of Wilmington, says: "Harvey was in a violent mood, and declared he was for assembling a convention independent of the Governor, and that he would lead the way and issue hand-bills over his own name." Later, leaders on the Cape Fear, acting on Har-

vey's suggestion, called on the people to choose their
deputies.

That Convention met, although the Governor forbade
it by proclamation. This was the first Revolutionary popular Convention that ever met in America without royal
authority, and in defiance of it. That Convention, and it
was a very able one, met in New Bern, and John Harvey
was its President. It passed resolutions denouncing the
claim of the Parliament to tax the colonies without representation, denounced the tax on tea and forbade its use
in North Carolina, denounced the Boston Port Bill, declared an import duty upon goods of English manufacture,
declared in favor of a Continental Congress of the colonies, and appointed delegates to that Congress in Philadelphia; and it authorized John Harvey, the President,
to call another Convention whenever he thought it expe-
dient.

That shows where North Carolina stood before there
was an overt act of revolution, before a gun was fired at
Lexington, and before Virginia showed her Revolutionary
teeth. That showed the blood that flowed through John
Harvey's veins.

Now, a word for John Harvey's memory. Blessed
memory! Heroic inheritance! First to hurl defiance at
royal authority in America! First to draw authority
from the people instead of the King. Before Henry first
uttered the slogan of "liberty or death" in the sacred
halls of old St. John's Church in Richmond, John Harvey had proclaimed the supremacy of the people of North
Carolina over kings and their representatives.

In the National capitol at Washington there is a hall
set apart for the statues of two of the great men of the
several States. North Carolina's niche in that hall is
empty. A bust of Harvey would not add an atom to his
heroic fame, but it would show the world that ingratitude
is a sin that does not tarnish the good name of North Carolina, and that John Harvey's name and fame is her priceless heritage.

THE RESOLUTIONS OF ST. PAUL'S VESTRY.

"Resistance to tyrants is obedience to God."

Many memorials of the patriotism of the citizens of North Carolina during the Revolutionary period exist and are preserved. Some have never had recognition, and some have slept the sleep of forgetfulness. Among those that have never had sufficient recognition are the resolutions of the vestrymen of old St. Paul's Church, Edenton, which are now preserved in the parish register of the church, and signed by Richard Hoskins, Wm. Boyd, David Rice, Thomas Benbury, Aaron Hill, Jacob Hunter, Pelatiah Walton, John Beasley, William Hinton, William Bennet, Thomas Bonner and William Roberts, on the 19th day of June, 1775.

These men are "apples of gold in pitchers of silver," and should be toasted on all our patriotic anniversaries, that tried men's souls in the dark days of those bloody times that bred heroes and tested the fidelity of men to home and country. Mecklenburg's pride glows with a warmer heart-beat when the names of Brevard, Avery, Polk, Alexander, Davidson, Graham, Balch, and the other immortals that made the 20th of May the day of days in Carolina's annals. Every true son of our dear old mother State joins hands and hearts with them in the loud acclaim of gratitude and honor. But who joins us in giving due honor to the Hoskins, the Benburys, the Beasleys, the Hills, the Hunters, the Hintons, the Bonners, and the other patriots who embalmed the 19th of June in our annals, a month after the "Mecklenburg Declaration of Independence"?

Read these immortal words by the vestrymen of St. Paul's Church, in Edenton, and take off your hats in honor of the great men who were true to their country when the die trembled in the doubtful balance. Listen, and bless and honor the vestry resolutions that have rung down the ages. Who dare challenge their heroism, their patriotism, their virtue. Listen, and be prouder of your heritage of renown:

"We, the undersigned, professing our allegiance to the King, and acknowledging the constitutional executive power of the government, do solemnly profess and declare that we do absolutely believe that neither the Parliament of Great Britain, nor any member, or any constituent branch thereof, have a right to impose taxes upon these colonies to regulate the internal policy thereof; and that all attempts, by fraud or force, to establish and exercise such claims and powers are violations of the peace and security of the people, and ought to be resisted to the utmost; and that the people of this Province, singly and collectively, are bound by the acts and resolutions of the Continental and Provincial Congress, because in both they are fully represented by persons chosen by themselves. And we do solemnly and sincerely promise and engage, under the sanctions of virtue, honor, and the sacred love of liberty and our country, to maintain and support all the acts and resolutions of the said Continental and Provincial Congress to the utmost of our power and ability.

"In testimony whereof, we have hereunto set our hands, this 19th day of June, 1775."

This protest of the vestrymen of St. Paul's Church, viewed in all its aspects, is most important, as indicative, of the spirit of our Revolutionary ancestors. Look at it: Edenton was the metropolis of the Royal Government in North Carolina. The agents of the British Government lived there. An atmosphere of royalty pervaded the community. Its most influential social element was among the representatives of the British Government. St. Paul's Church was a beneficiary of the Church of England's "Society for the Propagation of the Gospel." The vestry of St. Paul's Church represented both ecclesiastical and civil authority. They were evidently sturdy men. The strong language of their resolutions indicate their earnest and sincere purpose. They were carrying burdens social and official that the patriots of Mecklenburg knew not of. When they

declared that "neither the Parliament of Great Britain
nor any member or constituent branch thereof has a right
to impose taxes upon these colonies to regulate the internal policy thereof, and that any attempts to exercise such
claims by force or fraud ought to be resisted to the utmost," they rose to the full stature of stalwart manhood
and meant to sunder all ties in conflict with their love of
country.

THE REGULATORS.

THE BATTLE OF ALAMANCE.

For time at last sets all things even,
And if we do but watch the hour,
There never yet was human power,
That could evade, if unforgiven.

THERE are three events in North Carolina history that
have not been sufficiently commemorated: The Battle of
Alamance, the Proceedings of the Vestry of St. Paul's
Church of Edenton, and the Battle of Moore's Creek.
Mecklenburg has been more fortunate. Its position was
long contested, especially by the Virginia historians, but
it has fought its way to public recognition and now lifts its
head among the primal events of our Revolutionary history. Even that heroic event was long disputed, and
some of our most distinguished and faithful North Carolinians doubted its authenticity.

Alamance has been more unfortunate and longer in
having its claim as the germ-seed of the Revolution, planted before the Alexanders, the Polks, the Brevards, and the
other heroes of Mecklenburg had put on the toga of manhood, fully recognized by the predominance of testimony.
North Carolina is cautious, deliberative and slow, and Zeb
Vance, in that speech to the Army of Northern Virginia,
which General Lee declared was worth fifty thousand men
to the Confederate service, hit the nail squarely on the head

when he said the people of North Carolina were a race of "Tar Heels," and stuck when they put their heels down. Strange, too, because she has two sisters, on the south of us and north of us, one full of mercury, and jumps to a conclusion at the first flash; and the other, full of pompous stateliness and avarice of fame, folds her robes of dignity about her and says, "Stand back, we are better than them."

The sons of the State are now putting Alamance in its true and rightful position as a beacon light in the primal storms of that great event in the world's history that taught mankind the great lesson in free government and made the American mountaineer a marvel in the world's history. All honor to W. L. Saunders, the stout-hearted North Carolinian. Blessed be his memory. A worthy son of a worthy and reverend father, Rev. Joseph H. Saunders.

The Regulators were patriotic. They resisted oppression of British office-holders. They were outraged and oppressed by unlawful taxations, by the oppressor's scorn and the proud man's contumely. They protested again and again against these infamous acts of the British Government. At last, after their patience was exhausted, they resorted to force, and Tryon's soldiers overcame them on the bloody field of Alamance, subdued them in battle with death on both sides, hung them after a drum-head trial, and executed the prisoners without mercy. Their grievances were afterward acknowledged by Tryon, the "Wolf of North Carolina," as the Indians designated him, and his successor, Governor Martin. And now, the victims of this flagrant oppression by the British Government cry from the ground for justice from their countrymen who sprang from the seed their brave hearts had planted. Let their countrymen, who have reaped the fruits of their heroism and sufferings, make requital by justice and blessings, late but timely, on their long misrepresented memories.

The Battle of Alamance, on the soil of North Carolina,

on the 16th of May, 1771, was the reveille drum-beat of the Revolution, and the blood then shed, on the open battle-field and on the scaffold, was the blood of the martyrs of liberty; the germ-seed of Mecklenburg's Declaration, of the patriotic protest of old St. Paul's at Edenton, of the victorious fight at Moore's Creek, and of Guilford and Yorktown.

THE TUSCARORA MASSACRE.

"Man's inhumanity to man."

The saddest event in our history is the Indian massacre by the Tuscarora Tribe of Indians in 1711.

It was the most numerous of the Indian tribes in the colony at that time. They dominated the other smaller tribes, and were known for their ferocity and cruelty.

They had long shown unfriendliness to the white settlers, and with characteristic secretiveness were maturing their plans for an indiscriminate slaughter of all the colonists, without regard to age, sex or condition. Their end and aim was an utter extinction of the white settlers.

On the night of the agreement of the Tuscarora tribe, there was a general uprising, and the Indians massacred one hundred and thirty men, women and children with such inhuman barbarities that humanity shudders at the recital.

The population of the colony at this time did not probably exceed two thousand. There had been occasional Indian disturbances between the white settlers and the Indians. They were of a local character, but they were feeders of the general disturbance which resulted in the atrocious massacre of 1711, on the night of the 22d of September.

It was a well-laid scheme of the cruel Tuscaroras, in

which they had enlisted the smaller tribes then dwelling
in the colony—the Meherrins, the Corees, the Matamus-
keets, and others. The unsettled condition of public affairs favored them. The contest then raging between the
Church of England men and the Quakers for equal rights
in the government of the Province, represented by Cary and
Glover, the opposing claimants of the Governor's office,
and the angry feelings in which the contest was producing
its results of war and bloodshed and quasi war, invited
the Indians to the most cruel Indian massacre that sad-
dens our annals.

In one night, in the most perfect secrecy, with entire
accord, the Indians rose as one man on the night of September 22, 1711, and with inhuman desperation fell upon the
sleeping and defenceless population and slew them with
fiendish torture, at which our blood is curdled by the recital. Old men gray with age had their heads smashed
in and their white hairs bespattered with blood; helpless
infancy, with its pitiful cry for mercy, was cruelly murdered, and women in the presence of their children were
tortured and cruelly murdered.

The blow was a terrible one to the scattered inhabitants of the Albemarle settlements. It suspended for a
time the heart-burnings of intestine strife. Quaker and
Cavalier stood side by side in the presence of a common
danger, united by the ties of a common brotherhood.

Such was the dread scene of the 22d of September,
1711.

A promising colony of Swiss under De Graffenreid, of
Berne, Switzerland, had made a settlement in New Bern,
and were industriously engaged in laying off lands in the
vicinity. Lawson, the Surveyor-General of the colony,
accompanied by De Graffenreid and attendants, were on
a surveying expedition to locate the lands. While engaged in this peaceful business, they were attacked by a
party of Indians and captured. At an Indian council they
were sentenced to death, which order was inflicted upon
Lawson with great torture, and De Graffenreid was lib-

erated because he was supposed to be high in authority and that his death would be avenged.

Meanwhile messengers were dispatched to Virginia and South Carolina for assistance. Governor Spotswood, of Virginia, effected a treaty of peace with the Tuscaroras. Gen. James Moore, of South Carolina, came over with a body of troops, attacked the Indians with great bravery at Fort Barnwell near New Bern, with great slaughter, and drove them from the Province. They fled from the colony of North Carolina and joined the five Nations of the Iroquois Tribe in New York, forming what has been called the Six Nations in New York, where a remnant of them still live.

The smaller tribes who were led by the fierce Tuscaroras were left undisturbed.

THE HUGUENOT BLOOD IN NORTH CAROLINA.

The web of our life is of a mingled yarn, good and ill together.
—*Julius Cæsar.*

THE revocation of the Edict of Nantes is one of the most memorable events in French history, and is a most significant illustration of the mercurial disposition of the French people. The French people have more individuality than any people that have ever lived upon earth, and their individuality finds expression most frequently in scenes of revolution, violence and bloodshed. They are bright, vivacious, full of enterprise, energy and forecast, prone to take offence, sudden and quick in quarrel, and daring death at the cannon's mouth. They have given to history its greatest military heroes, its greatest statesmen, its greatest philosophers, its greatest writers, its greatest poets, and its greatest orators.

The first Napoleon said to one of his great Marshals who had followed him in his exile, and who stood by him in the

4

supreme hour of death: "Bertrand, there have been but three great captains, Cæsar, Alexander and myself." The world has furnished no greater warrior than Napoleon, no greater scientist than Cuvier, no greater poet than Bossuet, no greater philosopher than Fenelon, no greater novelist than Hugo, no greater dramatist, save Shakespeare, than Moliere; and France has made more history, both in its social and tragic features, than any other nation on earth.

They must have derived their fighting blood from Cain, their sagacious blood from Esau, their military blood and wise strategy from Joshua, their astronimic blood from Job, and their wisdom from Solomon.

This great blood, so compounded and intermingled, was cast upon the shores of Albemarle as a flotsam after the "Revocation of the Edict of Nantes." When that cruel and bloody persecution drove from France the best of its population, its most skilled artisans, the most cultured of its population, and enriched other lands with the best blood of France, the Albemarle country was newly settled and the Lords Proprietors invited, by liberal gifts and privileges, immigrants from all the world to come to the new-found land of Albemarle, subdue its forests and reduce to cultivation its rich "bottom lands."

Five brothers, Huguenots, skilled artisans, workers in metals, fabrics and leather, saw the invitation of the English Proprietors and determined to cast their lots in America. They were religious devotees, and left the land of their birth for freedom of conscience and freedom to worship God in obedience to its dictates. They had suffered persecution, and in the choice of recantation, destruction or exile, they chose the last.

In the latter years of the seventeenth century, about 1680, as the family tradition has handed down to us, five Huguenot brothers sailed from France to seek an asylum from persecution in the wild lands of America. They crossed the ocean in safety, and in seeking an entrance into Carolina's inland broad waters, they encountered the storm-swept shoals of Hatteras, that octopus of the sea, whose appetite for suffering and death has never been sated, and there they were wrecked and cast upon its then inhospitable shores, with nothing saved but life.

Soon after, they explored the lands on the headwaters of Albemarle Sound and settled there.   They settled in the counties adjacent to it.

John located in Tyrrell and engaged in the seafaring trade to Boston, and married in Boston.   Levi settled in Pasquotank County, owned the land on which Elizabeth City now stands, and is supposed to have engaged in commercial pursuits.   Thomas settled in Perquimans and became a farmer. Job settled in lower Chowan and became a successful farmer and worker in leather, which had been his business in his native home in France.   What became of the other brother is not known, but it is said in the old family traditions that he was drowned in Tennessee many years after.

These brothers were the germ-seed and origin of the numerous family of Creecys scattered over the counties contiguous to Albemarle Sound.

THE SCOTCH-IRISH ELEMENT IN OUR HISTORY

We tread upon the ashes of heroes, patriots and statesmen.

THE migration of races is one of the most interesting studies of history. It is one of the most potent influences in the complicated machinery of divine providence in preventing the decadence of the human race by the infusion of new blood, and thus preserving the unity of the race and its virile purity and strength.

North Carolina, though now the most homogeneous population of all the States, was originally a composite race, derived principally from the ancestral English stock, the Huguenot refugees, and the Scotch-Irish stock, impelled by the migratory instinct and by the unrest of the love of liberty, and the search for newer fields of enterprise.

Perhaps the most distinctive and enterprising element of our population was the Scotch-Irish element. It was the outgrowth of a Scotch colony who migrated from their parent hive and settled at first in the north of Ireland, where they became identified with the Celtic race by intermarriage and the adoption of their habits and customs. They were a combination of the warm blood of Ireland with the steadiness and tenacity of the Scotch Covenanter. It combined Irish wit, vivacity and impulse with Scotch sobriety and earnestness— a rare combination of contradictory qualities, resulting in wondrous alchemy.

This was a grand element in our population. The Irish element caused their migration to the new land beyond the sea, where broader fields, with less restraints of the rigid rule of government, invited them.

About the middle of the seventeenth century they landed upon the shores of Pennsylvania and there abided for permanent settlement; but the staid character of the Quaker population did not suit their progressive temperament and they sought a home in Carolina where lived the "freeest of the free," where the Irish blood could find vent for its hilarity and its Scotch stick and stubbornness could find a congenial home.

From Pennsylvania there came a stream of Scotch-Irish, and planted themselves in the sections of Alamance, Mecklenburg, and the adjacent counties, planted there by a wise Providence to await the unfolding of a great drama in which they were to bear a mighty part.

They brought with them their preachers and their school-masters, their creeds and their confessions; made the mountain section the garden of North Carolina, produced a stalwart population that gave us our greatest leaders in the crisis of our struggle for independence, and made their homes the pride of our State.

They gave us the martyrs of Alamance, whose patriotic blood was the germ-seed of the Revolution. They gave us Mecklenburg's immortal Declaration of Independence, whose primal bugle-note of freedom yet sounds in the grateful ears of the patriotic sons of our loved mother State. They gave us our beloved Vance, whose Irish nature found expression in his charming flow of wit and humor, and whose Scotch blood found expression in his heroic fortitude under suffering and his sturdy manhood under all the vicissitudes of his great, eventful life—a rare combination of two strains of blood that showed even in his broad religion. He was Father Ryan, the poet-priest, in the jollity of his Irish character, and John Knox, the sturdy Presbyterian, in his Scotch blood—an even-balanced monument of sturdiness and jollity. They gave us the Alexanders, the Brevards, the Polks, the Grahams, and others, whose blessed memories are an inspiration of patriotism, and they are giving us to-day a Queen City in the nest of the hornets of the Revolution, that will be the bright light of our whole country when New York and Boston and Chicago have become, like Persepolis and Palmyra, the buried cities of the plain.

TOM BROWN'S DOG TILDEN.

Who kicks
My dog,
He has got me to lick.
—*Burdette*.

Tom Brown was a Baptist preacher of Gates County. He was a master of the pulpit and made the gospel ring from the sacred desk. He was fond of field sports, and had a setter dog. The dog was named "Tilden," after the Democratic candidate for the Presidency in 1876. Tilden was given to him when a puppy by one of his brethren who lived in a distant part of his pastoral care. As a puppy Tilden showed remarkable sagacity. He was vigilant, affectionate and docile, and his bird instinct was apparent before his yelp was fully developed. He never forgot a friend or a foe, and his friends accumulated faster than his foes, for his disposition was most lovable. Before his molar teeth were grown he had learned all the language of dog pantomime, and the children, whose love he had won, were constantly learning him some new tricks. He would stand up on his hinder legs, try to stand on his head when bidden by a pantomimic waggle of the head, would bark before eating, with solemn gravity, and knew the names of his owner and of all the children. He loved field sports, and when brother Brown, who was a Nimrod indeed, forgot his gun and field sports, Tilden would pull at his trousers' legs until he made him get his gun, and Tilden would signify his approval and happiness by wild antics and capers.

Tilden grew to dog manhood and grew in wisdom every day. His learning in dogology was marvelous. He knew all the neighbors by face and name, would carry to any one of them whose name was called to him a message in writing in his mouth, and would wait for an answer. He would go to the post-office and bring the mail, and was never happier than when a party of sportsmen came with their guns to have a field-day with Tilden's owner. He was a perfect hunter, knew the haunts of birds, and would stay by a Bob White all day long, and would have died by him if the hunters did not come.

Tilden became a great pet in the community of upper Gates County, and they were a community who delighted in dog and gun. All of them loved him, and would send delicacies for Tilden to brother Brown's. His attainments in dog pantomime were a marvel of sagacity, and the tales that brother Brown told of him spread far and wide. At a Gates Court the tale was told to us. We thought it wonderful beyond parallel. When we got home we told the story of dog Tilden to our friends and neighbors, but they did not believe it, and some, bolder than the rest, intimated that brother Brown had formed a combination to manufacture a sensational story to interest and fool the public. It wounded our pride and damaged our character for truth, which we had always treasured as one of the purest jewels in our casket. So, when we next went to Gatesville, we met brother Brown, and said to him, said we, "Brother Brown, sir, you are a preacher, and under bonds to speak the truth, and we, all our life, have been striving to build up a character for truth. We must stop this talk about Tilden, or we will be put down as two of the biggest liars in North Carolina; and if it comes to that, we had better do as Judas Iscariot did." He then commenced snuffling his nose and wiping his weeping eyes, and said: "Tilden, poor, dear old Tilden, is dead." And thereby hangs a sad recital. We tell the tale as Tom Brown told it to us.

One day Tilden did not eat. His appetite failed more and more. He grew worse. His usual sleeping place was a comfortable dog-house in the yard. His eye grew dim, and his natural sprightliness left him. The Brown household were sad. Tom took him in his bed-room at night, made a comfortable rug bed for him on the floor, and he was watched over with the tenderest care. He lost flesh. Sometimes his lustreless eye would follow the children around the room. He seldom left his bed. He grew worse and worse. The neighbors would come in to enquire after Tilden. Tilden's time had come. Tom Brown put his hand over his heart and it was still. There was no pulsation. The children came around and called him, "Tilden, Tilden, poor Tilden!" but he gave no sign of life. Tom and his family then gave way to grief. Tom sent off for John Gatling, one of the neighbors. He came quickly. Tom met John at the door and told him Tilden was dead. John came in, felt of him and said there was no sign of life. After examining him over again, John said to Tom (they were brother hunters), "Tom, if he is dead, you get your gun and click the trigger by his ear, and he will give sign of life if he is not dead." Tom took a gun from a corner where he had several and clicked the trigger over his ear. He gave no sign. And then there was one universal outburst of grief. John turned to Tom and said, "Tom, that wer'nt the gun you use when you hunt with Tilden." Tom then went back and brought the gun that he commonly used, and stooping down over Tilden he cracked the trigger near his ear. The dear old fellow slowly opened his dying eyes, feebly wagged his tail, then closed them forever—Tilden was dead.

TEACH AND POTTER, CAROLINA'S OUTLAWS.

"'T is true, 't is pity,
And pity 't is, 't is true."
—*Macbeth*.

North Carolina is not a soil that produces great and good men alone. It produces good and bad men, but the good and patriotic men greatly predominate. We should be false to our record if we chronicled the good alone. We are all attracted by good men and are led by their deeds in the paths of virtue. We are warned by bad men and generally taught by their lives that the paths of lawless vice lead to dishonored graves. So, on the other hand, the paths of virtue lead to honor in life, peace and happiness at its close and perpetual blessedness in that eternal life to which we are all journeying.

The saying of the great poet that the evil which men do lives after them and the good is oft interred with them, is a poetic fiction with a modicum of truth. The good and the evil of our lives live after us and serve as beacons and buoys to warn and to guide us. No word or action dies in our lives, but lives on as still or clamorous monitors in the pilgrimage of life.

In turning over in our memory, in searching for the list of conspicuous bad men who have left their baleful influence upon our annals, we are gratified that we are unable to find but two men to hold up as beacons of warning to our countrymen. We do not regret their living, although the world is not the better for their having lived in it. They are the dark foils that make virtue more lustrous, and make us more grateful for our heritage of the great and good names that shine on every page of our blessed history.

Who were these two men, so conspicuous by their rarity? One lived in colonial days and was a sea pirate. His life was that of a desperado and his death was by violence in mortal combat, an outlaw, a refugee from justice, an

Ishmaelite indeed, who carried his life in his hand, which was lifted against mankind. His name was Edward Teach (Blackbeard), and he made the waters of Albemarle Sound and its tributaries his rendezvous and place of retreat for security from his enemies. Teach lived in the early years of the eighteenth century. He was not a native of North Carolina. He was born in Bristol, England. He entered on his career of piracy in 1716. Up to that time for several years he had been a private sailor. He was daring and adventurous, and a famous pirate, named Kornagold, put him in command of a sloop which he had captured. Teach sailed for the American coast, making many captures on the way, which he plundered. From that time he continued his piratical outrages along the Carolina, Virginia and Atlantic coast, and made the Carolina sounds his home.

Governor Spotswood, of Virginia, offered a reward of one hundred pounds for his capture.

At length, hearing that he was in Pamlico Sound, near Ocracoke Inlet, on the 17th of November, Governor Spotswood dispatched Lieutenant Maynard, of the British Navy, from James River in Virginia to search for Teach and capture him. On the 31st he came in sight of the pirate at Ocracoke Inlet. Blackbeard had heard of his coming, and when he saw him he prepared for a desperate resistance. Teach had seventeen desperate men under him. Maynard had more than thirty. The engagement was desperate. By a feint, Maynard's men were sent below and Teach was made to believe that Maynard declined the fight and was about to surrender. When Teach saw this, he sailed to Maynard's ship to take possession of her. As soon as he boarded, Maynard ordered his men on deck, and then it was a hand-to-hand fight, Maynard and Teach heading it with sabres. Teach was mortally wounded after he had wounded thirty of Maynard's men. After Maynard had captured Teach's sloop, he cut off his head, fastened it to his bowsprit and sailed up to Bath in Beaufort County, then Hyde.

The other "black sheep" in North Carolina's history was Bob Potter, who lived a century after Teach. He was a native of Virginia, and we first hear of him in the town of Halifax, where he became a notorious, brawling politician, antagonized J. R. J. Daniel, and became notorious for his street brawls and personal conflicts with that celebrated public man. They both had a following of friends. Potter was an attractive and brave man, and seemed to have the public sympathy. He was a ready writer, and in the printed controversies Potter's vocabulary was scathing and terrible. Bob brought over from Virginia his brother Hal, who was armed and not averse to a fight of any kind. In a street fight in Halifax, in which weapons were used on both sides. Hal came out of it with fifteen buck-shot in his groin.

This warfare was kept up for several years, when Daniel went to Louisiana and Potter settled in Granville County. Potter was a lawyer by profession, and a magnetic, ambitious and aggressive man. He had not been long in Granville before he was nominated for Congress and elected. Meanwhile, he had married a girl in Granville of prominent family connection. He went to Congress, where he passed a gay and voluptuous life and represented himself to be an unmarried man; and Governor Branch, who was his colleague in Congress, warned his young female friends against him. He returned home after the adjournment of Congress, brought criminal charges against his wife that were without foundation, committed the crime of mayhem upon two innocent men who were his wife's relatives, and one of them an old man. Notwithstanding this flagrant outrage, he announced himself a candidate for the Legislature from the county of Granville and was elected. He went to Raleigh at the meeting of the Legislature, and was expelled from that body for the infamous crime of mayhem which he had committed in Granville.

Soon after his expulsion from the Legislature, he left for Texas, then a Mexican province. We have heard that he went on foot, armed with a shot-gun and followed by two bloodhounds.

In Texas, where he settled, he led a vagrant and lawless life, and was soon involved in brawls with his neighbors. In one of these he was overpowered by his foes and sought safety in flight, after killing one of his antagonists. He was hotly and closely pursued, and to escape from his pursuers he plunged into a lake and dived under the water for safety. When he came to the surface he was fired upon from the shore and his head riddled with bullets. Teach and Potter both came to violent deaths -fit termination of lives of crime and violence.

OLD-TIME HAZING AT THE UNIVERSITY.

O, the boys; the boys.

HAZING is a college custom as old as the hills. Seventy years ago it was known as the ceremony of "Admission to the Ugly Club." In its origin it was a useful institution. It broke up the *mauvais honi* (so-called) which beset a green student, and made him miserable under the apprehension of doing something or doing the impolite thing. In process of time it developed into the modern "hazing," which has grown into such proportions as to call forth the discipline of the colleges, and has sometimes found its way into our law courts. Please tell us what "hazing" means, and what is its derivation?

The Ugly Club origin of hazing was a social institution of the University of North Carolina seventy years ago. It was presided over by the acknowledged ugliest member of the club, and was intended as a benevolent institution, to be used as an antidote for the disease of nostalgia (home-sickness), which was epidemic with freshmen. It counteracted the malady of longing for home, and introduced the new-comer to a home and familiar circle.

In 1831, we entered the Freshman class of the University, and for several days we suffered intolerably from the homing feeling. One day, Lumbus Battle, the only student and classmate with whom we had formed an intimate friendship, asked us if we had joined the "Ugly Club." We told him no, and that we had never heard of it. He then persuaded us to join, and told us that he had joined, and that Mr. John Gray Bynum, who was President of the Club, had told him to invite us to join them. We told Lumbus we would join if he would go with us. The night of the meeting came. The session was held in a room in the upper story of the South Building. At the appointed time, Lumbus and I went to the hall. Lumbus gave four raps at the outer door, and suggested that we needn't be scared. The door was opened by the ugliest specimen of a man we had ever seen, and dressed in the most uncouth style. He had on his head something like the old dunce cap of the public schools, except that it had horns to it. His cheeks and eyebrows were blacked with grease and soot. His sleeves were rolled up, and he looked like our ideal of the mythological Vulcan. He looked at us with one eye closed, and invited us in with his best bow. We went in, the President preceding us. Lumbus joined the brethren and put on his cap. President Bynum then marched around the room, mumbling some cabalistic words, while we stood alone in the middle of the hall, feeling very much like a fool.

Bynum came to us after his mummery and, in solemn manner, asked us if we could dance. We told him, "Not much." He said, "How much?" We told him timidly that we had danced some at "corn shuckings," and some little at girls' parties. He then pranced around us with a sort of "limber leg double shuffle," and asked us to join him. He then hummed "Sugar in the Gourd," and kept time to it with his feet. He then asked if we could sing. We said "Not much." He asked again, "How much?" and we told him we could sing "Up in the Morning Early" and "Three Blind Mice." But he couldn't get us to sing. Like poor Macbeth, the song "stuck in our throat."

Bynum then asked us, "Could we wrastle?" We told him, "Yes, some." No sooner was the word out of our throat than he pitched in and grappled us. The old war-horse was now roused in us. We caught him round the middle, and we had it round and round the room, the members of the club shouting, slapping hands and whooping, "Creecy, Creecy!" Some one cried out, "Tie old snake" on him. Old Gray Bynum took the hint, tied the "old snake" lock round our legs, and before we could say "Jack Robinson," we were flat of our back on the floor, and "Old Gray" on top of us. "Gray" had us down, but his tongue was out. After a few long breaths, "Gray," still holding us down, said, "What mout be your name?" "Dick," said we. He then asked us our other name.

"Creecy," said we. "Well, it's a funny name; you are greasy by name, and I'll make you greasy by favor," and, calling for a pot of grease and soot, he dabbed our cheeks with it. We then got up, and he introduced us to each one of the brethren, and then we were at home and all of the sheepishness was gone out of us.

Then Gray took the President's chair, made an address full of his old-time wit and humor, and then pronounced the meeting adjourned. He was our friend ever after, until his graduation, and when that famous controversy arose between the Di. and Phi. Societies, which for awhile threatened conflict, we were a Bynum man.

Lumbus and I slept under the same blanket that night. He was very happy, and during the night he said: "Dick, if old Gray hadn't tied 'old snake' on you, you'd have had him down in a few more rounds. You had his tongue out when he throwed you."

THE OLD-TIME QUAKER.

How dost thou do?

THE Quaker element in our population was prominent in the early settlement of Eastern Carolina, in the Colonial period, in the period of the Revolution, and subsequent thereto up to the half of the nineteenth century, when negro slavery had much to do with the large Quaker emigration from North Carolina to Indiana and Illinois, and the gregarious instinct of sectarian brotherhood swelled the tide of migration to other States until a genuine old-time Quaker is now almost an ethnological curiosity. Belvidere, in Perquimans County, and some scattered settlements in Northampton County, alone remain as representatives of a sturdy race that made their distinctive impress upon the character of Eastern Carolina, and even their peculiar dress and phraseology have almost disappeared.

A sturdy and stalwart race were the old-time Quakers; conservative, plain, direct in purpose as in language, averse to worldly vanities, poised, prudent, undaunted before authority, shrewd in business transactions, thrifty in business, in all things a Quaker. But the old-time Quaker has passed away, and the "old broad-brim" and the old "Quaker coat" are not seen on our streets and highways. But their memory is green.

The last old-time Quaker in Elizabeth City was friend Miles White, a wealthy old citizen, who, at his death in Baltimore about the year 1855, was worth over a million of dollars.

Miles White started in life as a poor one-horse farmer in the county of Perquimans. In early life he sometimes brought a load of pine wood or some product to town. He was industrious. W. C. Brooks, of Gates County, father of George W. Brooks, took notice of his industry and persevering ways, and proposed to him a mercantile co-partnership. It was accepted by White, and they opened a dry goods store on Road street, not far from the old Tisdale Building, midway between the Relf House (now Albemarle) and Leather Hill. They conducted the business for several years and prospered until the business was dissolved by mutual consent.

Having accumulated money by merchandise, White next entered upon a general business, which he conducted with such success that he became a wealthy man of the town. Everything that he touched prospered. But his success never altered the simplicity and geniality of his social life. His temper and disposition was sunny and unruffled, and he became very popular with all classes save those he had driven a hard bargain with. Persons sometimes complained of his shrewd ways of business, but his honesty was never impeached but once, when he had overreached a man of the town, who was also noted for his shrewd business ways, and was also noted for his irascibility. The excited townsman grew hissing hot in the collar, and began to denounce Miles as a wretch, a dishonest man, who loved money better than his God. He abused Miles in the most opprobrious terms of the language. Miles kept his temper and his tongue, and looked steadily into the eyes of the irate banker, and when he stopped his abuse from pure exhaustion, he replied with the utmost composure— "John, ditto." The scene was so ludicrous, and the reply of the old Quaker was so terse and comprehensive, and the contrast so great, that both of them broke into laughter and parted good friends.

Miles White never laughed, but often smiled, chuckled at any amusing incident, and enjoyed a modest joke wonderfully. In the latter years of his residence in the town, he divided his time between Elizabeth City and Baltimore, and was principally engaged in purchasing crops of corn. During this time our acquaintance was somewhat intimate, and we sometimes joined him of an evening in riding in different parts of the county, looking after his purchases of corn, and arranging for its shipment to markets in different parts of the country. These trips were very pleasant to us, and his conversation was instructive and

5

entertaining. On one of these occasions he amused us with an account of a business transaction he had with Mordecai Morris, a brother Quaker of the straightest sect. Mordecai was a wealthy man, a large farmer, shrewd on a bargain, and as sharp in trade as Miles. We knew that Miles wanted to buy Mordecai's crop of corn on Dry Ridge. He had made him what he thought was a liberal offer for it. Mordecai stood off to strain Miles up to a little advance on his offer. He had often complained to us of the dilatory tactics of Mordecai. On a Saturday evening, he told us that he was going down to spend the Sabbath with Mordecai, and if he did not take his offer for his corn he would stop. After a long chaffer over the bargain on Saturday night, the two stiff and wealthy "broad-brims," went to meeting on Sabbath day at the old "meeting-house" near Simon's Creek. The spirit didn't move much that day, and Mordecai fell into a comfortable snooze. In the sepulchral silence of the devotions, the devil, who was "walking up and down upon the earth" looking for a job, came up and whispered into Mordecai's ear as he slept, and the thought of the corn trade being uppermost, he burst out, as he slept, and said: "Miles, if thou wilt furnish the bags and bag strings, the corn is thine." This incident amused Miles greatly, but he never jested about sacred things.

THOMAS HART BENTON.

Render unto Cæsar the things that are Cæsar's.

No NATIVE-BORN Carolinian has been truer to his nativity than the illustrious United States Senator from Missouri. His steps had wandered far from home, but his heart always turned in affection to the "Haw Fields" of Orange County, North Carolina. He loved the old State with filial devotion, always treasured her sacred history with veneration, and her sons with honor, and emptied the cornucopia of his own well-earned laurels into her loving lap.

Nat. Macon was the Gamaliel of his politics. He learned his lessons of sturdy patriotism at his feet, not only for his personal admiration of the virtues of that firm "old Roman" but because he was a son and representative of "his native State."

To him belongs the honor of first giving to North Carolina's Guilford Battle Ground the just honor of being the great pivotal battle of the Revolution, and the distinction of making Yorktown the close of the struggle for independence. He first presented to our eyes the first true story of Guilford, and made us prouder of the heroes who obeyed the orders of their commander and fell back in order, after accomplishing his foreformed purpose.

The history of Thomas Hart Benton is full of the lessons of energy, industry, will force and heroic determination.

In the contests of life which were assigned to him, his back was never turned on friend or foe, and all who met him as friend or foeman, recognized a great gladiator in the arena. He lived in heroic times. There were "giants in those days," and he was one of them. He was a truly great man; great in heroic manhood, in sturdy friendship, in profound acquirements, in personal bravery, in moral bravery, and in the magnificent achievements of genius and industry.

In the many heroic events of the last century of our
civil life, there is none more so than the history of the
"Expunging Resolutions," of which Benton was the author. "Solitary and alone," against opposition such as
was never encountered before, he snatched victory from
defeat, humbled the Senate of the United States, triumphed over Calhoun, Clay, Webster, Mangum and Watkins Leigh, and made the Secretary, in the presence of the
Senate, draw black lines around and across their resolutions of condemnation of President Andrew Jackson for
his removal of the government deposits from the United
States Bank four years before. There has been no instance of such will force and determination in the parliamentary history of the world.

Thomas H. Benton was born in Orange County, North
Carolina, near Hillsboro, and emigrated to Tennessee in
the last years of the last century. He practised law in
that State for several years, and emigrated thence to the
State of Missouri, where he achieved his distinction and
represented Missouri in the Senate of the United States
for thirty consecutive years, and while in the Senate was
without a superior.

MECKLENBURG DECLARATION OF INDE-
PENDENCE.

THERE are few events in our National history more conclusively established by circumstantial testimony than the Declaration of Independence by the patriots of the county of Mecklenburg, on the 20th of May, 1775. There is no event in the history of North Carolina of which her people are prouder, or which they cherish with more filial loyalty. There is no event in her history of which they are more jealous, or that they defend with more persistence or more stubbornness. It is not the earliest germ-seed of the Revolution. John Ashe, in the Stamp Party of Wilmington, defied the authority of Great Britain ten years before with his drawn sword. John Harvey defied its authority before the Mecklenburg Declaration by assuming the authority of the Governor and convoking a Revolutionary Assembly. These acts were heroic. But Mecklenburg's Declaration is more conspicuous because it has been more assailed and more defended. But no one now denies its authenticity, but an idiot or an enemy.

It was a great event in our history American blood had been shed at Lexington and Concord. There was a meeting of citizens of a mountain county in North Carolina, principally peopled by that heroic Scotch-Irish race that has always been foremost in the struggles of history, in the hazards of war and the enterprises of peace a race that has never turned its back on friend or foe, and that now, in time of peace, is doing more for North Carolina than any other in the State. These hardy mountaineers met in the county-town of Charlotte on the 19th day of May, to consider the situation of affairs between the American colonies and Great Britain. The convention was addressed by the leaders of the county, men of intelligence and influence. The fire of liberty spread like a contagion. Finally, it adjourned to meet again the next day.

On the next day, the ever memorable 20th of May the spirit of independence burst into flame. The patriot leaders and a large concourse of people assembled, passed patriotic resolutions of independence of Great Britain, recognized the authority of Congress, organized an independent civil and military government, and pledged their lives, fortunes and sacred honor to maintain it, and sent the resolutions to the American Congress at Philadelphia by a special messenger.

All this was done more than a year before the National Declaration of Independence, before the public sentiment of the country was ripe for independence, before any State had suggested independence, and at a time when the author of the National Declaration of Independence was not in favor of secession from Great Britain.

DECLARATION OF INDEPENDENCE BY THE CITIZENS OF MECKLENBURG COUNTY, NORTH CAROLINA, MAY 20, 1775.

"In conformity to an order issued by the Colonel of Mecklenburg County, in North Carolina, a Convention, vested with unlimited powers, met at Charlotte, in said county, on the 19th day of May, 1775, when Abraham Alexander was chosen Chairman, and John McKnitt Alexander Secretary. After a free and full discussion of the object of the Convention, it was unanimously

"*Resolved* I. That whosoever, directly or indirectly, abetted, or in any way, form or manner, countenanced the unchartered and dangerous invasion of our rights, as claimed by Great Britain, is an enemy to this country, to America, and to the inherent and inalienable rights of man.

"II. *Resolved*, That we, the citizens of Mecklenburg County, do hereby dissolve the political bands which have connected us to the mother country, and hereby absolve ourselves from all allegiance to the British crown, and abjure all political connection, contract or association with that nation who have wantonly trampled on our rights and liberties, and inhumanly shed the innocent blood of American patriots at Lexington.

"III. *Resolved,* That we do hereby declare ourselves a free and independent people, are, and of right ought to be, a sovereign and self-governing association, under the control of no power other than that of our God, and the general government of Congress; to the maintenance of which independence we solemnly pledge to each other our mutual co-operation, our lives, our fortunes, and our most sacred honor.

"Abraham Alexander, Chairman; J. M. Alexander, Secretary; Adam Alexander, Hezekiah Alexander, Ezra Alexander, Charles Alexander, Waitstill Avery, Ephraim Brevard, Hezekiah J. Balch, Richard Barry, John Davidson, William Davidson, Henry Downs, John Flenniken, John Ford, William Graham, James Harris, Robert Irwin, William Kennon, Matthew McClure, Neill Morrison, Samuel Martin, Duncan Ochletree, John Phifer, Thomas Polk, Ezekiel Polk, Benjamin Patton, John Queary, David Reese, Zacheus Wilson, Sr., William Wilson."

THE STAMP PARTY IN WILMINGTON.

No braver soldier ever yet drew sword.

THROUGH the whole history of North Carolina, the Cape Fear section has been the fruitful nursery of heroes, patriots and statesmen. Wilmington is its business centre, and Wilmington has always been the home of men who were foremost in the race of distinction. On the roll of her great names the Ashes, the Waddells, the Swanns, the Moores, the Hoopers, the Howes, and the Hills are familiar to all who feel a just pride in the good name of North Carolina.

Among all these illustrious names there is no one more distinguished than Gen. John Ashe. He was a son of John Baptista Ashe, the founder of this distinguished family in North Carolina. He had, for some years, been a leading member of the Colonial Assembly, and in 1762 was chosen Speaker of that body. He soon became the most prominent man in the colony, and, by his position, was the most influential.

He was entitled to the unique distinction of having been the harbinger of the Revolution in North Carolina, and probably in America, the first to resist the authority of Great Britain, the first to defy it by an overt act, the first to triumph over its officers, and the first to compel royal officials to sign an act of disobedience to the sovereign authority of England's King.

This bold act was done in open day, in the presence of the Governor backed with a royal force, and has no parallel in the history of those trying times of the Stamp Act troubles. It was a controversy over the old question of taxation without representation that roused the resistance of our Revolutionary fathers ten years later, and the matter of contention was the same—the imposition of a tax stamp on paper.

The heroic act was thus:

Houston was the Stamp Master of the British govern-

The Patriots of the Cape Fear boarding the British ships of war to demand a redress of grievances.

ment, an official representative of the government who was to have the custody of the stamped paper used for official purposes, and distribute it for use among the people. There was a tax on the paper, not onerous, but offensive to the American people because it was a tax that they had no voice in its enactment.

A large quantity of this paper was expected every day to arrive and be handed over to the Stamp Master. About the middle of November, 1765, Houston came to Wilmington, and Colonel Ashe led the people with drums beating and colors flying to his lodgings, and took him out and carried him to the court-house, where he was forced to sign a resignation of his office.

A few days later the stamps arrived in the sloop-of-war "Diligence," but as there was now no Stamp Master to receive them, they remained boxed up on board that ship.

Two months later, two merchant vessels coming into port, were seized by the sloop-of-war Viper, commanded by Captain Lobb, because their papers were not stamped, and they were held by the war vessels off old Brunswick, where Governor Tryon had his residence, and where the ships of war lay at anchor. Colonel Ashe, as Speaker of the House of Commons, had warned Governor Tryon that any attempt to enforce the Stamp Act would be resisted to death. The release of the captured vessels was at once demanded: Governor Tryon, after some delay, refused to release them. In the meantime, Ashe and his associates had perfected their plans. He called out the militia of New Hanover, and, being joined by Colonel Waddell and the Brunswick militia, and detachments from Bladen and Duplin, he marched to Old Brunswick, determined to put an end to that act of Parliament in this Province. Arriving at the Governor's mansion on the evening of the 19th of February, they informed Governor Tryon that they had come to redress their grievances, and demanded to see Captain Lobb. But Captain Lobb was not there. A detachment then pushed on to Fort Johnston, at Smithville, to seize that fort and get possession

of the cannon; but Lobb was able to spike the guns before
the fort was taken. At noon the next day the Governor
and Captain Lobb, and the King's officers, held a council
on board the ship-of-war "Diligence," and Captain Lobb
declared his determination never to surrender the captured
merchant ships. Two hours later, Ashe and a band of Patriots boarded the "Diligence," and there, under the royal
flag, surrounded by the King's forces, they demanded
that Captain Lobb should give up the vessels and abandon
his purpose to enforce the Stamp Act.

Their blood was up, and they were resolved to fight to
the death. Their undaunted spirit brooked no opposition.
Lobb was compelled to yield. Within three hours after
the agreement was made in the council of King's officers
to hold the captured vessels, the British commander surrendered them up into the hands of the Patriot leaders.

But that was not enough.

Ashe and the people had come with arms in their hands
to put an end to the Stamp Act, and the work was not yet
finished. They now proposed to make the crown officers
swear never to issue any stamp paper in this colony. The
first officer they demanded was Colonel Pennington, His
Majesty's Comptroller of Customs. Pennington was then
in the Governor's mansion, and Tryon sought to protect
him. But the mansion was thoroughly surrounded by
armed and determined men, and every avenue of escape
was cut off. Pennington resigned his office to the Governor, and surrendered himself, and took the oath the
Patriots dictated. And so also, Mr. Day, the Collector of
the Port, and all the county clerks and other crown officers
were required to swear never to issue or to use any stamp
paper in the Province.

This heroic act was revolutionary seed that sprouted
ten years later, and for seven years produced through blood
and suffering the glorious fruit of independence.

JIMMY SUTTON AND ADMIRAL COCKBURN.

Jimmie, Oh! Jimmie was a Rider

JOHN GILPIN's ride is known through the length and breadth of the land, but Jimmy Sutton's ride is unknown. The difference is that Gilpin is embalmed in English verse, and Sutton's rests on uncertain traditions; but the one is historic and the other poetic fancy.

Jimmy Sutton lived at Sandy Point, on Albemarle Sound. It is a long projection into the Sound, and commands a view to the east as far as the human eye can reach.

In August, 1814, Admiral Cockburn, of the British Navy, came into the inlet at Cape Henry, attacked the town of Hampton, and committed outrages upon its defenceless population that were without parallel in the annals of civilized warfare.

After desolating Hampton, he gave out word that he would next attack the sound and river towns of North Carolina. This was a feint to conceal his purpose of attacking Washington City, which he afterwards did, and in the war then raging between the United States and Great Britain he added another wreath to his crown of infamy.

The report, which reached Edenton and New Bern, that he intended to make these towns his objective points in the raging fight, together with his outrages at Hampton, created a panic in these towns that was without precedent. The first Mrs. Gaston, of New Bern, died from fright under the apprehension of his coming. The population of Edenton was wrought up to a pitch of fear and excitement unknown to them before.

Col. Duncan McDonald, a young officer but a born military man, called out the county militia, drilled them for the fray, mounted eight smooth-bore cannon, and prepared to resist the British fleet when it came into Edenton Bay.

Jimmy Sutton, a squatty-built farmer who lived at Sandy Point, on Albemarle Sound, was directed by Colonel McDonald to station himself on the point of projection of Sandy Point, and to be on watch day and night, and if in the distance on Albemarle Sound he should descry the approach of Admiral Cockburn's British fleet, he should immediately report the fact at headquarters at Edenton, at post-haste.

Jimmy was a kindly but eccentric man, but firm, loyal and true to his country. Colonel McDonald could not have selected a better man for the work assigned him. For two days he watched at the Point for the enemy, with his fleetest horse saddled and bridled in the woods near by.

On the morning of the third day he descried a small object that loomed in the distance. It was not larger than your hand, but it grew bigger, as did Jimmy's eyes. At length the masts developed, and then a fleet of vessels. Jimmy took one last look at them, and then, murmuring "Gunboats! British gunboats, by George!" he jumped through brake and briar for his horse, jumped in his saddle, yelling as he went, "The Admiral! the Admiral!" He put his horse on the run, yelling as he sped, "The Admiral! the Admiral!" It was a windy day, and as he hastened for Edenton his hat blew off. But on he went, not caring for his hat. Some of his neighbors ran out to see what was to pay. To his shouting, "The Admiral!" he was asked, "What Admiral?" He gave but one answer, "The Admiral!"

When he reached town after his Gilpin ride, the air was vocal with his shouts and the people were in great alarm. Colonel McDonald was mounting his cannon, and the women of the town were making their escape in every way.

While this scene of turmoil prevailed, six small oyster boats came up to the wharf, laden with the luscious bivalves, and quiet was restored. About the same time Admiral Cockburn was burning Washington and President Madison was making his escape from the President's house; and Jimmy Sutton's flight from six little oyster boats haunted him through life.

BATTLE OF GUILFORD COURT HOUSE.

Oh! History! what falsehoods are written in thy name.

History sometimes repeats itself, but oftener corrects itself. Napoleon once said that history was a fable, and we sometimes have thought that he who made more history than any other life, spoke truly. It really is melancholy to think of the fables of history, the inaccuracies of history, the omissions of history and its misrepresentations. North Carolina has been a great sufferer in that way; probably the greatest of all the original thirteen. Why this is so, we know not; but we have a theory that may, perhaps, account for it.

The history factories of our country have been Boston and Richmond. Boston's market for its historical wares has been the North, and Richmond's market has been the South. Boston has never cared anything about us, any way; probably all the greatest of the original thirteen, had a swollen head and a morbid State pride than caused Virginia to think that history and its heroes belonged to them, and North Carolina, being their next door neighbor, was absorbed, and all its historic laurels torn from her modest brow and wreathed around Virginia's avaricious crown.

Time bringeth all things right, but often wears leaden shoes, and is rather tardy in putting in its work. Time took a hundred years and more to write aright the history of the Regulators of Alamance and for that long time it allowed the history factories to brand the heroes of that earliest bugle note of the Revolution as lawless brigands, instead of heralding them truly as patriots, heroes and martyrs to the sacred cause of liberty.

So with the Mecklenburg Declaration of Independence. It was a hundred years before that immortal event in the history of North Carolina and the whole country was given its just place in the annals of this country. And to this day it is sometimes spoken of as apocryphal.

And now we are engaged in a manly struggle to maintain, from contemporary authority and proofs that are incontestable, that the Battle of Guilford Court House, on North Carolina's sacred soil, rendered the British surrender at Yorktown a "foregone conclusion," that the retreat of the North Carolina troops, after two steady rifle volleys, was a strategic movement, ordered by General Greene and carried out in good order and without confusion.

The Battle of Guilford Court House was the beginning of the end of the Revolutionary War. It was the pivotal battle of the war. It was the Gettysburg of the fight. The enemy fell into our victorious arms at Yorktown, with heart and backbone broken by their stunning blow at Guilford.

The action of the North Carolina troops at Guilford was a military strategy that Morgan had successfully used at the Battle of Cowpens, and had recommended to General Greene to be used at Guilford. The troops were militia, and they were ordered by General Greene to deliver a rifle volley into the ranks of the British when they made a bayonet charge and got within rifle range. They obeyed orders. They delivered two volleys, mortally wounding Colonel Webster, of the British Army, who was in command of the charging party, and mowing down his men like autumn leaves. They then retreated in good order, as ordered by General Greene.

Colonel Tarleton, of the British Army, who was in the road to the rear of Webster's Brigade, and witnessed the charge, says of it: "The order and coolness of that part of Webster's brigade which advanced across the open ground exposed to the enemy's fire, can not be sufficiently extolled. The militia allowed the front line to approach within 150 yards before they gave their fire."

The Battle of Guilford Court House was fought on Thursday, March 15, 1781, between the American forces under Major-General Greene and the English forces under Lord Cornwallis, and in its character and consequences was second to no battle of the Revolution.

Lee and Campbell, who participated in the fight on the American side, and have written about it, have written disparagingly of the North Carolina troops, who were in the front line of General Greene's army. But they were Virginians, and their testimony has been criticised and contradicted by so many witnesses that truth has overtaken it after the lapse of many years.

On Saturday before the battle, Greene writes to Governor Jefferson, of Virginia, explaining his plan of battle, and his expectancy of General Caswell of the North Carolina militia and Colonel Campbell with the Virginia Regulars; and upon their arrival he expected to "dispose of the army in such a manner as, at least, to encumber the enemy with a number of wounded men." In General Greene's correspondence he refers to General Pickens' command of North Carolinians as troops "on whose services he could depend on from day to day." Johnson, who adopts the Virginia disparagement of the North Carolina militia, in speaking of the battle of Hobkirk's Hill, which took place on the 25th day of April, more than a month after the Battle of Guilford, says: "The only militia force then with the army consisted of 254 North Carolinians; 150 of these, under Colonel Read, had joined Greene soon after he crossed the Dan, and had faithfully adhered to him from that time." These men were in the Battle of Guilford.

There were 1,640 North Carolina troops in the Battle of Guilford. These were militia and volunteers whose names are not mentioned on the muster rolls. They obeyed the orders of General Greene, discharged two volleys at the bayonet charge of the English, doing great slaughter, and then retreated as General Greene had ordered. These facts are well established, while it is as well established that a militia company commanded by Lee left the field without orders from General Greene. (See Schenck's North Carolina, 1780-81.)

6

JOHN STANLY.

An eye like Mars.
To threaten and command.

Few men have lived in North Carolina of more conspicuous natural endowments than John Stanly, of New Bern, who was disabled for many years by a stroke of paralysis while speaking on the floor of the House of Commons of North Carolina. That was in 1825, and he died in 1834.

In the obituary notice of Stanly, written by his great rival at the bar in North Carolina, William Gaston, gives a graphic account of the sad close of the career of one of the most gifted men that North Carolina has ever produced. He was for many years a member of the Legislature of North Carolina, and by his aggressive and outspoken vehemence and sarcasm, he held the rod over that body.

Mr. Stanly was especially an Eastern man, and he held a rod pickled in his sarcasm over the Western North Carolina delegation in the Legislature of North Carolina. He kept them all completely "hacked," until Bartlett Yancey, of Caswell County, a fearless, fiery and impetuous speaker, came on the stage as a Representative in the Legislature.

As a lawyer, Mr. Stanly held the highest rank in the State, but he was more noted as an advocate before the jury than as a jurist, and his forte of sarcasm and invective gave him great power.

The misfortune of his life was his killing Governor Speight in a duel. The dispute between Speight and Stanly arose from some political controversy, and Stanly was challenged by Governor Speight to mortal combat. The challenge was accepted and the arrangements made for the meeting. The hostile meeting took place on the suburbs of the town of New Bern. They stood back to back at ten paces apart, and wheeled and fired when the word was given. The town turned out *en masse*. Several ineffectual shots were exchanged. There were propositions made for an amicable settlement, but Speight was obstinate, and refused all propositions for settlement. At length Stanly aimed the fatal shot and Speight fell, mortally wounded. Speight was an old and distinguished man, and had befriended Stanly in his early manhood. His death was a blow to the happiness of Stanly, from which he never entirely recovered.

Mr. Stanly was a man of great resource in emergency. An incident of his readiness and adroitness in legislation is given by his contemporaries in the Legislature. General Lafayette visited the United States from France in 1825. He was the guest of the country, and the honors that were paid to him were an outpouring of gratitude for his services in achieving our independence. He came to North Carolina during his journey, and the leading members of the Legislature were anxious for an appropriation from the State Treasury to defray the expenses of his visit to North Carolina. There was some opposition to the appropriation from some parsimonious members. The friends of the bill thought it would pass if the ayes and nays were not called. The vote on the final passage was at hand. The stillness of death pervaded the Assembly. Stanly was in the chair as Speaker. When about to put the question, a western member in homespun garb arose and said: "Mr. Speaker, I call for the ayes and nays." The house was dumb, and an awful stillness prevailed. Stanly called Iredell, of Edenton, to the chair, and rising, cast his "cerulean" eye over the Assembly and said: "Mr. Speaker, I thank the gentleman for his motion. I, too, desire to put every member on record, so that if any one votes against this bill he may be gibbeted high up on the pillory of infamy." Every man voted aye.

GASTON AT THE UNIVERSITY COMMENCE-
MENT OF 1832.

A proud day.

THE address of William Gaston at the University of North Carolina at the Commencement of 1832 was an event in the literary history of North Carolina. Gaston's Address at the University, Choate's Eulogy on Daniel Webster at Dartmouth College, and Grady's Address at Boston, were the three greatest rostrum addresses of the nineteenth century, so far as we have heard or read. Gaston's address was the grandest of them all, and no other of them would have won from their audience a rapture that rose above demonstrative applause, as Gaston's did.

When Gaston came to the University to deliver the annual address before the Dialectic and Philanthropic Societies, by invitation of the latter Society, of which he was an honorary member, he was on the high middle ground of life, being 53 years old. He had won fame in Congress and in the General Assembly of North Carolina. He had a State and a National reputation, and when the Phi.'s were enabled by the abrogation of an agreement which had existed to invite only regular members of the two Societies to deliver the annual address, it was regarded as a great triumph over the Di.'s, as it was thought that they did not have an equal to Gaston on their roll of membership, and he was already regarded as the Commencement orator.

The appointment of Gaston drew a large concourse of visitors from all parts of the State; the largest, it was said, that ever attended a Commencement before, especially of the prominent and distinguished men of the State. Gaston came during the Commencement exercises, a day or two before the delivery of the address. He was the guest of Dr. Caldwell, the President of the University. He became at once the cynosure of all eyes. His manner was grave, courteous and unostentatious. He was affable with dignity and companionable without familiarity. He visited the libraries occasionally, and sometimes walked with Dr. Caldwell to his astronomical observatory, and we once saw him with the austere and dignified President, who was a man somewhat in stature like him who climbed the sycamore tree to see Christ, and Gaston of large and imposing person, and the thought flitted through our mind that "Bolus" looked smaller by the comparison.

As the big day of the Commencement came, expectation grew as the time approached. The June day was auspicious. The students were arrayed in their best. All the arrangements had been made. Tom Ashe, of Wilmington, had been selected by the Phi. Society to walk on one side of Gaston in the procession to Person Hall, where he was to speak, and Thomas L. Clingman, selected by the Di. Society, on the other. With some difficulty, we procured a scholar's black silk gown large enough for Gaston to wear.

The procession was formed at the old South Building. The Richmond Cornet Band was in front. Next came Gaston, the orator, costumed in a black silk gown. On one side of him was Tom Ashe, with the trained step of an English grenadier, with the proud and grand visage that bespake his lineage. On the other side was Clingman, awkward and gawky as a plowman's prentice boy, but with a brain that Webster and Cuvier might have envied. Next to them came the Trustees of the University, marching two and two. Next the Faculty, then the student body, and last the concourse of visitors.

The procession started from the "Old South," right-flanked to the "Old East," and, when opposite Person Hall, wheeled on the left and faced for the Hall, the band, meanwhile, blowing their spirit-stirring airs "like mad."

The head of the column reached the threshhold of the old chapel, which, in a thousand years, will be a shrine for literary pilgrims. There was then and there a momentary pause. Then Gaston, with the bearing of

old John Kemble, entered on the left and right of him
Ashe and Clingman; Ashe with a military bearing
that would have done honor to the hero of a thousand
battles, Clingman throwing out his legs right and left like
he was stiff-kneed, and looking for all the world like he
thought all the crowd was looking at him, and that Gaston and Ashe were mere small kites dangling at his tail,
to give pomp to his pageantry. But "old Billy" had the
brains.

They marched to the rostrum, and as they were taking
their seats near a little table on which Gaston was about
placing his manuscript, Clingman, in moving his awkward
legs, knocked the table over, and but for Ashe's readiness,
the table, and perhaps Gaston himself, would have gone
sprawling on the floor below.

The Trustees followed, and with the Faculty, headed by
"old Bolus," took their seats on the rostrum like "potent,
grave and reverend seignors." The Seniors of the graduating class followed and took their accustomed seats, that
they were about to vacate forever for the rosy drama of
life. Then the Juniors, then the Sophs., and lastly the
Fresh., proudest of them all, because they were incipient
Sophs. and had thrown off the Freshman's toga.

The Fresh. had hardly taken their accustomed seats in
the chapel when the crowd of visitors broke ranks, as if
in panic, all pressing forward in eager haste to get seats
in the chapel. It was a madding crowd, heaving and
setting in a frantic mass that beggars description. Beavers were lifted above the crowd of surging humanity.
Beavers were crushed. Men were lifted from their feet
and borne along by the struggling and compact mass. They
were an hour pushing, tussling, heaving and setting to get
in and get seats. Tears of perspiration ran down their
rugged cheeks, and passion was painted on every lineament of that heaving mob. While they were heaving
near the door, we, a Freshman, full of admiration for
greatness, crept up to a standing place in the aisle near the
speaker, and waited there, standing within ten feet of
him.

At length the mob subsided and got standing places, and there was a great calm. The hall was jammed and crammed. Jack Haughton, of Tyrrell, a Senior friend, and we, stood near together, and gave the speech a rapt attention during the hour and twenty minutes of its delivery.

It was a grand effort, the grandest that Gaston ever made, and should now be in the hands of every school boy and every man of generous aspirations in the State. It should go down the generations as the companion piece of his State anthem—"The Old North State." It should be taught in our schools. It should be committed to memory in classes. It should be declaimed on our school boards. It should be adopted as a classic in our lessons of elocution. It would make us better boys, better men, better scholars, more accomplished gentlemen.

THE LAST OF THE ROMANS.

The Grand Old Man.

Mr. Jefferson said of Nathaniel Macon that he was the last of the Romans. John Randolph said in his will, he was the wisest man he had ever known. Mr. Benton speaks of him, in his "Thirty Years in the Senate," as his counsellor and friend in public life. Mr. Macon has passed into history as one of the purest and most incorruptible statesmen that has ever been on the stage of public life in these United States. He was a type of the old North Carolina character in the earlier and better days of the State. He was plain, straightforward and had great simplicity of character. His simplicity amounted to eccentricity. He was morally and physically courageous. He drew his knife to defend Mr. Randolph from personal assault in a theatre in Philadelphia. Against the unanimous sentiment of Congress and the people, he refused to vote for an appropriation in Congress to pay the traveling expenses of General Lafayette, when he visited this country in 1826 as the guest of the Nation. He was simple in his manners, ways, conversation and deportment. He wished his family and grandchildren to call him "Meekins," insisting that Macon was called Meekins by the old people, and they called him so until one of his devil boys, Bob, said to him at his table, "Grandpa Meekins, will you have some of the beekins" (bacon). He was elected to the General Assembly of North Carolina from Warren County when he was a private in the Revolutionary Army, with a musket on his shoulder. When his election was announced to him, he told the messenger that they meant somebody else, and refused the office until its acceptance was urged upon him by Governor Caswell. When he came to Raleigh in 1835 as a member of the Convention, Miss Betsy Gaddis, who kept a boarding-house for members of the Assembly, and with whom he had boarded when a young man in the Assembly, called to see him and embraced him. Mr. Macon did not know her at first, but after awhile he said that he remembered her, that "she made the best grog he ever drank." In the Convention of 1835, in a lull in the debate on the Catholic disability clause of the old Constitution, he called Jo Rhoullac, of Bertie, to the chair, and addressed the body on the subject. The danger of the Roman Catholic religion to our secular institutions had been much mentioned. Mr. Macon favored the removal of the disability, and among other things said, with great simplicity: "Gentlemen say they fear the Catholics will swallow up our liberties. There is some danger of it, but there's more danger of a mouse swallowing a buffalo;" and then he added, "I am not a member of any church, but I sometimes attend the Baptist and feel pretty sure the Baptists would swallow them before they swallowed our liberties."

We are probably now the only living North Carolinian who has a distinct impression of Mr. Macon's personality, and we are often applied to for information about him. We saw him once in 1831, when a boy of fifteen, in Warrenton at a Fourth-of-July banquet. Mr. Macon was then about eighty, and was evidently the "big dog in the pit" and a favorite of the people. He talked familiarly with any and everybody. He had on a chip hat and homespun plain clothes, with a long vest that covered his abdomen. They called him "Uncle Nat." Some one asked him where he got his hat from. He replied that his overseer's wife made it for him.

We next saw him for ten consecutive days as presiding officer of the Convention of 1835. He was then about eighty-three, apparently vigorous and having but little the marks of senility. His hair was short cut, not fleecy white, but a light sandy gray. He was apparently about 5 feet 8 inches in height; weight apparently about 165; complexion blonde, inclined to rosy. Dress, a brownly white suit of linen thread of apparently domestic manufacture. His eyes were gray, inclined to blue. He was stocky built; his eye was not dim, and his natural force

was well preserved. He was clean shaved. He was always
in his place, and did not vacate his place but once in the
ten days we attended the Convention in the Presbyterian
church, in Raleigh, and that was during the debate on the
thirty-second article of the old Constitution, above referred to.

BETSY DOWDY'S RIDE.

HISTORICAL TRADITIONS OF THE BATTLE AT GREAT BRIDGE.

"O, woman, timid as a child,
When skies are bright, serene and mild;
Let evil come, with angry brow,
A lion-hearted hero thou."

THE winter of 1775 was a dark and gloomy time for
the Revolutionary patriots of North Carolina. Governor
Tryon had left his "palace" in New Bern, secretly and
hurriedly had taken refuge on board the armed schooner
"Cruizer," and was stationed at the mouth of the Cape
Fear River, issuing orders, fortifying the Tory feeling
in the Colony, and inciting the slaves to servile insurrec-
tion. Lord Dunmore had been driven from Williamsburg, Va., by popular indignation, and had gone down to
Norfolk and intrenched himself there. From this position he was annoying the adjacent sections of Virginia
by hostile raids, and was expected to make incursions into
the adjacent sections of Carolina. The death of John
Harvey, of Perquimans County, in June, 1775, had cast
a gloom over the Colony, and especially over the northeast-
ern counties, where his patriotism and manly virtues were
best known. But the fires of liberty were kept burning.
Dunmore, with a few regulars who had accompanied him
in his flight from Williamsburg, Va., had ravaged Suf-
folk and some other places, and was preparing to extend
his ravages to the Albemarle section of Carolina. Our
leading men were on the alert, and couriers were keeping

Betsy Dowdy's ride.

them in close touch. John Harvey, of Perquimans, had joined his fathers across the great divide, but his mantle had fallen upon his kinsman and connection by marriage, Gen. William Skinner, of Yeopim Creek, and he was watching every movement of Dunmore. Col. Isaac Gregory, of Camden, was hurrying with a small militia force to join our Col. Robert Howe and meet the enemy at Great Bridge, in Virginia. Tom Benbury, of Chowan, then Speaker of the lower house of the General Assembly, had left his luxurious home at "Benbury Hall," that overlooked Albemarle Sound, and was hurrying to join the troops under Howe, with commissary stores. Excitement ran high, and the expected invasion of the Albemarle counties, and the probable collision at Great Bridge, where Dunmore was intrenched, was the universal subject of conversation. Howe was pushing by forced marches to the aid of Virginia with some regulars and the Hertford County militia under Colonel Wynns of that county. Public expectation was on tiptoe.

Joe Dowdy and old man Sammy Jarvis lived on the "banks" opposite to Knott's Island. They were near neighbors and intimate friends. Early in December, 1775, Jarvis went over to the "main" to hear the news of Colonel Howe's movement toward Great Bridge. When he returned home, late in the evening, he was greatly excited. He was impressed with the dangerous situation of the dwellers by the sea. He was constantly saying, "Dunmore and them blamed Britishers will come down the coast from Norfolk and steal all our 'banks' stock and burn our houses, ding 'em." After a short rest and a hasty bite of supper, old man Jarvis went over to Dowdy's to tell him the news.

Dowdy was a wrecker for the money that was in it, and a fisher for the food that was in it. He was always watching the sea. He was a devout man, always prayed for the safety of the poor sailor who was exposed to the perils of the deep, and always closed with a silent supplication that if there should be a wreck, it might be on the

Currituck beach. He had prospered in the business of
a wrecker, had saved many lives and much wreckage and
money. His visible store of chattels was beef cattle and
banker ponies. He herded them by the hundreds.

Uncle Sammy came in without ceremony and was cordially received. "Well, Uncle Sammy," said Dowdy,
"what are the news; tell us all." "Well, Joseph," said
Jarvis, "things is fogerty. Gregory, Colonel Isaac, is
hurrying up his Camden milish to join Howe, and Tom
Benbury, of Chowan, is pushing on his wagons of com-
missaries. If they don't reach Great Bridge in time to
bear a hand in the fight, they'll hurry on to Norfolk and
drive Dunmore out of the old town. But if Dunmore
beats our folks at Great Bridge then our goose is cooked,
and our property is all gone, all the gold and goods saved
in our hard life-work, and all our cattle and marsh ponies." "You don't tell me," said Dowdy. "Yes, it's so,
just as sure as 'old Tom.' The only thing that can save
us is General Skinner, of Perquimans, and the militia,
and he is too far away. We can't get word to him in
time." As Jarvis said these words slowly and with emphasis, Betsy Dowdy, Joe Dowdy's young and pretty
daughter, who was present with the family, said: "Uncle
Sammy, do you say the British will come and steal all our
ponies?" "Yes," said he. She replied: "I'd knock 'em
in the head with a conch shell first." Betsy soon left the
room. She went to the herding pen, and Black Bess was
not there. She then went to the marsh and called aloud,
"Bess! Bessie! Black Beauty!" The pretty pony heard
the old familiar voice and came to the call. Betsy took
her by her silk'n mane, led her to the shelter, went into the
house, brought out a blanket and also a small pouch of
coin. She placed the blanket on the round back of the
pony, sprang into the soft seat and galloped over the hills
and far away on her perilous journey. Down the beach
she went, Black Bess doing her accustomed work. She
reached the point opposite Church's Island, dashed into
the shallow ford of Currituck Sound and reached the

shore of the island. On they sped, Black Bess gaining new impulse from every kind and gentle word of Betsy. The wonderful endurance of the banker pony never failed, and Black Bess needed no spur but the cheering word of her rider. "Bessie, pretty Bess; my black, sleek beauty, the British thieves shan't have you. We are going after General Skinner and his milish. They'll beat 'em off of you." She almost sang to the docile pony as they went on their journey. Through the divide, on through Camden, the twinkling stars her only light, over Gid. Lamb's old ferry, into Pasquotank by the "Narrows" (now Elizabeth City), to Hartsford, up the highlands of Perquimans, on to Yeopim Creek, and General Skinner's hospitable home was reached. The morning sun was gilding the tree tops when she entered the gate. She was hospitably welcomed, and when she briefly told the story of her coming, cordial kindness followed. The General's daughters, the toast of the Albemarle, Dolly, Penelope and Lavinia, made her at home. He listened to her tale of danger and promised assistance.

Midday came, and with it Betsy's kind farewell. Filial duty bade her, and she hied her home. As she neared her sea-girt shore the notes of victory were in the air. "They are beaten, beaten, beaten, they are beaten at Great Bridge." The reports materialized as she went. The battle at Great Bridge had been fought and won. Howe had assumed command of the Virginia and Carolina troops upon his arrival, and was in hot pursuit of Dunmore toward Norfolk, where, after a short resistance, Norfolk was evacuated by the British troops, who sought refuge on board their ships, and, after a few cannon shot into the town, they departed for parts unknown.

Then, and long after, by bivouac and camp fire and in patriotic homes was told the story of Betsy Dowdy's Ride.

WHAT I KNOW ABOUT SHOCCO JONES.

Great wit to madness nearly is allied,
And thin partitions do the bounds divide.
—*Pope.*

LEAVING out the early chronicle of Lawson, we have had four formal histories of North Carolina, Lawson's being an account of his journeyings through the country, and the history written by Joseph Seawell Jones, of Warren County, North Carolina, being called "Jones' Defence of North Carolina." "Shocco" was a pseudonym, adopted probably because he was born near Shocco Springs, in Warren County, N. C., a place of fashionable resort then, and for some years after. Jones was a young man, full of enthusiasm, with an intellect of brilliant rather than substantial type, with eccentricity on the border line of insanity, sometimes considered the genuine article, and with a love of the sensational, which was the ruling passion of his soul. With the addition of that passion by which Wolsey and the "angels fell," you have a pen picture of a North Carolinian of the olden times, who filled a large space in the public eye of the State, and whose sad history was a romance and a failure.

"Jones' Defence of North Carolina" was a development of the period. Dr. Williamson's History of North Carolina had been a failure as a history and not a success as a medical disquisition upon the fevers of Eastern North Carolina.

Xavier Martin's History succeeded Williamson's, and but for his removal from the State in the first years of the nineteenth century, and the subsequent loss of his historical materials, his history would have supplied a great want.

Then came a long interval of quiescence about the State history, and its first revival was by the publication of some accounts referring to the Mecklenburg Declaration. It attracted considerable attention in the State, and the subject was given a new interest by the publication of a correspondence between ex-Presidents John Adams and

Thomas Jefferson, in which correspondence Mr. Jefferson had charged that the Mecklenburg Declaration was a fraud, and in connection with it had made some unjust imputations upon the patriotism and loyalty of the North Carolina representatives in the Congress of the Revolution. It excited a furor in the State. It touched our patriotism at the nerve centre. In this tide of popular sentiment of North Carolina, "Shocco" Jones was thrown upon the top of the wave of public indignation. He was fashionably connected, an habitue of the elite society of Shocco Springs, a native of the historic county of Warren, young, ardent and aggressive, and with an individuality of the most eccentric character. Voluble to a degree, his progress was not handicapped by modesty. The man and the occasion met. Jones had literary instincts, ambition, culture to some extent, and surely Mr. Jefferson was an antagonist worthy of his steel. He had the social feeling inordinately, travelled much, knew everybody, and wished to know everybody else, and his purpose to launch a shaft at the memory of the Sage of Monticello became widely known. He became a pet of the distinguished men in North Carolina, and men whose lineage ran back to the foundation of the State were fired by his patriotic enthusiasm, and made him the custodian of their valuable family records, which he had no talent for preserving. It was proclaimed that he would prove that Mr. Jefferson was a plagiarist and that he had the resolutions of Mecklenburg County on his table when he wrote the National Declaration of Independence.

"Jones' Defence" appeared, and it added fresh fuel to the flame of patriotism. It did not give entire satisfaction to the mature judgment of the State. Some said it was inaccurate in statement, and others that it was too "efflorescent in diction," but it fired the youthful mind and was the basis of many a college essay and declamation.

PERSONAL RECOLLECTIONS.

About the time that the "Defence" made its appearance, or while in the throes of expectancy, we were a Freshman or Sophomore at the University, and the news spread through the College that "Shocco" Jones was in the village and had come through the campus riding upon the shoulders of a stalwart negro. We were the librarian of the Philanthropic Society and on duty when the news reached us. Soon after, there came into the Library Hall a man, swarthy, tall, long-haired, wild-eyed, who introduced himself as Jo. Seawell Jones, of Shocco. He was attended by several students. The conversation was led by Mr. Jones, and soon it fell into the subject of his "Defence of North Carolina." His whole soul seemed absorbed in the subject. He was unsparing in his denunciations of Mr. Jefferson. He stated that he was then engaged in preparing a "Picturesque History of North Carolina," to follow the "Defence of North Carolina." We suppose now that he meant an "Illustrated History of North Carolina," as he casually referred to some of the historic scenes on Roanoke Island.

We neither saw nor heard any more of "Shocco" Jones, except occasional mention of his being in Washington, and his prominence in society circles, until about 1836. Meanwhile his "Defence of North Carolina" had been generally read, and it had various comments. It became a pyre at which the torch of patriotism was fired.

About 1836 it was reported in North Carolina that "Shocco" Jones had been involved in an angry personal dispute in Rhode Island, with a citizen of that State, about the Revolutionary history of North Carolina, which had resulted in a challenge from Jones to the field of honor. The challenge was said to have been accepted, and the fight was to come off at an early date. In a short time came a proclamation from the Governor of Rhode Island, forbidding the violation of the peace within the bounds of Rhode Island. A counter proclamation was promptly issued by Jones, in which he intimated that the fight could be had across the little State of Rhode Island without violating its laws. Meanwhile the public mind of North Carolina was on the *qui vive* of expectancy.

While the public interest was at its height, a Scotch schoolmaster of the town of Edenton, named McLochlin, raw, credulous, sympathizing, came from Norfolk, Va., by the canal-stage route to his home in Edenton. The stage stopped at the "Half-Way House" for dinner. While McLochlin was at dinner, there came from an inside door a man, wild-looking, haggard, nervous, abstracted, and took a seat beside him. He confided to McLochlin's credulous ear the story of the fatal duel he had just fought on the Virginia line, where he had killed his adversary, and all for North Carolina. He said he was pursued by the officers of the law, showed him a handkerchief saturated with blood with which he had staunched the blood of his dying adversary, begged his help in this time of his greatest need, asked McLochlin if there was any one in Edenton who would shelter a man who had shed the blood of his enemy for North Carolina. Jones took his new friend to a private room, where he opened the tale of the tragedy. After long deliberation, the name of Hugh Collins was suggested as the friend of the distressed. Oh, yes! Jones knew him well. Had met him in Washington society circles. The very man!

It was arranged that McLochlin should go on to Edenton, go at once to Hugh Collins, who was then fishing a large seine at the old Sandy Point fishery, and get him to meet Jones at the arrival of the stage in Edenton next day. McLochlin hied him home. Jones remained in hiding.

Jones came to Edenton next day. Collins was in waiting. Damon and Pythias were not more cordial than "Hugh" and "Shoc." A carriage was in waiting. Both were hurried in and off, and with rapid speed they were taken to the safe retreat of Sandy Point beach. When they arrived, Jones, for greater safety, asked Collins to put out pickets to provide against surprise and to keep his private yacht manned with four stalwart oarsmen, ready at a moment's notice to take Jones to the southern shore of Albemarle Sound. "Hugh," full of the responsibility of his great charge, had everything ready as requested. The oarsmen never left their rowlocks. After a few days Jones came out from hiding, and for ten days no man in North Carolina has been more lionized, petted and feasted. Jack Leary, a veteran wealthy seine fisherman, banqueted him with great and bounteous honor. Thomas Benbury, the oldest fisherman on the sound, claimed him as his honored guest. Others followed. If Jones had asked for $100,000, we believe he could have had an honored check for it in half an hour.

After some time spent in this round of festivity and honor, Jones went to Mississippi, where he hobnobbed with Sargent S. Prentis, "whom he had introduced into good society at Washington." Finally, in the wilds of Texas, in the days of the old Texan wars with Mexico, he died, a hermit, alone, deserted, unknown—with all his eccentricities, a patriot, a lover of his old home, having done some good in his day and generation, and left a name among its historians.

GOVERNOR JOHN M. MOREHEAD.

Good name in man and woman. dear my lord,
Is the immediate jewel of their souls
                                        —*Othello.*

GOVERNOR MOREHEAD, of Greensboro, was a typical,
representative North Carolinian. He was poised, conservative, unpretentious and plain. Large in person, dignified in bearing, courteous in deportment, he had the
"guinea stamp" of nature's nobility. We imagine he
was not a man of early educational advantages, and we
think he was not an alumnus of the University. We received that impression from hearing his inaugural address
as Governor in the capitol at Raleigh, after his election over
Gen. Romulus M. Saunders in the famous Harrison campaign of 1840. We were a younger man then than now,
and thought the whole educational duty of man was to know
the proper construction of a grammatical sentence and to
explain the difference between "done" and "did," and Governor Morehead, in his inaugural address, rose above the
littleness of tweedledum and tweedledee. It was an able
speech, strong, patriotic and masterful, but not elegant.

We did not then make allowance for the school of the
campaign with General Saunders, from which he had
recently emerged, and which had taught him that strength
was stronger than elegance. General Saunders was the
roughest of rough diamonds, and his phillipics were just
on the temperate side of the "cuss" belt.

In the campaign of 1840, Morehead was the Whig candidate, and Saunders the Democratic, and in Edenton,
before a cultured audience of ladies and gentlemen, there
was a dramatic scene in the court-house, in which Morehead was in the act of rebaptising Saunders with a huge
pitcher of water, in response to his inelegant language
of vituperation, and would have accomplished it but for
the timely interposition of friends who were sitting on
the platform with them.

Governor Morehead was a patriotic and influential citizen of North Carolina. His judgment was clear and his convictions courageous. His heart always beat true to the State and all its interests. He left a name of highest character and usefulness, at the mention of which our hearts have a warmer heart-beat of pride and gratitude.

While Governor Morehead was in active life, the popular cry and aspiration of all the leaders of thought in North Carolina was the building of a railroad running from the mountains to the seaboard of North Carolina at Beaufort harbor. The idea was first started by Dr. Joseph Caldwell about the year 1824.

The Doctor had travelled in Europe in the interest of the University in that year, and had witnessed the origin of railroad construction. He was a cold, cool, calculating man, and weighed things in icy scales before he endorsed them. He saw the beginning of the railroad era, saw the beginning of them in practical operation, and he came home thoroughly aroused to their great value in the development of new countries, and especially helpful to North Carolina.

Over the name of "Carleton," he published in the *Raleigh Register* and other State papers a series of railroad articles, urging the importance of a road running through the State from west to east and terminating at Beaufort harbor. The ablest and most influential leaders of the State welcomed the idea, took hold of it in a half-hearted way, talked about and spoke in public about it. It was the dream of a generation. But nothing of a practical character was done about it for many years.

The honor of giving a practical impulse to that patriotic State enterprise is due to William S. Ashe, of the distinguished Ashe family of Wilmington, who introduced in the Senate of North Carolina a bill chartering the North Carolina Railroad and giving State aid to the amount of two millions to that great object. This bill passed both houses of the General Assembly, and Governor Morehead then threw his whole energy into accomplishing the work, building it from Charlotte to Goldsboro. Later, Governor Morehead applied himself to giving full effect to Dr. Caldwell's idea of connecting the mountains and the sea.

What had long been the dream of Carolina's most distinguished and patriotic sons became a reality to him. The people looked to him as the great leader of public thought in practical matters. The people listened to him gladly, and his counsels fell upon good ground and produced its fruits. He rode down the contemplated road, worked up an enthusiasm that it had never known before, planted in the minds of the population along the route new seeds for contemplation that grew up, and in time Governor Morehead saw his work fully under way, and saw a new town started in Beaufort harbor that bore his name and was consecrated to his memory.

The good work inaugurated by our great Governor, and partly accomplished by him, has never yet emptied into the lap of North Carolina the rich fruits which at first were so confidently predicted; but in the cycles of time, in which a thousand years are as but a day, the time will come when a united North Carolina, with universal acclaim, will rise up as one man to bless anew the revered name of John M. Morehead.

AN EVENING WITH WILLIAM GASTON.

His life was gentle; and the elements
So mixed in him, that Nature might stand up.
And say to all the world, *This was a man.*
                                        —*Julius Cæsar.*

MATURED greatness has no feature more beautiful, and no ornament more attractive and graceful, than a condescending and amiable attention to youth. It is the Corinthian column of the Gothic temple, inviting by its graceful proportions the approach of its youthful votary in the flush of enthusiastic devotion. Without it, greatness is less great, and learning less comely; Hercules with his club, inspiring awe, but repelling affection. "Like some old tower dimly seen by starlight, it leaves the impression of power akin to the terrific and sublime; but wants the mild and softening light of this absent grace to make it lovely to the contemplation and dear to the heart."

Trusting to your defense from the charge of egotism, I will venture to incur the imputation by relating an incident connected with William Gaston, illustrative of his genial and kindly nature, which occurred at an early period of my life, when I had but recently divested my youthful habiliments, and had scarcely yet accommodated myself with becoming dignity to the *toga virilis* of American manhood.

Not very long after the Convention of 1835, I chanced to visit the city of Raleigh while the Supreme Court was in session in company with a young friend; and being detained longer than we had anticipated, I determined, if a suitable occasion presented, to turn the detention to account by satisfying what had long been a wish ungratified, of forming the personal acquaintance of William Gaston.

When a mere boy I had received a kind of parenthetical introduction to the great man, during a moment of leisure, while he was engaged in the trial of some cause before the Supreme Court, of which he was then an

attorney; but I did not feel justified in renewing my acquaintance, after the lapse of several years, upon the basis of such an impromptu introduction.

As my youth ripened into manhood, this ungratified wish had grown until it had become, indeed, an ardent passion of my heart. It was natural.

It had been my good fortune to witness the exhibition of his wondrous power in some of its sharpest intellectual conflicts, and its most signal intellectual triumphs; to witness it at that most impressible period of life when the heart, alive to every sympathy, yields its spontaneous homage to the magic mastery of genius.

When, on my way to college, an aspirant to the honors of Freshmanship, I tarried a little in Raleigh: not as at Jericho, "until my beard should grow," for that would have detained me too long—but in order to keep company with a party of "gay young fellows" who were going up the same way I was, and who persuaded me to wait and join them and have a nice time altogether.

The Legislature was in session. All Raleigh was aflame. Legislative combinations had been formed, and antagonistic elements had been moulded into a homogeneous mass to remove the capitol and rob her of her birthright.

For want of something to do, I spent much of my time in the lobby of the Governor's house, then used as a temporary legislative hall, in consequence of the destruction of the capitol by fire. It was then and there I first observed William Gaston. He was the centre of general attention, the cynosure of all eyes. So distinct is my recollection of him, I can see him now, as it were yesterday, sitting in front, a little to the left of the Speaker's chair, a grand old man, just touching the verge of venerable age, with finely chiseled, classic features, calm, contemplative thoughtful brow, and manly person: the scholarly stoop increasing rather than marring the effect of the *tout ensemble*. Personation of intellectual intelligence.

"A combination, and a form, indeed,
  Where every god did seem to set his seal,
  To give the world assurance of a man."

I heard both his speeches upon the "appropriation bill," as it was then called; the bill which raised the question of the removal of the seat of government from Raleigh. His second speech was a master-piece of brilliant, elaborate, finished oratory. It was the first great speech to which I had ever listened, and I was borne on the top of the tide of admiration with which it was universally received. That speech, unfortunately, is not now preserved, and its reputation rests upon the insecure traditions of those who are fast passing away.

His first speech was a *ruse de guerre;* what, in the language of Isaac Walton, would be "a bait for a nibbler"; in fowling phrase, "a coy duck"; in the language of the "ring," a "feint," to be followed by a stunning blow. It was a good speech, not remarkable; going just far enough, and not too far, for its purpose; sometimes leaving a "castle exposed," and then carrying the war barely far enough to say "check your queen."

There sat his antagonist, a dangerous man, an adversary not to be trifled with, who, by the preconcerted arrangement of his party friends, was the champion who was not to expend his ammunition upon small birds, but to reserve his fire for the larger game.

> "His hook was baited with a dragon's tail,
> He sat upon a rock and bobbed for whale."

According to legislative etiquette, it was said that Gaston was entitled to reply to this keen sportsman; why, I do not know, not being learned in parliamentary dialectics; but it was apparent that his antagonist was determined not to move until Gaston showed his hand.

After the conclusion of Gaston's first speech, the member from Fayetteville proceeded to his work with the consummate skill of an accomplished dialectician, using with admirable dexterity all the weapons of his well-furnished armory, dissecting and eviscerating his opponent, to the infinite satisfaction of himself and his friends. But Gaston's rejoinder gave him a Roland for his Oliver, and made Raleigh the permanent seat of government of North Carolina.

I next saw William Gaston about a year later upon the literary rostrum, and heard his admirable address to the graduating class at the University; an address which has become a recognized standard of its class of literature, and which, apart from its wise and salutary counsel, may be studied to advantage by those who wish to acquire "an English style, familiar but not coarse, elegant but not ostentatious."

I next heard him, a few years later, upon perhaps the most memorable occasion of his life. It was in the Convention of 1835, in the debate upon what is known as the "thirty-second article." That discussion enlisted not only his patriotic, but his most earnest personal sympathies. One of the objects for which the Convention had been called was to consider the propriety of removing this article from the Constitution of the State. Although inoperative, it was regarded as a blur upon the charter, an odious imputation, if not a political disfranchisement of a meritorious class of citizens for their religious opinions; and it was pointed to by the envious detractors of Gaston, who had high office under the Constitution with that article in it, as proof that his lust of place was stronger than his sense of honor.

With these considerations weighing upon him, he arose to address an assembly distinguished for wisdom, gravity and age, and for two days bound them as with a spell by a production which, in all that can convince the understanding, charm the senses or move the heart, is unsurpassed in the annals of uninspired eloquence.

I am altogether unable to convey an idea of the impression made upon my mind, then just budding into maturity, by that great effort. "Demosthenes for the crown," "Cicero against Cataline," were familiar from recent study; "Burke against Warren Hastings" had been the delight of my boyhood; "Webster in reply to Hayne" was yet ringing throughout the length and breadth of the land; but they had all failed to tell me what "the Old Man Eloquent" signified. Never till then did I know what Gray meant when he sang,

" The applause of listening Senates to command."

Not till then did I know the gift which

" Touched Isaiah's hallowed lips with fire."

Not till then the wand which genius waves over men. It is now more than a third of a century since my heart-chords were swept by that master-hand; and many a touch from eloquent lips since then those chords have felt, but they vibrate still with the notes of that wondrous melody, and will vibrate ever

"—till my last of lines are penned
And life's hopes, joys and sorrows at an end."

The companion of my casual visit to Raleigh, above alluded to, was the fortunate heir of one of Gaston's old friendships, and had received many proofs of his friendly regard. In one of his visits during our sojourn, he observed that he had a young friend with him who was a warm admirer of his, and, if agreeable, he would be glad to introduce him at some moment of leisure.

"Make my respects," said Gaston politely, "and I shall be pleased to see you both at my office this evening at 8 o'clock."

Prompt to the time "as lovers to their vows," we presented ourselves at the appointed place, and I was formally introduced to him whose magic power had wakened first my youthful dream of glory.

We found there with Gaston a distinguished citizen of the State; a man who, under any other circumstances and other association, would have been a recognized great man; one to whom nature had been niggard of her gifts of physical graces, but to whom an ample atonement had

been made for an ungainly person by bestowing some of
her rarest intellectual gems and imparting to them addi-
tional lustre by contrast with the rough ore in which they
had been cast.

But all greatness is comparative. He bore to Gaston
the same relation, to use the language of the smithery,
that an excellent "striker" does to the head blacksmith.
And most opportunely for us was he there. For without
him, who would have done the *striking?* Without him,
the evening, instead of being to us a life-memory, would
have been a dumb show, performed by one player and
two mutes. But as it was, we had a most brilliant performance, a kind of duet, one playing upon "a harp of a
thousand strings," and the other striking the triangle
with musical taste and judgment.

If this opportune friend was there by invitation, from
kindness to us, it was most kind; if there by invitation
to take part in the exercises, it was most considerate of
some one's reputation; if there by accident, it was most
fortunate.

The conversation was at first upon general topics, the
proceedings of the Legislature, then in session; the effect
of certain measures then under consideration; the character of its members, with occasional reference to those who
had been prominent in the past legislative history of the
State; the practical operation and effect of certain amend-
ments to the Constitution made by the Convention of
1835 and then but recently adopted; the growing tendency
of our people to abandon their calm, conservative character, and to be carried away by the wild strife of political
parties, and which, at the moment, impressed me with the
idea that he was not quite up with the progressive spirit of
the age.

His style of conversation was peculiarly attractive:
easy, graceful, tasteful and unostentatious; sometimes
addressing himself to us and making us feel that we were
a part, though not *magna pars*, of the performance. Our
friend who came so opportunely, bestowed upon us, too,

an occasional look from the corner of his eye, as if saying, "and what are you doing here, you spalpeens?"

From an examination of the characteristics of our own people, and comparison of their social condition with that of the population of some of our sister States, resulting from the influence of long-continued strife, the conversation passed, by natural connection, to an examination of the condition, peculiarities and institutions of those States.

Gaston had passed the preceding summer in a lengthened tour through the Northern States and Canada, and the conclusions at which he had arrived from personal observation, and his description of natural scenery, were exceedingly interesting.

Niagara Falls had long been a living picture to my mind: by fancy, by personal description, and by the painter and the poet's art. I had read innumerable descriptions of it: from Halleck's grand anthem (I think it is Halleck's) to him of the shears and goose,

> " Who had but one unending note,
> Gods, what a place to sponge a coat!"

But none like Gaston's had impressed my mind so forcibly with the grandeur of this great work of the Omnipotent; none had been so easy, so natural, so grand and yet so simple, so like the great work itself. His graphic description impressed an animal vitality into the storied stream, as with easy self-possession he pictured the placid water moving smoothly on, and, just at the brink of the precipice, making a pause, as if unexpectedly encountering a foe it could not conquer, and then writhing in the agony of a moment's desperate determination before taking the awful plunge.

He related an incident of the effect produced upon an untutored mind by this stupendous work of nature. He met at the falls an old college class-mate whom he had not seen for many years—Judge Berrien, of Georgia—accompanied by his two daughters and a faithful old family servant whom the young ladies called "Mammy."

"We had all," said Gaston, "been standing for some time near the cataract, gazing in silence upon the mighty work. The silence was broken by the old servant.

" 'Missis,' said she to one of the young ladies, 'how long has this water been running here?'

" 'Since the foundation of the world, Mammy.'

"And then pausing for a moment, the old woman continued, 'and how long will it keep on running here, missis?'

" 'Until the end of the world.'

"Raising her hands and eyes to heaven, with a manner which no art can imitate, she simply exclaimed, 'Great God Almighty!' "

Many other subjects and incidents of his travels, dwelt upon by Gaston, were most delightful and instructive: his personal descriptions and delineations of character of the men of note he met, his contrast of society in Canada and the United States, his reflections upon the vanity of human greatness, suggested by certain amusing incidents of travel which occurred in his journey, and his recital of interviews and conversations with distinguished people.

But I have already exceeded my original design, and must bring this paper to a close.

I fear I have left the impression that my friend and I performed the part of simple mutes in the entertainments of the evening. If so, that impression is most erroneous and most unjust to our reputations. We were not conspicuous, and we would not have been so. But we bore our part. We twain spoke *one* word. It was thus:

During the summer at some watering-place Gaston had met with Martin Van Buren, then in the zenith of his popularity and greatness, and wearing in triumph the hereditary honors of his "illustrious predecessor." He had much to say of the distinguished man, his political and personal character: mentioning, among other things, that, in conversation with Chancellor Kent in reference to Van Buren's intellectual ability, he had contended that his public career furnished no evidence of superior intellectual endowments, but had been distinguished rather for the exhibition of those qualities of mind which are rarely, if ever, associated with executive ability; that he had cited the opinion of David B. Ogden expressed to him in conversation, as corroborative of his own.   ,

"Oh," said the Chancellor in reply, "Davy is warped by his political prejudices. Van Buren is a man of very superior, positive ability. He practiced law before me for twenty years, and he always seized the strong points of his own case and the weak points of his adversary, and I take that to be proof of ability in any man."

Gaston then proceeded to give his own estimate of Van Buren's character, pointing out some good features, but regarding him as distinguished by that quality which estimated the value of men according to their uses to himself.

"He regards men," said he, "as I do these snuffers, valuable when needed, but after being used of no further value, until wanted again."

Proceeding in his narrative, he referred to a toast sent by Van Buren in reply to an invitation to be present at some political demonstration. He was unable to recall the language of the toast. His inability to remember a certain word interrupted his narrative, and for a moment seemed to annoy him. Turning to our opportune friend, he said, "What was the word he used about 'hostility to the United States Bank?' You remember the toast." No response came. He turned unsatisfied away.

He then turned toward us. As his eye traveled by me, I caught it, saw his troubled expression, and in a "still, small voice" I said—"Uncompromising."

"Yes," said he, addressing himself directly to me with a most benevolent expression which I can never forget, "uncompromising hostility to the United States Bank," and then, in a tone and manner which made me feel as if my father spoke it, he added, "we should be uncompromising with nothing but vice."

One word more. William Gaston has now been dead many years. While he lived his position among his countrymen was as that of the son of Kish among the Philistines. In any association he was truly a great man. I speak of him not as a lawyer, not as a judge, nor a states- man, nor an orator, writer, philosopher, or poet; but as a great representative man; representative of the excel- lencies of his race, the dignity of learning, the beauty of virtue, the worth of integrity and honor and uprightness of character; the Christian graces, the kindly sympathies, the fraternal impulses of life, which alone impart to man his real manhood, and make him a reflex "image of his Maker." Yet, great as he was, no literary memorial com- mensurate with his real magnitude has yet been dedicated to his memory.

There are those living who were his compeers; who knew him best and admired him most, men every way com- petent to tell the story of his life; men distinguished by some of the same qualities which made up the sum of his exceeding greatness. Let them not by longer neglect inflict a foul wrong upon posterity. Let them look to it, as men who desire a place in the recollection of those who must pronounce their eulogy.

INTERESTING NORTH CAROLINA HISTORY FOR OUR YOUTHFUL READERS.

ON North Carolina soil Virginia Dare, the first child of English parents in America, was born.

The first print of English footsteps ever made in America was made in North Carolina in 1584, in the brightest period of English history.

The first prayer of Christian worship ever uttered by English lips in America was uttered on Roanoke Island, in Dare County, North Carolina. The first ordinance of the Christian religion ever celebrated by the English-speaking race in America was celebrated on North Carolina soil.

The first popular Legislative Assembly in America called by the authority of the people, in defiance of royal authority and against its protest, met in North Carolina, at New Bern, in August, 1774.

The first blood shed by the people in America, in resistance with arms against the oppressive acts, power and authority of Great Britain, under a Governor appointed by King George of England, was North Carolina blood, at Alamance, in North Carolina.

The first open Declaration of Independence of Great Britain made in America was the Declaration of Independence made by the people of Mecklenburg County, at Charlotte, on the 20th of May, 1775.

The first purchaser, in America, of Indian lands for a valuable consideration was made in Perquimans County by George Durant from Kuskatanew, King of the Yeopim Indians, in 1663, nearly fifty years before the purchase by William Penn of the Pennsylvania Indians.

After these distinguished first historical events, is it not a just claim of North Carolina that she is "the rightful mother of the States?" Sir Walter Raleigh stands sentinel at the gateway of her history, and following him she has an illustrious lineage down through her long history. From Mosely to Vance her sons have lighted the beacon fires of freedom. Her eminence in the Pantheon of history is only equalled by the modesty that accompanies true greatness. True greatness never seeks fame. The greatest North Carolinian was the most modest and diffident of men. He was a lawyer, and to the close of a long life always trembled when he first got up to speak. General Washington was our greatest citizen, the most distinguished and the most beloved. After the Revolutionary War Congress passed resolutions of compliment and thanks to him for his public service. He was present, and got up to reply, but his modesty overcame him, and he could not get along. Mr. Witherspoon, of New Jersey, an old Scotch preacher, who was in Congress, rose and said: "Sit down, young man; your valor is only equalled by your modesty"- -and then he replied for Washington. Distinction sits not gracefully on him who seeks it. "Office sought me; I sought not office," was the proud and just remark of William Gaston, when discussing the question of Catholic disability in its personal application to himself in the Convention of North Carolina of 1835. Once when she was taunted by some noisy politicians with being a plain and slow State, that great man replied that he hoped it would be long before she exchanged that for a more equivocal characteristic. The taunt came from our sister State of South Carolina, and the reply was in some respects a deserved rejoinder. Let us cling to our grand old State. Let us cherish her homely virtues, and let us also cherish the splendid position she deserves as "the Mother of the States."

PASQUOTANK RIVER.

A thing of beauty is a joy forever.
—*Keats.*

"No man is a hero to his valet," saith the old saw. To a great extent it is true, but it is nevertheless true also that propinquity and familiarity make the most brilliant objects stale. Familiarity breeds contempt, saith another old saw that is kindred to the first.

We have known men in North Carolina that lost their legitimate claim to the dignity of greatness simply because they were genial, vivacious and witty. George E. Badger was a many-sided great man, but threw away the major part of his grand heritage by his doggerel buffoonery.

Chief Justice Smith, who was an observant man, as well as a big lawyer in his time, once told us when we were young lawyers together, that Mr. Badger was a brilliant and superior man, a great lawyer and an astute logician, but there was some flaw in the material or manufacture of his greatness that marred its symmetry. We suggested that the defect was that he was too good an actor in low comedy for a matured great man. Webster, who was fond of Badger when they were in the United States Senate together, once told Badger, when he was playing buffoon for the entertainment of Webster and a little circle of Senators, that he was the "most magnificent trifler that he had ever known." The remark of Webster was a ten-strike, and a word photograph of Mr. Badger.

A young friend who was the greatest genius as a boy and young man we ever met, could say more funny and witty and smart things than we ever heard from human lips. He had the gift of greatness in a remarkable degree. He said to us in the last conversation we ever had with him that he had been a failure in life, and he knew why. He made men laugh too much; that dull men laughed at and pitied him; that if he had his life to work over, he would put an owl on his mantel to be an object-lesson to him to look wise and say little; that Cowper's "Jackdaw in a Church Steeple" did not fill the bill half as well as a big-eyed, wise-looking, far-seeing and reflective screech owl.

Pardonnez-moi. Au menton; which means, halt; you're off your head, come back to the first station. You set out to tell us about the Pasquotank River, and you wandered to George Badger and your young friend, and they never saw Pasquotank River. We have paused to consider the connection between the river and the great men marred by the frivolities of genius. We've got it. It all turned on familiarity, and how it belittles men and things.

We have known Pasquotank River from our earliest manhood. We have bathed in its amber waters. We have swallowed the nectar of its ambrosial current. We have gazed listlessly upon the shadows of the magnificent cypress giants that guard its banks. We have wreathed fancy stories from the weird pictures drawn by the setting sun. But we saw it every day, went up and down it many times, until we became its valet, and the evening shadows and the glowing sunrise and the weird pictures cast by the dying sun made no more impression upon us than any every-day object of nature.

Once, it has now been fifteen or twenty years, we were sitting alone in our editorial sanctum, enjoying a pleasant surcease of toil, when a handsome boy of apparently ten or twelve summers came in and asked for a copy of the city paper. After giving him the paper, we fell into conversation, and he told us that his father and mother and himself were from Lexington, Ky., where his father published a magazine called the *Kentucky Stock Farm,* and that they were on a visit to this part of North Carolina to see the country. As he left, we sent word to his father to call in and see us.

During the day his father called. He was courtly, intelligent and interesting. He had come from Kentucky to Norfolk, and thence via the canal and the Pasquotank

River to Elizabeth City. He had come over the evening
before. He was enthusiastic in his admiration of Pasquotank River, its grand weird scenery, the gigantic forest growth of cypress trees, the varied aspects of serpen-
tine bends, succeeded by long sweeps of straight currents.
He had traveled much, and he compared it with the historic rivers at home and abroad. He said that its floral
beauties (it was in May) were unrivalled in the world.
He dwelt upon its amber crested waves and its dense solitudes in which nature maintained its supremacy. He
compared it with the famed Hudson, and gave the superiority to the Carolina river that was the pan-handle and
reservoir of the Great Dismal Swamp.

And then we recounted to him some of the strange
legends of its history. How it was the favorite rendezvous
of Teach, the famous Carolina pirate, who was the terror
of the Carolina and Virginia coasts in the early years of
the eighteenth century, and who made his headquarters at
the head of one of those long straight stretches of the river
that commanded a lengthened view and gave notice of the
approach of an enemy. And when we told him of the
"Old Brick House," its history, and its date of 1700 on
the old bricks, and of the blood spots on the floors of
two rooms of the house, mute and ineffaceable witnesses of
the tragic scenes that they commemorated, his curiosity
was excited as we had not seen before, and he expressed
great desire to see with his own eyes the scene of the dread
orgies.

Since then we have seen the river much and often in
its varied aspects of scenery, and have thought more and
more that it is distance which gives enchantment to a
view, and that familiarity robs it of its gorgeous plumage.
The eye that looks daily upon Niagara and hears its lion
roar, thinks of it as a good site for a laundry or a cotton
factory, while the unfamiliar eye exclaims, "Great God
Almighty!" and turns in mute adoration toward the Almighty Architect and Builder.

GASTON IN THE CONVENTION OF 1835.

When he speaks, the air, a chartered libertine, is still.
                                        —*Shakespear.*

THE name of Judge Gaston awakens in our memory a reminder of that great man, and recalls to us some events in his distinguished career. His life was an eminent success, a succession of brilliant achievements in civil life, won by genius, character and assiduous labor, without the adventitious aids of revolutions or arms. His triumphs were truly the triumphs of peace, the triumphs of intellectual contest, and we purpose to briefly recall one of those occasions which probably summoned all the weapons of his well-equipped intellectual armory.

Judge Gaston was the central figure of the Convention of 1835, confessedly the ablest and most distinguished body of men that has ever assembled in North Carolina to deliberate upon the affairs of State. Nat. Macon was President, having retired from long and distinguished public service in the National councils. Judge Daniel, of the Supreme Bench of North Carolina, and several Judges of the Superior Courts, were also members, and ex-members of Congress were in large number. Crudup, of Granville, and Sam Carson, of Burke, both of whom were distinguished in public life. Jesse Wilson was one of the delegates from Perquimans, Joseph B. Skinner from Chowan, Judge Bailey from Pasquotank, Governor Swain from Buncombe, and indeed, the most conspicuous men were sent from all the counties. The State was greatly excited over the basis of representation, the eastern part of the State holding the control of power by the property qualification, and the west complaining violently that population was not made the basis. The Convention was a body of limited political powers, but there were other questions submitted to its consideration besides the basis of representation.

Not the least attractive of these questions to which the Convention was limited, was the religious disability ques-

tion, which was embraced in the thirty-second article of
the old Constitution, which was adopted in 1776. That
article disqualified for office in North Carolina "all who
denied the existence of God or the truth of the Protestant
religion." That article doubtless interested Judge Gaston more than any subject that was to be brought before
the Convention. The design of the article unquestionably
was to disqualify Roman Catholics from holding office in
North Carolina. It was to Judge Gaston a delicate personal
question, a question of conscience and honor. He was a
devoted Catholic in religious faith. He was a Judge of
the Supreme Court of the State, and in assuming the duties
of his high office had sworn to support the Constitution of
North Carolina, with the thirty-second article excluding
from office those who "denied the truth of the Protestant
religion" in it. Gaston was sensitive to honor and chivalrous in character. He was of distinguished ancestry,
and nurtured in the most cultured, refined and distinguished circles of New Bern's elegant society. His own personal honor was on trial, and was involved in the decision
of the Convention. The thirty-second article must have
been to him the great question before the Convention, and
it was natural that he should have been, as he was, grave,
thoughtful, absorbed, wrapped in the communings of his
own thoughts as the deliberations of the Convention went
on.

For the ten days that we, then a youth just returning
from the University, attended the sessions of the Convention, in the Presbyterian church in Raleigh, Judge Gaston always occupied the same seat, a little to the right and
not far removed from the chair of the President. To our
youthful imagination, he was the embodiment of intellectual greatness. He seemed apart. He was courteous,
but not familiar, exchanged few words with those near
him, and never indulged in pleasantry. The thirty-second article was not taken up early in the session. The
suffrage question had been up, and Gaston had been conspicuous, able and conciliatory in the debate.

When we came to Raleigh and went to the sessions of
the Convention with our boy friends, C. C. Battle and
Henry W. Miller, both deceased, the thirty-second article
was under discussion, and public interest was greatly excited.   The hall of the Convention was crowded with visitors and ladies.   Distinguished men and the *oi polloi*
were all out.   Judge Sewell, Dr. Smith of Orange, Crudup
of Granville, Judge Daniel, and several others, had spoken
as the days wore on; Gaston sat in profound thought,
head bent down, arms sometimes folded, always vigilant.   We well remember the indignant rebuke he once
launched upon Judge Sewell, who was his enemy and unsuccessful rival for the honor of the Supreme Court, at a
personal reference to Mr. Gaston and his occupancy of a
place on the Bench.   Most of the speeches had been in
favor of retaining the thirty-second article, and the sentiment of the Convention was apparently the same way.

When the subject had become somewhat exhausted, Gaston arose slowly, with great deliberation, amid breathless
silence, and for two days riveted the attention of all present by a speech which is unequalled in our memory.   He
showed fatigue after speaking the first day, and a motion
was made by Mr. Wilson, of Perquimans, for adjournment, but upon some manifestation of opposition to the
motion, on account of the rapt attention, Mr. Gaston commenced to resume his speech ; but the motion was renewed
when it was seen that Gaston needed rest. The next day the
speech was resumed and continued to the regular adjournment.   The fate of the thirty-second article was seen
before the speech was concluded ; and upon the question of
amendment being submitted, it was carried, we think,
very largely.

Had that speech never been made the thirty-second article would probably now be a stain upon our Constitution.
The speech was a masterly one, and probably the most
labored effort of Gaston's life.   All his powers were
worked up to their utmost energy, and every power of
moving men's minds by speech was brought into requi-

sition. It was powerful in argument. His position that one could disbelieve in Protestantism and yet believe the "truth of the Protestant religion," was exceedingly fine and ingenious, and also his position that the thirty-second article, when rigidly interpreted, would exclude Dunkards and Quakers as well as Catholics. His humor, in illustrating the common ignorance of the Catholic religion, by a conversation about the meaning of a "fetheral" (a Federalist) was inimitable, and placed him in the foremost rank of great actors. His appeal to all Christians for charity in the name of a common Christianity, was equal to any of the masterpieces of English composition.

But to our mind, when the speech was delivered and now, the most captivating and stirring passages were the personal parts relating to himself, and which do not appear in the reported and published speech as taken down in shorthand by Joe Gales at the time.

After adducing conclusive proof that the article under consideration was obscure, if not positively inoperative, he turned to the Convention and made a most powerful appeal to them to make the Constitution of the "good old State" clear and explicit. And then, addressing himself to the proposition that they should make the article a clear and plain disqualification of Catholics, he said, in tones that touched all hearts, that he had not determined what he should do, but he could not move among his countrymen, to whom he had devoted his heart's affections and the best years of his life, "with an infamous brand upon his forehead": and as he closed the sentence he slapped his hand upon his forehead and marched with a step that was the personation of majesty a short distance among the members near him.

It was a grand scene that time can never efface.

GAVIN HOGG.

THE Bar in the Edenton district has always held a distinguished place in the history of North Carolina. Before the Revolution Mosely had a reputation as a leading lawyer, and before and after the Revolution Governor Johnston had the name of a great jurist. Doubtless there were others whose names do not occur to us. After the Revolution came the Iredells, father and son, names long honored in our district and the State: the Blairs, the Cummings, and others. Some of these are mentioned by the first Waightstil Avery, the founder of the Avery family, in his diary, when he passed through this section of the State, from Connecticut, before the Revolution. In his diary he chronicles the fact that those members of the bar in Edenton to whom he had letters of introduction were sceptics, or free-thinkers, in religious matters; in which respect we are glad to chronicle that our Edenton brethren of the present day are not their counterpart, but contrariwise are very proper men.

Later down into the post-revolutionary period, we reach the time in the early nineteenth century when Gavin Hogg commenced his career at the bar in Bertie County, then a poor and briefless barrister, afterward an acknowledged chief, and a formidable rival of Gaston, not in culture and acquirements, but in rugged, stalwart power as a great lawyer. It may encourage some of our younger brethren who are disposed to repine at their hard lot and to shrink from the rugged pathway of early professional life, to give a little incident of Hogg's entrance upon the profession. It was related to us by the venerable Jonathan Tayloe, when over eighty years of age, as having come under his personal observation. Hogg was born, we have understood, at Chapel Hill of poor parentage. He was of Irish lineage. Having his law license, he went down into the eastern part of North Carolina in search of a place to "locate." He drove up to the tavern in Windsor in a single-stick gig, after a long and fatiguing day's ride, without money and without the acquaintance of any one in the place. He interviewed the landlord pretty soon, told him his business, told him he had no money and no friends, showed him his license, said he meant work, and wanted board and would pay him if he got work, and if not he would not pay him. The landlord, whose name we regret that we can not recall, upon the faith of his mission and his candor, welcomed him cordially, gave him his board until he could pay, invited him, as was the custom of the period, to take something, which he declined; and Hogg commenced his life-work, which knew no step backward, until in old age he retired from the profession, the peer of the great ones, wealthy, respected and honored.

Gavin Hogg was of large person, with a fine, massive head that would have made Fowler and Wells happy, and an eye like Mars. In manner he was grave, reserved, austere and forbidding, wrapped in the solitude of his own meditations. According to the testimony of our best lawyers, the ablest brief that the Supreme Court Reports of North Carolina show was prepared by Gavin Hogg. Personally he was unpopular. But in the war of 1812 he raised a company in Bertie, of which he was Captain, and was at the "Battle of Craney Island," near Norfolk, Va., and he was a very popular officer. It is related that in his old age, after he had retired from the bar and was a wealthy and honored man, he went to Windsor from Raleigh, to which place he had removed when his reputation was established and acknowledged, and strove to be affable and familiar with his old friends and clients among whom he had settled when poor and briefless, but they could not be familiar with him. He died in Raleigh at an advanced age about the year 1837.

JAMES ALLEN.

JAMES ALLEN, of Windsor, Bertie County, has left a greater impression upon the public mind for gigantic intellect than any man who has been at the bar of the Edenton circuit. His head was the embodiment of intellect, high, massive base, rising like a dome, with an eye of remarkable brilliancy, and a person below the medium height, but of considerable rotundity, not unlike the celebrated Judge Douglas, of Illinois. He was a poor boy in the town of Windsor, neglected, untrained, his father following the sea and taking but little care of his son. His brightness and remarkable head attracted the attention of Thomas A. Turner, an eccentric but intellectual and observant old bachelor of Windsor, who persuaded him to go to school at his expense. He probably made rapid proficiency at school, for at an early age he walked to Washington City, during the administration of General Jackson, to solicit an appointment as cadet at the Military Academy at West Point, having a letter to Governor Branch, who was then Secretary of the Navy in the Cabinet of General Jackson. Governor Branch introduced him to the President, who, it is said, looked at him, asked him some few questions, and, upon the faith of his pluck in walking to Washington and, doubtless, his intellectual head, old Hickory appointed him a cadet-at-large. He went to West Point, where he took the very highest stand, being in the class with General Lee, of the Confederate service, and graduating equal first with Henry Clay, who fell in the Mexican War, son of the illustrious Kentuckian. The on dit of the time was that Allen was a better mathematician and a better scholar than Clay but that his father's influence made him Allen's equal. It is said that General Lee enquired for his old classmate during the Confederate War, but he was dead some years before.

After graduating, Allen remained in the army a few years, and there appearing no prospect in the profession of arms but a life of inglorious ease, he resigned and returned to Windsor, to enter upon the legal profession. Having obtained his license, he rose at once to the front rank and acquired a good practice. He was a purely logical speaker, speaking in a plain, unostentatious manner, but with most convincing effect. He dealt in pure reason, but no man was more convincing to a jury. His speeches showed a powerful mind. He had in some degree the humorous faculty, which he sometimes indulged and with great effect. In the Harrison campaign of 1840, he sometimes took part as a Whig, and always spoke with convincing power. He was at a large district convention of the Whig party, at Edenton, in 1840, which was attended by Outlaw, Cherry, Paine and other prominent leaders, and no one spoke with more effect, or was a greater favorite with the audience, than James Allen.

ETHNOLOGY.

For we are the same our fathers have been,
We see the same sights our fathers have seen,
We drink the same streams, and view the same sun,
And run the same course our fathers have run.
—*Anon.*

PERHAPS no subject in the vast range of thought possesses more interest for man than the history of man. The poet was right when he announced, "The proper study of mankind is man." Man is man's most favorite and interesting study, and mysterious as is his moral and intellectual nature, his physical nature and history is as much or more so. Whence he came, or how he came, whether he sprang into existence with all his faculties perfect and entire at the fiat of the Omnipotent; whether coeval with the earth which is his dwelling-place, or subsequently placed there to till and dress it and to be monarch of the vast domain; whether starting from the lichens and the mosses, he has gone on in the slow progress of improvement until he has developed into a Cæsar or Napoleon; whether one man and one woman "created He them," or whether of many types and races; are still questions puzzling and mysterious, taxing to their utmost power, and beyond their power, the philosophic acumen of the learned and the curious, and will ever remain mysterious, until by a new development and a higher and holier and more intelligent existence our eyes shall be opened and all things be made plain.

Leaving the question of man's origin, other questions as mysterious crowd upon the imagination and tax the burdened thought. The origin of races, the migration of races, the extinction of races, the amalgamation of races; whether the progress of the human race is the great purpose of God, or progress and retrocession be the law of His mysterious providence; whether in our enlightened period we have not forgotten as well as learned; whether the age of Pericles and the Athenians was not superior in

arts, in letters, in physical development and manhood to
the vaunted developments of the twentieth century;
whether the mechanical skill which reared the Pyramids
in the desert as a mausoleum for the Ptolemys, thousands
on thousands of years gone by, has ever been equalled in
the long line of ages since—these perplexing questions,
full of mystery and doubt, leave us as they found us,
groping blindly, bewildered and unsatisfied.

Turning to our own country we find new and equally
mysterious pages in the history of man's unlearned lesson
of man. Our nursery books tell us that Christopher
Columbus discovered America in the year 1492, and that he
found the country peopled by an aboriginal and strange
race whom he called Indians. The Indians the aboriginal
race! They were the creatures of yesterday. Ages before
them there existed on this continent a race that lived in
towns and cities, that cultivated the arts of a superior civilization peculiar to themselves, a race that has left no written memorials, but whose unwritten history is traced in its
fortifications that show engineering skill, in its walls of
masonry, and its tumuli, in which were deposited the remains and relics of the dead. How long this race ante-
dated the discovery of Columbus is left to conjecture to
determine. They probably existed at a very remote period of history, or belonged to the pre-historic period.
Their principal settlements were in the valleys of the
Ohio and Mississippi and along the great lakes, where
they lived in fortified towns, constructed walls and raised
mounds for the sepulture of their dead. There is little
doubt that many of them dwelt in North Carolina, but
the indications are, from the absence of fortifications,
that they did not make it their permanent dwelling place,
or that the other races were subjugated to their will.

The evidences of the existence of this ancient race in
North Carolina are found chiefly in the county of Mitchell. In the forests of this county, in the valleys, along
the crests of the hills, are found numerous pits, generally

about ten feet in diameter, now nearly filled up and upon many of them a large full-grown forest growth. These pits have been excavated, and the examinations made have given the conclusion that they were unsuccessful explorations in search of precious metals. Other pits of larger size are also found in the same county. One, called the Sink Hole, near the North Toe River, eight miles from Bakersville, forty feet deep and about the same diameter, has been opened and worked beyond is original depth, and mica found in sufficient quantities to make the labor remunerative During the excavation some of the tools used in the original excavation were found, and also a tunnel connecting with other shafts. The tunnel was only fourteen inches wide, indicating that it was worked by a diminutive race of men.

A series of these pits is found in the same county on Cane Creek, and also on North Toe River, near the Turnpike. All of these pits have been profitably worked for mica during the last few years.

These are the forest records of a race of whom history or tradition has furnished us no mementoes, a race that had made some progress in the arts of civilized life —a race that had some knowledge of engineering, who built cities, raised fortifications, waged wars, mined into the bowels of the earth to procure the means of carrying on the peaceful traffic of commerce a race fashioned after the same Maker and endowed with the same passions with ourselves, who mourned their dead and laid them with sepulchral honors in mounds reared to their memories, where they too were laid, and all have passed away without a trace to tell the story of their being, save the mysterious record of their labors dug by their strong arms into the eternal hills.

"When I consider Thy heavens, the work of Thy fingers: the moon and stars which Thou hast ordained;

"What is man, that Thou art mindful of him? and the son of man, that Thou visitest him?"

9

THE CONVENTION OF 1835.

The earth hath bubbles as the water hath.
—*Banquo.*

THE North Carolina Constitutional Convention of 1835 is generally acknowledged to have been the ablest body of men that ever met in the State. It was probably as important a body as ever met. It was the climax of a controversy that had long agitated the whole State, and of the angry feeling that was engendered between Eastern and Western North Carolina, which at one time threatened civil convulsion. The subject of controversy that gave rise to the Convention was the basis of representation, the west contending that population should be more largely represented, and the east that a conservative constitution should make property largely the basis. In 1823 and '24 the agitation was most intense. Under the old post-revolutionary constitution at Halifax, the eastern representation was largely predominant, based as it was upon property, and they persistently resisted all increase of western representation. The west was constantly applying to the Legislature for a division of their large counties, which was as frequently refused by the eastern majority. The direct object was to make the business of the west more convenient to the people of the counties, the indirect object was to give Western North Carolina the majority in the General Assembly, and thereby call a Convention to change the basis of representation. Western North Carolina was then chiefly composed of a hardy race of rough bear hunters, without property and without culture. Their representatives generally were men like themselves. Their applications for redress were unheeded, and their representatives were objects of derision; but they increased in numbers, and their numbers were a constant menace to their more wealthy and more cultured eastern brethren. John Stanly, of New Bern, was the champion of the east, and was unsparing in the use of all the weapons of sarcasm in his well equipped armory, upon the western members who came to Raleigh in their best cow-colored homespun clothes. But in 1824 western Carolina issued a protest, signed by Charles Fisher, Bartlett Yancey and other leading western men, which thrilled the State by threats of revolutionary separation, and ultimately led the east to pass the act calling a Convention to amend the Constitution.

That Convention was a stormy one. It made changes in the basis of representation and other articles of the old Constitution. It was composed of able men, antagonistic in sectional interests, and it came to represent opposite sectional ideas. The west was armed in the justness of their claim, and their delegates were more aggressive and violent in the expression of their opinions. Sometimes, while the Convention was in session, secession from the body by western men was imminent. But for the kind, moderate and fraternal words of that great Carolinian, William Gaston, of New Bern, we think that violent and revolutionary methods would have been resorted to. His words, heard when a youth, addressed to western men aflame with passion, yet ring in our ears—"My friends—and surely mine to you is no unfriendly voice—" and how well do we remember his rejoinder to Governor Swain, who gave Scriptural illustration to western revolutionary sentiment. Governor Swain, in a closing burst of passionate eloquence, said: "Unless our demands are granted, unless our wrongs are righted, we will rise like the strong man in his unshorn might and pull down the pillars of the political temple." The allusion was a happy one and happily applied, and appreciated, and the western delegates "rolled it," in their speeches "under their tongues," as a "sweet morsel," always giving credit to the "distinguished gentleman from Buncombe." After some days, Gaston, who had been silent in the debate on the "basis," rose to speak, and after ably discussing the subject at length, paused and said, substantially: "The distinguished member from Buncombe has said that unless the wrongs of our western brethren are redressed, they will rise like the strong man in his unshorn might and

pull down the pillars of the political temple.' The strong
man, the son of Manoah, was brought out to make sport
for the enemies of his country at the impious feast of
Dagon. He tugged and pulled the massive pillars of the
temple and buried *all* in one hideous ruin. It was a great
and a glorious deed. He fell a martyr and a hero, victorious among the slain." Gaston had read the Bible
more thoughtfully than Swain.

JOSEPH B. SKINNER.

An all-round man.
--*Old Saw.*

PERHAPS the most distinguished lawyer in the district
after Hogg, and contemporary with him in his early professional life except the younger James Iredell, whose his
tory Wheeler has already written, was Joseph B. Skinner,
of Edenton. There are remarkable men that float along on
the tide of time that are without a parallel. Mr. Skinner
was such a man. He was born in Perquimans County,
in Harvey's Neck, and was the son of Joshua Skinner, a
hard-working and well-to-do farmer, who raised his sons
to hard work and plain living. He gave indications at an
early period of uncommon brightness, and an uncle of
his determined that he should have the advantage of mental
training. He had already learned the elements of education at the common schools. In a conversation that
this uncle had with his brother Joshua, he was heard to
say: "I see in this boy the future hope of our family."
Through the influence of his uncle he was, after proper
preparation, sent to Princeton College, where he graduated at an early age, and where he was the contemporary of
Gaston. After graduation he studied law, at Hayes, the
seat of Governor Johnston, and after obtaining his law
license, entered upon the practice of his profession with

diligence. He was devoted to business, at all times in his office, early and late, making his business his sole pursuit, making all things secondary to it—the social courtesies of life, the demands of pleasure, the calls of wealthy or distinguished persons. In the town of Edenton, where he practiced law, his attention to business attracted universal attention. Mr. Collins, the wealthiest man in the place, called at his office for a social call while Mr. Skinner was engaged in business, and he did not notice Mr. Collins. He left unnoticed, and always after employed Skinner in all his business. His attention to business won the rich man. Mr. Skinner did a large and lucrative practice from Currituck to Chowan, and over the sound. He acquired fortune by his practice. At about fifty-five years of age he retired from practice and went on a farm one mile from Edenton, where he passed the remainder of his life in the enjoyment of all the comforts which ample fortune could give. It was said by some that the rivalry and superior attainments of the younger Iredell drove him from the bar. However this may have been, Mr. Skinner was in the full enjoyment of a large practice when he retired.

He was not an eloquent speaker, in the popular sense, but no man spoke more lucidly; in fact, that was the striking characteristic of his mind, the clearness with which he conceived any subject and his plain manner of stating any proposition. His humor was also a striking characteristic, and he was master of the whole armor of ridicule. His judgment was unerring, and his confidence in it gave a boldness to his operations in business that surprised every one with his success. He engaged largely in fishing on both sides of the Albemarle Sound with eminent success. He was probably the best and most progressive farmer in the counties of Chowan and Perquimans, where he owned large possessions. He was an aristocrat, and exclusive in his social intercourse; but he was kind and liberal to the poor, aided meritorious young men who needed assistance, and his knowledge of men

was so accurate that his judgment never failed in his estimate of men.

Mr. Skinner was a man of rare humor and foresight,
and his humor frequently entered into his business cal-
culations.

On one occasion he was very anxious that the minister
in charge of old "St. Paul's" Church, in Edenton, of
which he was a member, should have an increase of salary.
At that time the salary of the minister was made up by
the renting of the pews. He attended the renting, and
finding that the bids were low and would not realize such
a salary as he wished, he commenced running up the bids
on all that were put up to such a sum as he thought necessary to make up the salary of the clergyman. When he
had bid off some dozen or more, some one, in surprise,
ventured to ask him what he was bidding off so many pews
for. He said he bid them off for his negroes, and intended that they should attend church and occupy them.
They knew that he would do it, and the white members
of the church soon took them off his hands and bid higher
on the others.

He was once sitting in his parlor writing a letter of
instructions to a manager of one of his farms in Perquimans, and his overseer, Jas. Cannon, was waiting in the
room for Mr. Skinner to finish writing, when a knock was
heard at the outer door. The visitor was invited into the
room. It was the period of clock-peddlers, a class of men
that were the persistent representatives of the book agents
of our time. The visitor was a clock peddler. He came
into the parlor, bringing his clock with him. "Buy a
clock this morning, sir?" asked the peddler, before offering the customary salutation. "Don't wish one," said
Skinner, without raising his head from his writing. "First-
rate time-keeper," said the peddler, setting his clock to
striking: "Double pendulum, brass mounting, full ring,
no cheat, let me put her up for you, sir." "Don't want
your clock, sir," said Skinner, continuing to write. "Come,
now, do buy, keep good time, all right for fifteen dollars,"
said the peddler, the clock all the time ringing out, "ting,

ting, ting, ting"—"No mistake in her, sir." Mr Skinner slowly raised his head from his paper, and in his slow and deliberate tones, said: "Cannon, tell Eden, and Little Jack, and Big Bob, and Peter Mike, and Slab Foot Jim, to come here." Meanwhile the peddler kept on an endless fusilade of recommendations, the clock all the while keeping music, "ting, ting, ting." The order was no sooner given than obeyed. The five strapping negro fellows came in to receive the order, the clock and the peddler in full cry. "Boys," said Mr. Skinner, "take that clock peddler and put him in his wagon and send him off." No sooner was the order given than it was obeyed, to the peddler's utter astonishment and despite his violent struggles to release himself. Skinner, looking at Cannon with an arch expression, said: "Cannon, d—n the fellow, how he kicks."

Mr. Skinner died about the year 1850, being over seventy years old, of rheumatic gout. He had been a great sufferer for years. He left a large estate. He requested that the Book of Common Prayer should be placed upon his breast, and the Bible, open at the Book of Job, by his side, before his burial.

JUDGE R. R. HEATH.

If we knew the woe and heartache
Waiting for us down the road,
Would we waste the day in wishing
For a time that ne'er can be?

—*Anon.*

THERE arrived in Edenton from New Hampshire, on a schooner from Boston, a young man, a stranger, without pecuniary means, slender of person, modest and retiring in demeanor, seeking employment. He was an educated man, and appeared to have graduated at Dartmouth College. The Trustees of Edenton Academy, hospitable to merit, employed him as an assistant in that institution, to Jos. H. Saunders, who was principal in the flourishing institution. That man was Robt. R. Heath, afterward a Judge of the Superior Court of North Carolina. He remained in that employment for three or four years, exhibiting a social and agreeable disposition and becoming a favorite in the community. During this period he was engaged, in an irregular and desultory manner, in studying law with George W. Barney, who had, some years before, come to Edenton from New Hampshire, and had acquired wealth by his law practice and by marriage, and who, later, dishonored the profession of which he was a conspicuous member. One fine morning the boys who were his pupils were startled by the news that their teacher had gone to Raleigh to be made a lawyer. They whistled aloud and put their fingers on their nose, for none of them knew that their schoolmaster was studying law. However, at that period "honors were easy," and the Supreme Court ground all the grist that was brought to the mill. He came back, after some days, a lawyer, and the boys, always on the lookout for knowledge, heard that all the law that he carried to the mill was stuffed into him by Barney, who was a good lawyer, as they rode together to Raleigh.

After obtaining his license, he left the school and took

a law office, but was not much in it. He, however, attended to his business irregularly, and Thos. B. Haughton, an old lawyer, whose daughter Mr. Heath subsequently married, sometimes said, to the surprise of others, that Heath was one of the best lawyers in the town, but no one believed it. After his marriage, and while Mr. Haughton lived, he did but little, a sort of *flotsam* of the profession. But when Mr. Haughton was drowned, leaving a very large estate, heavily involved and ultimately bankrupt, Mr. Heath waked up to the reality of his situation, poor, the son-in-law of a bankrupt father, dependent upon himself, with nothing but his law books, a family looking to him for bread; and he became a man. He removed to Edenton from the country. He was diligent in business. He made friends. He won clients. He gained causes. He was a plain man. Plain in his attire. Plain in his manners. Plain and free and simple in his intercourse. He followed the courts from Currituck to Hyde, and was everywhere a favorite. In politics he was an unterrified Democrat, at a time when it was thought not to be decent to be other than a Whig. Democrats recognized him as an able leader in whom there was "no variableness nor shadow of turning." He was everywhere their trusted leader, counsellor and guide. He was a thorough, well-posted politician and Democrat, not a speaker of the first class, but eminently wise in counsel.

Mr. Heath was now a leader in the profession, with a leading practice in all the courts, the peer of the ablest in a bar that presented a galaxy of talent, and that numbered among its members Moore, and Kinney, and Outlaw, and Cherry, and Bragg, and Jim Allen, and Tom Jones, and Jas. Jones, and Haughton, and Jesse Wilson, and Bailey, and Sheppard, and Smith, and Elliott and Paine, and Brooks, and Martin. Among this array of talent Mr. Heath held high rank, as a ready, astute and profound lawyer. His memory of authority and precedent was a marvel. At a moment's notice he would cite cases by name and page and in point.

In Edenton, where he lived, he was the acknowledged rival of Judge Moore, and in their conventional courtesy there was too much rivalry for cordial friendship. Moore was laborious, painstaking, cautious, earnest. Heath was ready, quick, alert, surprising. Moore was earnest, and his earnestness sometimes arose to eloquence. Heath was calm, easy, placable, even tempered. Moore was impassioned and vehement. Generally Moore was the more successful lawyer. He never trusted himself. He never "went off half-cocked." He was always thoroughly prepared. In mental characteristics he was very much like Chief Justice Smith. Heath too often trusted to the chances.

About the year 1850 Mr. Heath was elected to the Bench by the Legislature, without his seeking. He made an able Judge, and has left a reputation that is a credit to the Bench of North Carolina. After the war Judge Heath removed to Tennessee, and resumed his profession. He was never satisfied. In letters to Bat. Moore who was his intimate friend, he spoke of the Albemarle country of North Carolina as the best country to live in that he had ever seen, and that he regretted his having left it.

We heard the late Judge Brooks say that while in Edenton at the trial of the Johnston Will case, Judge Heath took a walk with him to his old house and home on Main street, and it was apparent to him that his mind was shadowed by a cloud of despondency. The past and its memories brooded over him as a pall.

About the year 1875 Judge Heath returned to North Carolina, where he married a lady of wealth in the western part of the State.

And here we would gladly pause and cast the veil over the memory of our old school-master; but biography, like history, must be true to itself.

After living in North Carolina a few years, in a time of great mental depression and bodily sickness, in a moment of despair, he shrank from the troubles of the world, which seemed of old to sit so lightly upon him, and took by violence his useful life.

Judge Heath was large in person, with a face of a most kind, benign and winning expression. He was especially kind and social with the young members of the profession assisting them with advice and looking, perhaps, too gently upon any of their irregularities. In religious faith he was a Roman Catholic. He died at about sixty-five years of age.

GENERAL WILLIAM GREGORY

A genius of eccentricity.

ONE of the most remarkable men in the whole history of Elizabeth City was Gen. William Gregory. In the posthumous collections of old North Carolina families by J. H. Wheeler, General Gregory, of Elizabeth City, is spoken of as an old citizen of North Carolina who, early in life, was known as "Beau Gregory." He was a conspicuous figure in his town for many years. He had great courtesy and style of manner, and was a punctilious observer of all the ceremonials of polite society up to his death in 1846. In personal appearance he strikingly resembled General La Fayette, so famous in our Revolutionary history. His father was a Revolutionary officer of large wealth, whose son William was his only son; and he gave him the advantages of educational culture and polite association, and after completing his general education, placed him under the tuition of Gen. William R. Davie, of Halifax, to be trained in the profession of the law. General Davie was the most eminent lawyer in North Carolina, and was distinguished for elegant accomplishments and courteous bearing, acquired by diplomatic association at the Court of France, where he had been a representative of our Government.

After completing his education and obtaining his license, General Gregory, for a time, opened a law office in Elizabeth City, but his large expectations of wealth and fondness for the pleasures of society interfered with his legal studies, and he was not a success at the bar. In fact, it was a long-current statement that he never appeared before a court and jury but once. It was said that he arose to address the jury, when the case was on trial, and said: "Gentlemen of the jury, I conceive that my client." He then looked confused and sheepish, and said again, "Gentlemen of the jury, I conceive." He then paused, looked foolish and dazed, and after a little while he proceeded and said again, "Gentlemen of the jury, I conceive," and then sat down. Mr. Goodman, the leader of the bar, who appeared on the opposite side, arose and said: "Gentlemen of the jury, brother Gregory has conceived three times and brought forth nothing," and then went on to argue the case. It was Gregory's first and last effort. He always kept up his association with the members of the law profession, always attended the courts, and was treated with marked attention and consideration by the members of the bar.

In his old age, when nearing eighty, he was a conspicuous figure on our streets, and was a specimen of vigorous old age, erect and sturdy looking. He was companionable with young men and old, and was a favorite with every one. He became very poor in his old age, and was kindly cared for by his relatives and friends. He dressed plainly, but with scrupulous neatness.

General Gregory had a singular constitutional defect in his intellectual organization. He had no conception of the proper use of words or their application, and the blunders which he made were a perennial fountain of jest for the town. He was utterly unconscious of his inaccuracies. Bill Butler, the wag of the town, was never happier than when he could get General Gregory to explain to him something relating to military matters. Butler would listen to him with apparent earnestness, while Gregory would go through all the details of military drill and evolution, and then Butler would go through the movements with the most ludicrous blundering. The

General would repeat it, saying "——d—n it, Butler (he would cuss sometimes), why don't you do like I show you!" While they enjoyed the joke, our old people were always respectful to the General. He was a militia General, and knew no more about military matters than a militia muster captain with a cornstalk sword.

General Gregory was utterly without business capacity, not for want of general intelligence, but for an impatience of the details of business, because he was dandled in the lap of luxury in his early days and could never bring himself down to the drudgery of labor.

He was postmaster of the town, and soon the business got awry, and his administration of post-office affairs was examined by an expert examiner of the office, who found a shortage in his accounts. His bondsmen promptly settled the delinquency and there was no attempt at concealment. After the matter was settled and the post-office had passed out of his hands, one of his bondsmen, an old and comidential friend, said to him -"Gregory, what did you do with all the money that came into your hands?" "What did I do with it? Why, I spent it like a gentleman, sir," said the General.

While he was postmaster a weekly mail came through the Dismal Swamp Canal from Norfolk. and generally arrived at night. Its arrival was announced by firing an old cannon on the wharf where the mail boat landed. One very dark night the cannon was fired some time before the arrival of the mail, and the postmaster, the landlord of the hotel, old Billy Albertson, and several citizens went down to the wharf to get the mail and the passengers, and some from mere curiosity. Dr. Mathews, then in his prime and ever on the alert for a practical joke, had stretched a rope across lower Main street on the route to the mail-boat landing. The rope was about the height of a man's knees from the ground. Gregory hurried down for his mail, and was the first to be tripped heels over head by the rope. While he was lying prostrate on the ground, Albertson came hurrying down to meet his passengers, and was tripped and fell, and he gave vent to his ire by cursing and threatening. Gregory spoke out in the darkness— "Billy, don't cuss; I am down, too. It's that damn Sam. Mathews."

— —

ANECDOTES OF MR. BADGER.

Still the wonder grew,
That one big head
Could carry all he knew.
                                        —*Goldsmith.*

LET us place upon the grave of Mr. Badger some few offerings illustrative of his eccentricities and of his wonderful versatility of talent, for, after all, his versatility of talent and acquirements were the most distinguished features of his character.

We once heard Chief Justice Smith say that if Mr. Badger talked about a horse one would suppose he had devoted his whole life to the study of horses, and so if he talked of anything else, one would think he had made that subject a special study. He seemed to have an intuitive knowledge of things foreign to his pursuits, and he had a fondness for displaying it that was almost a weakness. We once heard Colonel Ferebee say that in the Secession Convention, Mr. Badger discoursed to Wm. Pettigrew and himself, who were members of that Convention, about the relative merits of different kinds of liquor at a length and learning that was wonderful; concluding with a tribute to the value of whiskey over all other liquors.

Mr. Badger was in this town to argue a case of usury, in which the State Bank of North Carolina was plaintiff and Horatio Williams was defendant, at the Spring Term of the Superior Court of 1844, Judge W. H. Battle presiding. He was in the full vigor of his faculties and manhood. He was exuberant of health and spirits. He was full and running over with playfulness and vivacity. And he was looking anxiously forward to a place in the United States Senate, which was depending on his individual personal popularity and upon the success of the Whig Party in North Carolina during that canvass. We had heard of Judge Badger as an austere man, haughty, supercilious, proud, inconsiderate. We had heard him, when a boy, speak with contempt of popular government. We had heard of his contemptuous reference to the Legislature of North Carolina, of his contemptuous reference to the voters of Wake County, when he was an indifferent candidate for their suffrages in opposition to Wm. H. Haywood. We had observed when a boy that he never attended the sessions of the Convention of 1835. We took this as an expression of his contempt for that distinguished body. We had therefore concluded that the same intercourse would be shown here. How greatly we were mistaken. He was introduced to his professional brethren by Colonel Outlaw. He was courteous, kind and familiar. He became easy and playful with all the young members of the profession. The ink on our license was hardly dry, but we can remember with what happiness we felt the pressure of his great hand upon our youthful shoulders. He was familiar with all the people of the town. Tom, Richard and Harry, he would hail across the street by their familiar names and go tripping across to talk familiarly with them. He was at the time the most accomplished demagogue that we ever saw.

His speech was a masterly effort. He was assisted by Wm. B. Shepard and General Ehringhaus; the defence was supported by Chas. R. Kinney and Augustus Moore. The principal arguments were made by Mr. Badger and Mr. Kinney. Each foeman worthy of the other's steel. Mr. Kinney was in declining health but the knowledge of the foeman brought out the full measure of his strength. He overtaxed his physical power, and the next day he was prostrated by a hemorrhage.

Mr. Badger came to the court through the country in an elegant turn out with a pair of beautiful bays, which was every day at the door of the hotel at the service of the ladies who were boarding at the hotel.

The day before Mr. Badger was to leave in the evening, he was standing on the corner opposite the hotel, the gay centre of an admiring crowd of listeners, when Mr. Ehringhaus, the cashier of the bank, a venerable man of nearly seventy years, a great admirer of Mr. Badger, and especially pleased with attentions from the distinguished man, was passing on the other side. Mr. Badger hailed him aloud, familiarly: "House (as he called him) come over here." Mr. Ehringhaus came over, and after a few words of pleasant conversation, said to Mr. Badger, pointing to his handsome carriage and horses standing before the door of the hotel: "Badger, I wish you would leave that pair of horses down here for me when you go away to-morrow!" Mr. Badger looked at him for a moment, and, assuming a most grave manner, said: "House, I like you. I have another pair of fine horses at home, and I would like to give you that pair of horses. I would like very much to do so. But, House, suppose I was to give you that carriage and horses, how shall I carry away that nice lunch you will put up for me to-morrow to carry with me? How should I carry that old French brandy, that two or three bottles of old Port, that oyster sauce and pickles, that nice turkey and chicken salad, that cold lemon pudding, and the other nice and appetizing delicacies that you are going to fix up so kindly for me?" House put on the dry grins. Mr. Badger extemporized a thirty-dollar lunch in a few minutes.

The morning Mr. Badger left to speak in Perquimans, he was invited to breakfast with Mr. Ehringhaus, and ordered his carriage to leave from there. He was accompanied by Thos. F. Jones, of Perquimans, and it is from Mr. Jones' narrative that we take the account of that visit. Mr. Ehringhaus' family were society people, and Mr. Badger was received with marked and ceremonious courtesy. Nothing was omitted that was due to one so distinguished. All the ceremonial observances were strictly followed. The servants were trained to the observance of the most minute etiquette of fashion.

When breakfast was announced, Mr. Badger was ushered in with every mark of respect and deference. The guests were assigned to their several places; and as the distinguished guest was about being seated, the servant girl, as by direction, removed the chair to replace it when seated. When lo! Mr. Badger, not observing that the chair had been removed, attempted to take his seat before it was replaced, and fell sprawling upon the floor in a most mortifying manner. The whole family were in a condition of utter bewilderment. The servant girl was frightened and mortified, and things presented a most pitiable sight. Mr. Badger laid there till the tempest had subsided, and then, raising himself up on his elbows and looking at Mrs. Ehringhaus, said, with the most satisfied expression, "Well, Madam, what comes next?" as if it were a part of the ceremony for him to be tripped up and thrown upon the floor.

10

THE PEN AND THE SWORD.

Beneath the rule of man entirely great.
The pen is mightier than the sword.
—*Richelieu.*

THE question is often asked, Who was the greater, Napoleon Bonaparte or Sir Walter Scott? Scott wrote the life of Napoleon, and it was the first elaborate biography of that man of destiny. Who was the greater, Homer, author of the great epic poem, or Achilles, the hero of the great drama of history upon which that epic was founded? Who was the greater, Patrick Henry, the orator and tribune of the Revolution, or Wirt, who crystalized that oratory into biographical history? Unquestionably, the pen of the historian is mightier than the sword of the warrior. So likewise, *a fortiori* (as lawyers say) the pen is mightier than the "root of all evil."

To illustrate these propositions: North Carolina has made enough history to make a large-sized library. It has furnished enough orators to fill all the mausoleums of history. Wm. R. Davie was the orator, statesman and diplomatist of the Revolution. He was the Patrick Henry of North Carolina. Why was not Henry the Wm. R. Davie of Virginia? Davie was a superior man to Henry. Davie was a courtly gentleman of the old school, a good lawyer, an able debater, a representative of our government at the polished Court of France, and wore a gentleman's queue, manufactured in Paris. Henry was a barkeeper, a hook and-line fisherman, a fox hunter, and, as Mr. Jefferson told Mr. Webster at Monticello in 1820, associated with rowdies in intimate companionship. Why then, is it, that Henry rides down the lines of history as the "silver-tongued orator" of the Revolution, and Davie is hardly known to our school children? Simply because Wirt's pen was mightier than Davie's tongue or sword. All along the line from Davie down, orators have been indigenous to North Carolina soil, and at every period of her history. Why do we not know that history by heart?

Simply because our pens have been silent amid the clash of arms and the progress of great events. Now, this is all wrong. He that raises his arm on the ramparts of history should ride like a panoplied knight down its lines. If North Carolina has made history, as she doubtless has, then it is right and just that the laurels of history should be twined around her brow. How can the wrong be righted? How can it be condoned before the august tribunal of history? Let "North Carolina Day" be set apart in all our schools in the State as sacred to our history. Let each pupil select some event in our annals and write a historical essay upon the event, or some one be assigned to him for study and composition. Let the teacher select the best essay and preserve it and the next generation of North Carolina's sons will know more and be prouder of the grand old State of their birth and its achievements in the roll of history.

THE GIANTS OF 1840.

Green be the turf above thee,
Friends of my better days.
                —*Drake.*

THE year 1840 was the most memorable date in the political history of the United States. It was a great crisis in our party contests. The Whig Party had been maintaining an unequal contest with the Democratic party for several years, sometimes gaining a victory in sporadic cases, and always maintaining its intellectual ascendency in the National Congress, and always an overmatch for the great leaders of Democracy.

The Whig National Convention met in Harrisburg, and after a tumultuous session nominated a man who had been much of his life in the public service, had made no distinguished name as a statesman, but had made some reputation as a military man and had won one battle—the battle of Tippecanoe.

That convention at Harrisburg adopted no platform of principles. Its candidate was unknown, but he was heralded as a good old man of plain and honest character, of humble aspirations, and held the humble office of county clerk in a county town of Ohio, and lived in an unpretentious way at North Bend, on the Ohio River.

At Harrisburg he was nominated over Clay, Webster and General Scott. The nomination took the country by surprise, but it was backed by a vast deal of enthusiasm. In the National Convention the First District of North Carolina was represented by Kenneth Rayner, of Hertford County, our representative in the lower house of Congress, Charles R. Kinney, leading lawyer of Elizabeth City, and William W. Cherry, of Bertie County. There may have been some others. The nomination was received with derision by the Democrats and by some prominent Whigs, with coldness. Wm. B. Shepard, of Elizabeth City, who had been in Congress with Harrison for several years, said he could not vote for him, that he was an "old granny," and while in the Senate of the United States had been conspicuous for his stupidity. Mr. Shepard made no concealment of his opinions, and his influence was creating a local public sentiment against the Whig nominee for President. Charles R. Kinney, brimfull of enthusiasm for the chief whom he had helped to put in nomination, assailed the opinions of Mr. Shepard in the local newspapers and he was replied to by Mr. Shepard through the same newspaper medium. The controversy was kept up for some time with ability and acrimony that was leading to personal conflict. The matter was finally adjusted by mutual friends, and Mr. Shepard gradually fell into the surging Harrison tide and did yeoman service with ringing speeches, from Bertie to Currituck.

Kenneth Rayner was then the Whig leader of the First District, an earnest, ambitious and popular idol of the party. He came home from Harrisburg some days after the adjournment of the Convention, at which time the Harrison tide was rising and sweeping the people before it, and log cabins and hard cider were becoming the object lessons of the campaign.

The people of the town of Edenton had erected a capacious cabin on the green, in front of the court-house, and they would have Rayner to speak in it first. He seemed unusually thoughtful. When he rose to speak he was thoughtful to austerity. During his speech he used these words: "We must drive the Democrats from power, peaceably, if we can, if not, forcibly." The words were uttered with a deep-toned earnestness that thrilled the audience. There was no applause, but the solemn silence that attended it showed the deep thoughts that choked their utterance.

While Rayner was speaking there came into the cabin a little man of rather ungainly appearance, and whose attire and bearing indicated his indifference to those important objects. Some of his friends crowded around him with cordial greeting. We had never seen him before. He was invited and taken to the platform with

Rayner. He and Rayner met with the cordialty of intimate friendship. The little man's size and appearance
was against him. His bearing was wanting in dignity.
An intellectual smile played between his eyes and his
broad mouth. When examined carefully his physiognomy represented two qualities. His chin and lower jaw
stood for kindliness, humor, amiability and good fellow-
ship. His upper head was a capacious dome, enlarging
from base to summit. It was a symmetrical dome of
thought, the domicile of a brain power that made a great
master among men. It was William W. Cherry—one of
the most genial, gifted, eloquent, forceful speakers that
the Albemarle section has ever given to North Carolina,
perhaps the most so. He was the soul of wit, humor and
conviviality. His powers of repartee were as sharp as a
"two-edged sword," but left no wound. As a *raconteur* he
was the superior of Ham Jones. His benevolence was
broad as humanity, and he was as pure as a Vestal Virgin,
with an exquisite geniality that was never stained by a
bad habit.

When Rayner finished speaking, "Cherry! Cherry!" was
vociferously called for. He came in response to the cordial call. He had scarce uttered a few sentences before
everybody recognized a great orator. With electric argument that convinced, words that thrilled fell from him as
seldom before had fallen from human lips.

O, the ironies of fate!

Cherry died young; scarce turned forty. Fate had
emptied its cornucopia of honors in his lap, and his future
was a sunnil' prospect. He had not an enemy in the
world, and his friends were loving and true. He fell
before the relentless reaper, all unexpected, when the people were casting their honors, all unsought by him, at his
feet.

When we were in the court-house at Edenton where the
Whig convention met that unanimously nominated him
for Congress to succeed Kenneth Rayner, who had resigned the place, we were assigned the place of secretary

of the convention, over which Augustus Moore, Sr., of Edenton, presided. It was an easy task to nominate Cherry. It was prearranged. A committee was appointed to notify him, and they soon came in with him.

His speech of acceptance was in his usual style. We took it down stenographically as he spoke. When the convention adjourned, toward night we went out and in the early night wrote it out and then looked for Mr. Cherry to submit it to him for revision. After some search, we found him in the old Club House at the Edenton Hotel, in his stocking feet and shirt sleeves, sitting in a chair with his feet doubled up under him, and cracking jokes with a crowd of admiring friends. He was recounting to them a story of a Western county, North Carolina constable who went to Charleston, S. C., on horseback to purchase a piece of land in North Carolina from a rich nabob who was a titled colonel, which we had heard Ham Jones tell in Raleigh some years before. He beat glorious old Ham, far away.

After he had finished, we submitted our report to him. He pronounced it good, and with thanks gave every word his approval. We sent the proceedings and speech to the *Raleigh Register*, and the same number of the paper contained his death. The touching obituary by Weston R. Gales had under the headlines Burke's famous apothegm:

"What shadows we are, and what shadows we pursue."

THE DEATH OF WILLIAM GASTON.

O death! where is thy sting.

WHEN Judge Gaston departed this life in Raleigh, January 23, 1844, at 65 years, a great man left us, and Carolina was in mourning for her most distinguished son. Distinguished as his life had been, rounded, patriotic and useful, when he departed this life nothing became him like the leaving of it. He was a grand old man, and was beckoned away at the green old age of sixty-five years, full of honor, distinction, usefulness and the love and gratitude of his countrymen.

While the Supreme Court of North Carolina, of which he was one of the Justices, was in session in the morning, he was attacked with giddiness in the head, with symptoms of apoplexy. The Court adjourned immediately, and he was taken in a carriage to his office at Mrs. Taylor's. He rallied from the attack during the evening, and at night several distinguished friends called in to see him. He talked with them, and the conversation turned naturally upon the uncertainty of life and kindred religious subjects. As he became interested in the subject, Judge Gaston rose up on his elbow and then sat up in bed. He spoke on infidelity and its influence upon character, and referred to Tobias Watkins, a distinguished public officer, who was an avowed infidel, and whom he had known while a member of Congress in Washington. He said he always distrusted him, and then he added: "I do not say that an infidel may not from education and high motives be an honorable man, but I dare not trust him. A belief in an all-ruling Providence, who shapes our ends and will reward us according to our deeds, is necessary. We must believe and feel that there is a God, Alwise and Almighty." As he pronounced this last word, he raised himself up in bed and fell back a lifeless corpse. A grand and dramatic close of an illustrious life.

Mr. Gaston was a great favorite in New Bern, where

he had lived all his life. He was beloved for his courtesy, his kindness, his benevolence, and for his great ability and usefulness in public and private. He was the central figure in the group of distinguished men that illustrated the history of New Bern as no town in the State had been. It seemed at one time that every big man in North Carolina had been born or lived at some time in that "Athens" of the State, as the noble old town used to be lovingly called. Stanly, Gaston, Taylor, Shepard, Hawks, Daves, Badger, Manly, Graham, Henry, Nash, Speight, Backus, Bryan and a crowd of other great men, were all born or lived there.

The negroes joined in the general distress at Judge Gaston's death. He was always their friend. He always deplored the existence of slavery in North Carolina, and regarded it as "the worst evil that afflicted the Southern portion of our Confederacy," and in his famous address at the University in 1832, asked if it was too much "to hope for its ultimate extirpation in North Carolina." When he was a candidate for the Legislature, when the old "State House" in Raleigh was burned, and he was elected over Charles Shepard by one majority, all the free negroes voted for him.

His memory is yet green in the hearts of his countrymen, and the patriotic ode written by him in a moment of inspiration — "Carolina! Carolina! Heaven's blessings attend her" — yet wakens the love of our people for the dear old State we love so well.

MAMMY ELLEN.

Full many hearts in lowly bosoms dwell
The world knows not of, or cares not to tell.

We tell the story of the heroism of the lowly. There are heroes of domestic life that have found but little space in history. It is a picture of Southern life, and we hope it will not be out of place to rescue it from oblivion, without drawing on the imagination for its simple "annals of the poor." It is the picture of the old black mammy of Southern society before that cruel "war between the States," that, whatever may have been its benefits (and there are doubtless many) developed some of the most fiendish traits of our poor human nature and ruthlessly sundered ties that were heaven-born, earth-blessed, and nurtured in love.

It is the story of Mammy Ellen, a faithful old black mammy, to whose pure and loving memory we would now like to raise a monument of pure black marble to commemorate the virtues of a black slave who had been the fostermother of the children, had nursed them in childhood, had followed them in manhood with kindly words of counsel when the world's gilded temptations lured them from duty. But that coveted work has been denied us by an inexorable necessity that has dogged the heels of our *res angusta demi*.

Mammy Ellen's is a plain picture, true to life. She had her home by day and a lowly cot at night, in a loving household. She was always with the family and the children that she loved with unselfish devotion; intelligent, watchful, patient and forbearing. From a little girl she had been an intimate associate of the family. As she grew to womanhood she became their loved counsellor and friend. Her patience and good humor was a marvel of loveliness. She always kept her temper, even when it was subjected to the innocent provocations of childhood's love of fun. Sometimes "tired nature," wearied with watching at night, would seek relief in a short "cat-nap" by day, and healthy and bright children, always watchful for jobs in the field of fun, would poke straws into Mammy Ellen's closed eyelids, and she would always come to consciousness with a happy smile and a kindly word of chiding.

A little incident occurs of Mammy Ellen's faithful watching, mixed a little with the supernatural. A sick chamber, a little boy, of that interesting age when "sweet is the voice of childhood and its earliest words," is sick unto death. His mother, worn with watching, broken with grief, had left him in despair, to commune with God. His father and Mammy Ellen watched by his dying bed, both weeping. Death, with its inverted torch, we both thought had come to beckon him away. Every childish prattle of his was crowded into a moment. The critical moment, we thought, had come. At length the father gave way, and telling Mammy Ellen to close his eyes after death, sought the anguished mother. She was in an upper chamber, night clothed, pacing up and down the floor, sad but silent. The agonized father said: "My dear, we've got to give up our little boy. He can not live half an hour." She turned to the half-crazed father and said, as if in words of inspiration, "No, no; he will not die. I have been in prayerful communion with our Heavenly Father, and he has given me assurance that our dear little boy would be spared to us." We went back below. Faithful Mammy Ellen was watching over him. The little fellow roused for a moment from a comatose sleep. Mammy Ellen leaned over him and said, "How do you feel now?" He answered quickly, "I'm better, do you know, now." He turned over, went to sleep, recovered rapidly and was restored to his parents.

And now let us turn to the dark side of this shield. In the fall of 1863 there came to Elizabeth City an armed General, who wore and dishonored the epaulettes of the United States Army, and occupied the town. He brought with him five thousand negro soldiers. He established a reign of horror here for about a month. He imprisoned innocent and delicate women, placed them under a guard of negro soldiers, who watched all their movements by day and night. He threatened old men and non-combatants with fire and death. He had but one instinct — cruelty —and he gratified his thirst for desolation. He swept away every vestige of property and made us a land of wretched paupers. When he was leaving, he sent a squad of negro soldiers to take away all the negroes that were left. Some Buffaloes with whom he consorted, directed him to homes where some yet remained. They came to the home where Mammy Ellen lived. She did not want to go. They tried to persuade her away, and called her "sissy." She still refused to go. At length they told her she must go and made a show of force; the children came to them and, weeping, begged them not to take away Mammy Ellen. Their hearts of steel did not relent before the supplications of childhood in tears. At length Mammy Ellen, weeping, took from her pocket an old purse, and taking some silver coin, distributed it among them, and embracing them and calling them "her children," took her departure with the soldiers, and her body now rests somewhere among the sand dunes of Roanoke Island, and her blessed spirit still hovers over and follows the children that she loved and watched over in life.

HENRY W. MILLER.

Where every god did seem to set his seal,
To give the world assurance of a man.
—*Hamlet.*

NORTH CAROLINA has had many men in its citizenship that illustrate the touching lines in "Grey's Elegy in a Country Churchyard"—

"Some mute inglorious Milton
Here may rest,
Some Cromwell, guiltless of his country's blood."

They sleep unhonored because no pen has made record of their deeds—that handmaid of immortality, mightier than the sword, most potent of all the agencies in the preservation of glorious and inglorious deeds, the index finger of the art preservative, that marks the sign-boards in the pathway of time.

Among those "mute inglorious Miltons," whose grand march to greatness, witnessed by his wondering contemporaries, and whose magic words of eloquence and wisdom are fast fading from the memories of men, was Henry Watkins Miller, of Raleigh. He bore upon his august brow nature's guinea stamp of nobility. He was born to greatness, and the shadow of his wonderful intellectual gifts was cast before him before his entrance upon the arena of life.

He was our school friend. We for two years occupied adjacent rooms in the old historic "South Building" of the University of North Carolina, separated only by a narrow passage way. That passage way was the dividing line between the Di. and Phi. brotherhoods, but it did not divide our friendship, which was of a somewhat intimate character.

Much is said of the mastery of men, and Miller's mastery at the University was the mastery of men. His intellectuality as a boy was a marvel. His personality was charming. His eye was like a sloe; but the aspect of

Mars was softened by a glance of kindness that won all hearts by its sincerity and benevolence. Seldom he laughed, but when he did it was a musical ripple of a placid river on a pebbly bottom.

One word more and we will dispose of his boyhood. He was at the head of his class as an intellectual man, but he was not a "first-mite" man. His genius was too universal to be "cribbed, cabined and confined," to be bound around by the technicalities of the scholar. He was an all-round intellectual prodigy. His field of triumph was too broad for the struggles of logarithms, hydrostatics and optics, and he gave all his strength to the struggles of mankind. Another word, and we give up his boyhood and turn to the graver and sadder period of his life.

Miller graduated in 1834. He spoke the third speech in the order of distinction. It was a grand effort, full of the afflatus of oratory in its grandest type. His father, a plain old man, in the sixties, homespun clothed, a Virginian, of Buckingham County, came to the University at the Commencement of 1834, to see his son graduate. We stood by the old man in the aisle of Gerrard Hall. Young Henry Miller carried the audience along with him by the magic thrill of his eloquence. The old man wept like a child as young Henry swept the heart-strings of the audience, and when he sat down the old man, with streaming eyes, went upon the rostrum, took his gifted son in his arms, and wept aloud. All college distinctions paled before the grand triumph of that proud day.

While at the University he was a model of every propriety. He had no excesses, was a member of the Presbyterian Church, and was in all respects moderate, circumspect and exemplary. But let him who stands and of whom "all speak well," beware lest he fall!

He returned to his home in Raleigh after graduation. His fame of greatness had preceded him. Friends on every side met him with open arms and were profuse of compliment and congratulation. George E. Badger, the head of the law profession in Raleigh, and a leader in its

distinguished social life, took him by the hand, took him
up as "his boy," took him in his office as a law student,
flattered him, praised him, and predicted his future distinction. Weston R. Gales received him and made him
a pet in his charmed circle of social life, with its brilliant
baits of temptation and pleasure. His head was turned,
the proprieties of his past life were thrown to the winds,
he fell before the tempter and his life is now the best
temperance lecture in the whole history of North Carolina.

His life afterward was a fall, and a staggering, repentant
recovery. Sometimes, yea often, the old his old time
brilliancy would flame out with unwonted power. In the
Harrison storm of 1840, he was a power, and his campaign newspaper articles —"A Plain Man and One of the
People"--were read throughout the State and had a an
influence. He acquired the reputation of a great but uncertain lawyer. He had a leading practice in important
cases, and at his best was regarded as an unrivalled advocate.

About 1858 he was appointed by the "Ladies of the
Mount Vernon Association," with Edward Everett, the
great Massachusetts orator, to deliver lectures throughout the United States for the purpose of purchasing Mount
Vernon and dedicating it to the memory of Washington.
It was a distinguished honor, and much appreciated by
Carolina's talented son. For a time it exercised a salutary influence over his life, and he entered the service
assigned him with an earnestness and ability that eclipsed
the fame of Everett.

Miller's lecture was never published, but we had the
pleasure of reading the manuscript some years after, and
it was strikingly elegant, original and forceful.

As a graceful orator and elocutionist, he could not have
been excelled by Everett; for Miller was the equal of
Daniel Webster in magisterial face and bearing, and his
superior in person and in the sweet musical cadence of
his tones.

Once, in 1862, we were on a railroad bound for Raleigh. We were sitting by a friend, and while in conversation with him, we heard a voice full of melody and sweetness coming from behind us far down in the car. We said to the friend near us, "Surely we've heard that voice before. It sounds like Henry Miller's." He replied, "Mr. Miller is on the train." We had not met Miller for thirty years.

We turned and looked over the dense crowd. Far down we recognized the majestic brow and eye of "Old Coal" of the University. I went at once to him. He met me as I him, with the old-time heartiness, known only to school-day friendship.. We turned to the past, and gave some space to the present. He lamented the war then raging; and the stoppage of his work in the lecture field with Edward Everett added to his personal regrets.

We suggested that he devote some part of his life to preparing an elaborate biography of William Gaston. He said no man appreciated the character of the great Carolinian more than he did, but he was poor, and the demands of his family took all his time. He then passed his hand through our hair and made some comment upon the footprints of time with both of us. He got off at the next station, and we parted never to meet again.

JUDGE THOMAS RUFFIN.

" A good name is rather to be chosen than great riches." It gives weight to reproof, force to counsel and point to example.

—*Grier.*

As long as magistracy exists, the name of Thomas Ruffin, of North Carolina, will be conspicuous among her great sons. He was specially a great lawyer, and the monument that he reared to his memory was acquired by long and laborious service in her legal ranks.

From the ranks, amid difficulties, without family influence, without patronage, with the encumbrance of constitutional diffidence, in the face of eminent legal practitioners and rivals at the bar, he rose to be the acknowledged leader on his circuit of courts, and in the progress of his career came to be the chief minister at its altars.

His distinguished life and character is full of practical lessons to the young aspirant for forensic distinction who longs to inscribe his name upon the pillars of the legal temple.

It is a lesson of struggle under difficulties, of intense labor, of indefatigable perseverance, of resolute determination, of patience, of self-reliance, of triumph.

When Demosthenes, the great Grecian orator, and assigned the highest place in the Pantheon of oratory, was asked what was the main constituent of oratory, he said action; and when asked for the next element, he repeated action; and when asked for the third constituent, he repeated the same answer. The lesson of Thomas Ruffin's life was that labor, thrice repeated, was the grand element in the life of a successful, great lawyer. He was no orator as Brutus or Cicero. He was without the graces of manner. He had no honeyed words of rhetoric that won the hearts of men. His voice brought no reminder of the Eolian harp. His countenance was austere, and his limbs were not cast in the mould of an Appollo Belvidere. He probably never told a joke in

11

his life, and probably but seldom relaxed into pleasantry.
But he was a man of character, upright, earnest, sincere
and laborious. He had duty for his guide-star, and was
in every fiber of his constitution a grand model of God's
masterwork—an honest man. He was equal to all the
positions he occupied in life. He had been a legislator
in the General Assembly, had been a Judge on the Circuit
and Supreme Bench, and was a master in each. On the
Circuit Bench he was earnest, pure, able, and dispatched
business with great diligence, promptness and firmness.
On the Supreme Bench he was probably unequalled in
our judicial annals. His opinions on the Supreme Bench
were distinguished for learning, clearness and profound
research. They were universally commended, and were
quoted with approval in the courts of Westminster Hall,
in England.

If there was any weakness in the panoply of his acquirements, it was in his literary character. He was not at
home on the literary rostrum. He addressed the graduating class of 1835 at the University of North Carolina,
and we thought it too direct and practical for a graceful
literary occasion. There are some occasions in which wisdom is not wise when unadorned, when a "spade" must be
described, and not called by its homely cognomen.

Judge Ruffin was a Virginian by birth, a Carolinian
by education and adoption. His Virginia lineage em-
braces much distinction in the judicial line—a maternal
ancestor being Judge Spencer Roane, who was Chief Justice of that State.

His preparatory education was in the town of Warrenton, N. C., where he formed school-mate friendships with
many Carolinians, who in after life were his warm friends.
He graduated at Princeton College with distinction in his
class, and while there was the room-mate and class-mate
of Gov. James Iredell, of North Carolina. Soon after his
maturity he removed to Hillsboro, N. C., where he passed
his honored and successful life, and departed this life at
eighty-three years, full of honor and reverence.

A MONSTER SNAKE.

[A STORY OF THE SEA.]

SOME boys were on an outing to the "Fresh Ponds" at Nags Head, a favorite resort of sportsmen, and as they journeyed on through brake and briar, they saw an immense snake's head protruding through a hole in the body of a live oak tree. One of them, who carried the commissary basket, pointed to the monster's head, and was amazed. He was about to run home in fright, but another boy, larger than himself, shook him vigorously by the shoulders until his nerves were recovered.

While this athletic pantomine was going on, his snake-hood was looking on with serene composure. The boy was considering the Scriptural injunction to bruise that serpent's head. He recovered from his Scriptural reverie, seized his breech-loader and bruised his head with twenty-four heavy buckshot. In fact, he blew off his snakeship's head, and left him a monster off his head.

Nearer the bottom of the tree there was another hole, a sort of back door to the snake's sanctum (so to speak). In a little while the snake's tail began slowly to protrude itself through that snakely back door. One of the boys, recognizing his opportunity, dragged out five feet of his headless body through that hole, threw the head part over a boy's shoulder and the tail over his own, and then, forgetting the Fresh Ponds and the big black bass, marched back to the hotel as proud as an army with banners.

On their way back they discovered a protuberance in the snake's abdomen that alarmed them. Finally, they reached the hotel, and everybody came up and marvelled at the great triumph. They examined the egg, which the boys had dissected from the snake's body, and wondered still the more. They examined the egg, and each examiner had his own theory.

At length some one suggested that they should form an

organized body to deliberate on the mystery of the snake and the egg. Agreed. John G. Wood, of Hayes, was called to the chair, and Moses Blackstock, of Bertie, was called on to express his sentiments. He kindly responded. "This," said he, "is a venomous species of the *angulus dioscnus*. It is an amphibious animal, and is always found near the sea. It has a thousand legs, which are used as paddles in the sea and propellers on land. It can outrun the swiftest race-horse, and can jump twenty feet at a bound. As to the egg, it is the property of some thrifty old housewife, which she used as a nest egg to fool her hens with and make them lay when they don't want to." Others shook their heads, and said it was nothing but a story which the boys had hatched from a stone they had picked up on the beach.

In the confusion of their conflicting opinions, some one suggested that if any one could explain the mystery it was Bill Jones, an exotic banker; that Bill was a funny man, and when in his funny mood he could not tell his right leg from a powder-horn; but set two cocktails before him with a straw in each, and let him draw, and in ten minutes he would tell you more of the past, present and future than all the wise men from Cape Hatteras to Collington Bay. Two cocktails of John Ward's best were ordered, and a committee appointed to invite Bill Jones's presence at the conclave. He soon came, and, looking around, saw two cocktails staring him in his face, that was beaming with happiness. He addressed himself to them, and for five minutes discussed first one and then the other. Then, turning to the crowd, he said, "Gents, for what want ye me?" The chairman answered: "We want your learning as to this snake and this egg." He bowed his best bow, and then, pointing to the monster reptile, said: "That snake belongs to the *angadusa* family—venomous, destructive and rabid. Its jaws turn upon a pivot and hinge, and it can take in a hog, a possum, or a puppy, and sometimes swallows a baby, without distinction of color, race or previous condition. This one is well known here. He was the terror of these banks. He ate Betsy Barker's baby at one gulp. He ran off with Nancy Dowdy's two twins, and has eaten various and sundry others. From examination of his fangs, he is thirty years old. The boys were fortunate in shooting him as quick as they did, for when his head was thrust through that hole he was preparing for a spring, and would have wrapped his head around one of the boy's neck and stuck his tail in his nostrils, strangled him in less time than a minute, and devoured him at his next meal."

Turning to the egg, Bill J. eyed it from every standpoint and said: "This is an ossified egg of the Great Auk, a mammoth bird of the torrid regions that existed in prehistoric ages, just prior to the death of Abel. There is only one Auk egg in the world. It is preserved in the British Museum, and a million dollars has been refused for it."

BATTLE OF MOORE'S CREEK BRIDGE.

I have no words :
My voice is in my sword.
—*Macbeth.*

PERHAPS no battle of the Revolution had greater effect in rousing the Patriots of the Revolution in its earlier stages and inspiring their hearts with the enthusiasm of independence than the battle of Moore's Creek Bridge. It was the first regular pitched battle of the Revolution in any of the States. It was fought by the regular colonial troops of North Carolina, in Cumberland County, on a branch of Cape Fear River, on the 27th of February, 1776. The forces engaged in the campaign were the North Carolina troops, commanded by Col. James Moore, Colonels Lillington, Caswell, Martin and Ashe; and, on the other side, the Scotch Highlanders, commanded by Gen. Donald MacDonald, who was a Tory, and had been commissioned as General of North Carolina troops by the Colonial Governor. The Patriots consisted of about 1,100, being Colonel Moore's Continentals, and the minute men from New Bern and New Hanover and militia from the counties of Duplin, Craven, Dobbs and Bladen, under Colonel Caswell; a hundred "volunteer independent yagers" from Wilmington, commanded by Colonel Ashe, and a hundred and fifty minute men from Wilmington under Colonel Lillington. The opposing force of Tory Highlanders, under the command of General MacDonald, consisted of about 1,500 men, chiefly Scotch Highlanders.

As soon as the Loyalists began to embody at Campbelton, Colonel Moore took position at Rockfish Creek, seven miles down the river, and was watching the movement of the force under General MacDonald, and had determined to attack them at the first suitable opportunity. But the enemy, whose object was to get to Wilmington and join the British fleet in the harbor, evaded him by crossing the river and passing to the eastward to another road. Moore, however, directed Lillington and Caswell to concentrate their forces on that road near the widow Moore's bridge, on a creek that emptied into Black River, about thirty miles from Wilmington, while he hurried down to close in on the Highlanders. During the day and night of the 26th of February, Colonel Lillington, who was the first to reach the bridge, had thrown up a breastwork commanding the crossing, while the Highlanders were rapidly approaching from the opposite side. Colonel Caswell came just in time, and during the night Lillington also destroyed part of the bridge, removing the planks so as to impede the attacking party if they attempted to cross the bridge.

On the early morning of the 27th of February the Highlanders, seeing an embankment apparently unoccupied, and supposing that the Americans had abandoned or were about abandoning their position, determined to attack them. They fired a morning gun and then charged furiously over the bridge, not knowing the impediment of its partial destruction. The patriots attacked them with great impetuosity while on the bridge, and totally disorganized them. Then Captain Slocumb's company crossed the creek lower down and attacked them in the flank, and the Highlanders broke and retreated. The Patriots killed about seventy of the enemy and took many prisoners, among whom was General MacDonald himself. It was a complete victory for the Patriots and broke the formidable Tory outbreak among the Scotch Highlanders, who had fled from Scotland after the disastrous battle of Culloden in their home country, and made their new home in the Cape Fear region of North Carolina.

In this first pitched battle of the Revolution, that is hardly known to our own people, the Patriots, under General Moore, had two wounded, one of whom died. The Tories, under General MacDonald, lost seventy. Captain McLeod and Captain Campbell, of the Highlanders, were killed early in the fight on the bridge, the former of whom received upwards of twenty bullets through his body. A very few minutes after the fall of these leaders the whole army was in flight. Many were drowned and many prisoners were taken, General MacDonald being taken the next day. He was commissioned as Brigadier-General and Commander-in-Chief in North Carolina. There were twenty-six prisoners taken, all of whom were sent on to the American General Congress in Philadelphia.

The importance of this signal victory of the Americans is fully recognized in the scant contemporary letters and publications. They speak of the great joy that it had diffused in the Province, and how great a disappointment it was to Clinton and Lord William Campbell, who were in Cape Fear River in British ships of war, "in sanguine expectation of being joined by the defeated and routed Tory troops." If the fight at Moore's Creek Bridge had been won by the Tories under General MacDonald, all East Carolina would have been overrun and probably the whole South would have been subdued.

And yet, when Senator Butler introduced a resolution in the United States Senate proposing an appropriation to aid in raising a monument at the site of this first pitched battle of the Revolution, some Senator asked, with lamentable simplicity, where the battle of Moore's Creek Bridge was fought. Alas! alas! the schoolmaster is abroad, but where are the pens that are "mightier than the sword."

It is sometimes asked why the Highlanders, who had sustained so signal a defeat in a contest with the British Government at the disastrous battle of Culloden in 1745, should have taken up arms for the British Government against the citizens of their new home in North Carolina. It is the old story of the "burnt child." They had felt the fire of the British arm in their old home, and with the true instinct of a canny Scot they feared a repetition of Culloden.

But time has redeemed their mistake in the struggle for independence, and the State of North Carolina now points with pride to the descendants of the Macs who fell at Moore's Creek Bridge, who have since brought and emptied into her loving lap laurels won in field and forum.

THE BANKER PONY.

"The War Horse Sniffeth the Battle from afar."

THE horse is man's best friend. In peace he is man's best agent in subduing the forest to the plow. He is the great agent of transportation and intercommunication. He was a factor in the progress of the human race from the earliest period of time. He is as prominent as man in the chronicles of Holy Writ.

Why, then, should he not have a place in history? He has won battles. He has subdued forests. He has been the faithful companion of man in all his enterprises. He has been the inspiration of song and story and art. The artist has made him the emblem of death, and "Death on the Pale Horse" has immortalized the easel of West. The Arab loveth his steed. Civilized man cherishes his horse, gives ear to his intuitive knowledge of past, present and future events. Had the Great Creator denied man the power of speech, as he has the horse, the horse would have been his superior. Without speech man's reasoning would have been inferior to the horse's instinct. He has more strength, more sagacity without speech, more valuable instincts and forecasts than man, and in the outset of the race of life he starts in the race far ahead. His self-reliance, that great factor in human progress, is earlier developed and is more tenacious. But he is denied the vocal power, hence he takes rank next to head in the roll of creation.

Why, then, deny him a place in history to which he has contributed so much in sacred and profane records? Why close the doors of fame to him who has oftimes turned the tide of battle and changed the pathway of nations?

From Job to Pharaoh the horse is a conspicuous subject.

The earliest horse known in North Carolina is probably the banker pony, and in all the crossings of breeds and

the training of thoroughbreds, he has retained and never
been surpassed in his peculiar characteristics of endurance and docility. When Amadas and Barlowe came to
Roanoke Island in 1584 the pony was probably here on
the shores of the Atlantic Ocean, and was sometimes
used by the Indians in the chase and for transportation
purposes. He was self-supporting on the salt marshes,
and was sometimes subjugated by the aborigines for the
purposes of the chase.

How he came there, whence he came, and how long he
had been there are still unsolved problems in the speculations of naturalists and philosophers.

Some claim that he was brought over to America in
the migrations of the "Lost Tribes" of Israel after their
escape from the horsemen and chariots of the Egyptians in
the flood-tide of the Red Sea; and that our banker ponies
were the remnants of the Egyptian hosts who perished
in the Red Sea.

This remnant of wild horses escaped the general destruction and were taken by the Israelites and preserved
by them as memorials of their preservation. When the
lost tribes were lost in the forty years of wandering in the
wilderness and found a home in North Carolina, long
before Sir Walter Raleigh conceived the idea of trans-
atlantic exploration, they brought the Egyptian ponies
with them, and ever after preserved them as memorials of
a beneficent Providence.

Others claim that the banker pony is a development of
the sand fiddler from the long evolution of the ages.
They trace the marks of a remote lineage in their resem-
blances and characteristics, as the remote ancestry of the
blooded horse can be traced by white spots reappearing
among his descendants at intervals in the genealogy of the
blood. The "fiddler," they say, is tenacious of his habi-
tat and combatative in its defence. So is the banker pony.
The "fiddler" is remarkable for the strength of his spinal
column. So the banker pony. The spinal column of
the "fiddler" is as tough and sinewy as a "razor-back"

porker. The spinal column of the banker pony is phe-
nomenally tough and strong. He will pull with ease
a burden attached to his tail that he could not move when
attached to his shoulders. The "fiddler" is a burrower
in the sand, and makes his hole an asylum of refuge and
a castle of defence. The pony will paw the sand until
it will make a hole as deep as his body.

But we discard all these theories as philosophical vaga-
ries of a diseased fancy, and adopt another which has less
imagination but more wisdom.

When Ponce de Leon, the Spanish explorer, came back
to America, after accompanying Columbus on his first
voyage, he came in small ships; and to economize storage
he brought with him a few small Spanish mustang horses.
His object was to use them in his search for that marvelous "Fountain of Youth," which was to transmute the
dull and wasted materials of age into the vital principle
of youth, and enable old age to put on the vigor of youth
and retain the experience of age. De Leon landed on the
coast of Florida in the early years of the sixteenth century, to accomplish his original and glorious mission, but he
found much mosquitoes, tarantulas and alligators, but no
Fountain of Youth; and he went back to Spain and left
the little mustangs to shift for themselves. They, having
the instinct of wisdom, and not liking the sunny land in
which insects abounded and only man was dwarfed, sought
a more salubrious clime, migrated slowly northward, until
they came to the coast of Carolina, where food was abundant and insects scarce, and there, with a wisdom superior to man's they have ever since remained, docile when
domesticated and helpful to his human colaborer.

DARE COUNTY

Aye, call it holy ground,
The soil where first they trod
Mrs. Hemans.

. . . ty of Dare was . . . ed by . . . or rik taken
. . . . . . the co. . . . Car. . . ., Tyrrell and
Py . . . . 'en . . . . inha. . nts
. . . . s, . . lth
. . . . p. . . . . hou. . . . . wti h lways
. . . st. . . . . he ca. . Ma. . . . . e m v
t. . . . . d . . . ot Roa. . . . . . the
. . . . S. . 'ow Ba. B. . . . 'lo . . h . pres. . . own
. . . . . pre. . . s o. . . . ay, . . h . . r . . . . seat
. . . . ow . . . . lave
w. . . . . h 'he . . rich

A. sea
. . . C. . . . . H . . . . ew
. . . . . e . . . l . . . . of
. . . . B . . l . . Seven
. . . . . . C. . . . . M. . . . . Roanoke
. . . . hari-
. . . . 'is
. . . . tes
. . . . R. an
. . . . M . M . . . . . the
. . . . ne
. . . . ne
. . . . sh
. . . . oits
. . . . n ls,
. . . . ear-
. . . . N. . ber.
. . . . C. . te. . y, and
. . . . . C. . . l . . . . . ws 'he
. . . . l w. . d

repeats the circuit from Cape Hatteras. They are the terror of the sea. The bull dogs of the ocean. As ravenous as ... Woe to the man or beast ... fowl that comes within reach of ... Woe to ... Poor ...

... Waters of Roanoke ...

... "Menhaden," and ... when they reach the Albemarle coast they are recognized as "Fat Back," and welcomed with bloody teeth ...

... Sometimes, frightened almost to death by their pursuers ...

... with bloody ... the ocean all around ...

... somebody "shot," or could ... "much ..." ... rear up in the ... of the fish, and come up to the top of the oar ... around the ...

head, with three cheers for Tilden, Hendricks and Vance. All Dare, now, is on the rampage for the blue-fish fray, and though the terror of the sea, when they meet the daring men of Dare they'll meet an enemy they can not conquer.

— — - ·

NAGS HEAD.

"The Land of the Blest."

WE write amid historic associations. Our eye takes in at a glance the scenes and places where the first white men landed in America of whom history has preserved an authentic narrative. The now closed inlet through which Sir Walter Raleigh's colonists, under the command of Amadas and Barlowe, entered Roanoke Sound; "Ballast Point," where they cast anchor, where the white man and the red man first met face to face, with that strange and mysterious color line of race that hath not and can not be blended in harmonious unity; the waters where they chaffered and traded with the Indians; the spot where was born Virginia Dare, the first white child of American birth, and where was first administered the rite of Christian baptism upon American soil; the rude fort or embankment thrown up by the ill-fated colonists as a protection against the attacks of hostile Indians; Croatan to which they went when they abandoned the fort, never to return or be heard of more; Roanoke Island with its old and recent sanguinary historical memories; and the new town of Manteo, consecrated by name and locality to the memory of him who through all the vicissitudes of adverse fortune was the true and steadfast friend of the pale-faced colonists--another illustration that

> "Little deeds of kindness.
> Little words of love,"

graven by humanity upon the tablet of the heart outlive the proudest memorials blazoned by ambition upon the records of fame—all these lie spread out before us as a vast panorama.

Nags Head has also a history, not gray with age and "rich with the spoils of time," but attractive in its social and domestic aspects, and in its more public character, connecting itself with events which have shaped the destinies of peoples, and to which time will give the enchantment that distance imparts.

It was here, in the war of 1812, that troops under the command of Captain Bell, of Currituck, were stationed to guard the coast and prevent the landing of the British forces. And here, too, in the war of 1812 lived some of a class of men incident to all wars, who were typified by that animal to which nature has denied the natural weapons with which it has armed its kind, which never "locks horns" with an enemy. It was here, in the war of 1861-1865, that Gen. H. A. Wise, of Virginia, had his headquarters while in command of the troops stationed on Roanoke Island, in the Spring of 1862, holding, when the disastrous battle ended, the post of safety, if not of danger, and illustrating in his safe and precipitate personal retreat by the light of buildings and stores himself had fired, that discretion is an important element in the estimate of valor.

But it is in its social and hygienic aspects that Nags Head is chiefly known and has become identified with the local history of this part of Eastern North Carolina. From that time when "the memory of man runneth not to the contrary" it has been the resort for health of persons and families living in the adjacent section. From time immemorial it has been the nursery of the Albemarle country. For many years families came down and passed much of the months from June to October, living in rude and primitive style, with such accommodations as could be obtained among the dwellers along the coast, a plain and peculiar people who obtained a precarious support from the supply of fish which the waters afforded and from the wrecks cast by the dangerous tempests upon the coast. From its accessibility and from its being a narrow part of the sand bank separating the sound from the ocean, Nags Head became the resort most frequented by the visitors, and about the year 1830 some advance was made in its summer comforts by some of the visitors putting up small one-story houses near the sound, upon the sand hills which dotted the shore in every direction. These simple shanty structures added greatly to the number and comfort of visitors. They possessed an expansive elasticity without limit, and by the addition of curtains were infinitesimally subdivided for the accommodation of friends.

The erection of a hotel building capable of accommodating some 200 persons in 1838, by a company composed of citizens of Elizabeth City, constitutes an epoch in the history of Nags Head. This event gave it a new character and a new departure. Hitherto it had been the resort of families and their friends, occupying isolated rude tenements, with no common centre of union, but now fashion and gayety were to attract with their enchantment a new class of visitors. Youth and beauty, belles and beaux, with the romance of love and flirtation, added a new feature, and every season had its tale of matches made or broken. "Engagement Hill," about this time, derived its name from circumstances that its name suggests, and its tradition and history excel those of "Kill Devil Hills" or "Nags Head Hill" in romantic and tender incidents.

The career of Nags Head was an unbroken progress of prosperity until the war of 1861, which desolated the place. Elegant structures, the seats of social refinement and happiness, were given over to the ruthless hands of half-savage negroes and a fanatic soldiery. The private residences were torn down. The little church, around which clustered so many sacred associations, shared the same fate at the hands of the spoilers, and when peace came with its healing wings, scenes once bright with the mingled happiness of childhood, manhood and age were naught but a mournful desolation, with the wild winds chanting the requiem of the dead past amid the solitude of the eternal hills.

But time will heal and tears will dry, and after an absence of many years, with their mournful vicissitudes, we have come again to revisit old scenes peopled with memories of the departed, with the old familiar land-marks swept off by the sand drift. The old ocean is still here with the huge billows still echoing the great voice of the Almighty. We have buffeted again the same grand old mountain waves, swam out again beyond the breakers, and rested again in poise upon the bosom of the briny deep. That old ocean trick out of the strong swimmer acquired in boyhood, clings to us through life with the same tenacity that it clings to a bull frog. All of scene changed, some vestige of the old hotel, built in 1838 and burned in 1862 are still visible.

12

GOVERNOR SWAIN.

" Speak of me as I am; nothing extenuate;
Nor set down aught in malice."

If we were asked who was more distinguished in the public life of North Carolina for patriotism, usefulness, and State love, we would reply, after Zeb. Vance, our beloved war governor—Governor David L. Swain—the long-popular President of the University of North Carolina, both natives and residents of the county of Buncombe.

Strange to say, Governor Swain was a surprise and a disappointment to the whole State of North Carolina when he was selected as President of the University. He was a malformation in person, out of proportion in physical conformation, apparently thrown together in haste and manufactured from scattered debris of material that had been used in other work. Nature had been a most unkind mother to him; gawky, lanky, with a nasal twang that proclaimed him an alien, and a pedal propulsion that often awakened derision and offended nobody's self-love. In addition to all these unjust gifts of nature, he was an unlettered man and owed nothing to the primary or higher schools, and so far as scholastic training goes, he was an ignorant man.

And yet he was elected to the Presidency of the oldest and best institution of learning in the Southern States, and administered its affairs longer and with more wisdom than any of his distinguished predecessors; and by precept and example during his long administration, he impressed himself upon the sons of North Carolina as no other man in the State has ever done— an impression that is shown in our mature manhood at this day, and will be felt in North Carolina as long as time lasts.

It was President David L. Swain that helped much to give us Zeb. Vance and make that most loved Carolinian the great man that he was. It was President Swain's bounty that enabled Vance to secure an education at the

University of North Carolina, where he laid the foundation of his future greatness.

When the bee of the University first buzzed in Governor Swain's bonnet, so to speak, he was himself in doubt as to his fitness for the Presidency of the University. He had been prominent in politics, had acquired some distinction as a lawyer, had been a leading member of the Legislature, and was sometimes spoken of as a popular speaker and parliamentarian. He had been elected Governor of the State, and when Dr. Caldwell, President of the University, died in 1835, Swain's administration of the State Government was about expiring.

One fine fall evening the Governor was sitting alone in his official office on the capitol grounds in Raleigh. Judge Nash passed through the grounds, and seeing Governor Swain sitting alone in the door of his office stopped in to talk with him. The Governor was in a confiding mood and explained to the kind Judge his situation. He said his term of office as Governor of the State was drawing to a close, and he was puzzled to know what he was going to do for a living; that it would take a long time for him to reestablish himself in his law practice; that he was never fond of law practice; that there was no vacancy in the United States Senate from North Carolina, and would not be for several years, and that he thought of being a candidate for the Presidency of the University. He asked Judge Nash, who was a man of literary accomplishments and legal learning, what he thought of it. The Judge did not reply promptly and it was evident he did not think well of it. Before Judge Nash replied the Governor said to him: "Well, Judge Nash, if you will mention the matter to Judge Duncan Cameron, who loves the University, and he disapproves of it, I will say no more about it." Judge Nash replied that he was then on his way to Judge Cameron's to tea, and would mention the subject to him. Judge Nash during the evening at Judge Cameron's said to him that Governor Swain wanted the appointment of President of the University, and asked him what he thought of it.

Judge Cameron, after a moment's reflection, said:
"Well, I never thought of it, but Swain is the very man
for the place; a man who has proven himself such a great
manager of men would make a good manager of boys."
The Governor was told this opinion of Judge Cameron,
and forthwith announced himself as a candidate for the
place.

When the intelligence of Governor Swain's candidacy
for President of the University reached Chapel Hill the
faculty was astounded. Dr. Mitchell, familiarly called
"Old Mike," who was a pushing man, anxious for a
place, and had an unbridled tongue, ridiculed the subject.
Dr. Hooper, familiarly called "Old Billy," also hankered
after the place. He was a proud man, of exquisite wit
and humor, and his pride of ancestry was sharpened by
the current of his blood that ran through nobles ever since
the flood. He was quiet, but in an unguarded moment let
drop the remark that "the people of North Carolina had
done everything they could for their ignorant Governor and
now they wanted to send him to the University to be educated."

We had seen Governor Swain twice before he became
President of the University. Once when he was Governor, and once when he was a member of the Convention
of 1835, representing Buncombe County.

In that Convention, which was torn by antagonistic
factions in the State on the basis of representation in the
General Assembly, Swain was the leader of the forces of
Western North Carolina. He made a great speech on
that subject, which at one time threatened the unity of
the State, and we listened to it with delight. He presented
all the points in the case from the western point of view.
It was bold, defiant, logical, argumentative and sometimes
eloquent. He was fond of Scriptural quotations, and often
used them with great effect. Once, towering in his wrath
and raising his index finger as in defiance of Eastern
Carolina, he said: "Let our Eastern brethren beware. If
they do not grant our peaceful appeal for a change in the

basis of representation, we will rise like the strong man in his unshorn might and pull down the pillars of the political temple."

The subject was under discussion in the Convention for several days, and every Western member that spoke referred to the Scriptural quotation of the "eloquent gentleman from Buncombe." At length, Mr. Gaston addressed the Convention on the same subject. After speaking about an hour, he turned round and said: "The gentleman from Buncombe has said that if the East does not grant the peaceful demands of the West, they will rise like the strong man in his unshorn might and pull down the pillars of the political temple. The strong man, the son of Manoah, was brought out from his prison to make sport for the enemies of his country, and do honor to the impious feast of Dagon. He tugged and heaved at the massive pillars of the temple, and all were crushed in one hideous ruin. It was a great and a glorious deed. He fell a martyr and a hero, victorious among the slain."

No more was heard of the eloquent gentleman's Scriptural quotation. Gaston had spiked Swain's Scriptural gun.

JAMES IREDELL--W. B. SHEPARD — KENNETH RAYNER—W. N. H. SMITH—COL. HENRY M. SHAW.

"Like the mother of the Gracchi, when asked for her jewels, she pointed to her sons."

The First District of North Carolina has always been proud of her Representatives in the National councils. Looking to the Senate of the United States first, she has had but one member of that august body during the existence of the Government—James Iredell, Jr.

Mr. Iredell was the son of Justice James Iredell, of the Supreme Court of the United States, under the administration of Washington. Descended from an intellectual ancestry, born to distinction, and being endowed by nature with great genius and ability, he reached manhood with much promise of distinction in his legal profession. He soon acquired distinction and popularity with his fellow citizens, and public life sought him as a Representative in the General Assembly.

He took high rank in debate in the General Assembly, and was the peer of Gaston, Drew, Cameron and Alfred Moore, and the other great men who adorned our State councils at that time. He was at the head of the law profession in the First Judicial District, and at an early age was transferred to the Circuit Bench.

Some years after, he was elected Governor of North Carolina by the Legislature. At the expiration of his term as Governor, he was elected to the United States Senate, to succeed Nat. Macon; and in that body he maintained a high position. It is said that he was selected to reply to Mr. Webster, in the celebrated debate on nullification, and his place was, in consequence of Iredell's sickness, supplied by Hayne, of South Carolina. He died at the age of sixty-five, when attending the Courts of the First District.

William B. Shepard was a native of New Bern, N. C. After coming of age, he removed to Camden County, where he had large landed estates, and after obtaining his law license he practiced his profession in that county with great success for several years.

After living some time in Camden, he made his home in Elizabeth City. Always interested in public affairs, studying politics from its highest standpoint, he took part in public discussions and became known to the people of the District as an able and accomplished man.

Lemuel Sawyer then represented the District in Congress, and had been in Congress for several years. Shepard was put in nomination by his friends as an opponent of Sawyer, and was elected over him in 1829, and continued in office for eight years; and while a member of Congress for eight years he became the undisputed leader of the North Carolina delegation in Congress. He was gifted as an orator, conservative as a statesman, and a gentleman in all his instincts and intercourse. He voluntarily retired from Congress.

He then, with ample means and leisure, led the life of a gentleman of leisure, attending the Courts of the local bar, and often elected to the Legislature as Senator and Representative.

He was often spoken of for United States Senator from North Carolina, and aspired to the position, and was fitted for it. In 1845 he was the competing candidate before the Legislature with George E. Badger, and his friends always thought that he would have been chosen if his speech accepting the situation had been made before his defeat. After that, his interest in public affairs diminished, and it seemed to be looked at by him from afar. He occasionally was elected to the Legislature, and some time in the fifties his health gave way, after the death of his second wife, and he departed for the "undiscovered country" with the love and admiration of his countrymen.

Kenneth Rayner was a lion in his early manhood. In its maturity his "vaulting ambition o'erleaped itself," and he fell, and in age he was poor and disappointed, forgotten by his old friends, having deserted them for new friends that he had always despised. At his death, his life became the burden of a moral and a tale. His memory is full of sadness, and recalls the words of the preacher, "Vanity of vanities! vanity of vanities! all is vanity!" Alas! once the popular idol, honored, loved, flattered and caressed. A great leader, bold, daring, unflinching. True to his friends, defiant to his enemies, loving North Carolina with his heart's devotion.

"Cromwell, I charge thee, fling away ambition. By that sin fell the angels." By that sin fell Kenneth Rayner. "Oh! what a fall was there, my countrymen!"

William N. H. Smith, of Murfreesboro, was a good and a great lawyer. He stood at the head of his profession. He rose to the Chief Justiceship of North Carolina. He took high rank in social position. In private life he was without reproach. In public and official life he was without a superior. He died in harness, in advanced age, with honors thick upon him, and left a memory that was without spot or blemish.

Col. Henry M. Shaw was a native of Rhode Island, but a citizen of North Carolina all of his mature life. At an early age he became an inmate of the family of Dr. Gideon Merchant, of Currituck County, and from that Gamaliel of Democracy he imbibed those political principles with which he was always identified.

From the time when he commenced the practice of medicine, he rose rapidly in practice and became very successful. But he was always an ardent politician, and soon became a leader in the Democratic councils and a public speaker in political campaigns.

He had great readiness as a public speaker, and was the most logical, forceful and deliberate that we ever listened to. He was thoroughly posted upon political and general subjects. He became prominent for Congressional honors, and was put in nomination as the candidate of the Democratic party.

His election followed his nomination, and he made a most excellent, obliging and able Representative. He went to Congress in a stormy period. The cloud-burst that drenched our country in blood was already portentous with forked lightning and rumbling thunder. Soon after, he left Congress to cast his lot with his troubled countrymen.

At the outbreak of the war, Colonel Shaw was tendered the command of the 8th Regiment of North Carolina Troops, which he promptly accepted. He entered the field at once. He was captured in the defence of Roanoke Island, where, after a gallant defence in a fight with over-powering numbers, he surrendered to a hopeless fate, after being flanked on both sides.

After his parol was out, he returned to his post of duty and danger, and at the battle of Bachelor's Creek, near New Bern, on the 1st of February, 1864, Colonel Shaw sealed his devotion to his country with his life. He was killed by a rifle ball while reconnoitering the enemy.

WILLIAM W. CHERRY.

" Friend of my youth,
Great mind of wondrous gifts "

CHERRY was distinguished at the University more for his rollicking disposition and for making the "Old South" ring with the echo of his voice, than for his studious habits. He was seldom on time at the beginning of a session, and once, on his way to the University, at the beginning of a session, he fell in with a party of companionable friends, not students, and went down to Fayetteville with them, reaching the University to join his class when the session was well advanced. But he managed by his genius and good nature to keep up with the class until his graduation.

Leaving the University, he returned to his home in Windsor, Bertie County, and after some delay entered upon the legal profession, of which he became a leading member. He was a great advocate, remarkable for his readiness, his admirable presentation of the facts of a case, and had a most magnetic influence with a jury. He was not a great lawyer, a profound lawyer, with a thorough and accurate and comprehensive knowledge of precedent and authority, versed in the deep subtleties of the law, its intricacies and discriminations, and capable of dividing a hair " 'twixt north and northwest side," but he was a thorough master of the facts of a case. He could turn and twist them, presenting them in every shade and complexion and aspect, and making them luminous to the plainest understanding. His language, the vehicle of his thought, was wonderful, and the play of his changing expression of countenance gave great force to it. His manner was natural and easy, his action perfectly unaffected and suited to the word, and his voice was charming to listen to, not the mellow deep toned voice of the trained elocutionist, but one that won by its sympathetic and kindly tones. It was a voice that drew his hearers to him and made them kin. When he was about to use a pleasantry, his face was lighted from afar, and his voice changed and his audience was led along and prepared for it.

Mr. Cherry was an active politician of the Whig school. He was a partisan without bitterness. When the Whig party was first known by that name, the Democratic, Jackson party, was largely in the ascendant in Bertie. Cherry took his fiddle, on which he was an expert, and canvassed the county in all the highways and by-ways, and by his pleasantry and *bonhommie* won them largely over into the Whig ranks.

In the Harrison campaign of 1840, he was a great power. He attended the Whig National Convention at Harrisburg that nominated General Harrison, and it is believed that he first turned to account for General Harrison the "hard-cider and coon-skin" jeer, upon which the campaign so largely turned in that political storm. He certainly was the first that used it in Eastern North Carolina, stating in a log-cabin speech in Edenton, soon after his return from Harrisburg, that he had first seen the taunt in Baltimore on his return from the National Convention, and used it in the campaign. In that campaign Cherry was the great bulwark of Whiggery in the First District. He spoke everywhere to large crowds, and gained votes. Shepard, and Rayner, and Outlaw, and Speed, and Allen, and Tom Jones were his compeers and supporters. He was elected from the county of Bertie to the Legislature of North Carolina for the first time in the public service in that year. He was then but little known out of the District, but we heard Judge Moore say, about that time, that Cherry would be a thorn in the side of the Democrats in the Legislature.

A little incident may be mentioned illustrating his readiness. He went to Raleigh to the Legislature by way of Warrenton. Arriving in Warrenton at night, a stranger, he joined a group of Warrentonians around the fire of the public room of the hotel and soon joined them in a political talk, they being all Democrats of the Warren County type, he taking the Whig side. The stranger, plainly clad, and not imposing in person, got the best of the argument, and the Warrentonians looked at him with some astonishment. Failing in argument, they fell back on an authority which settled all questions in Warren County. They quoted Nat. Macon in confirmation of their opinions, supposing that no one would dare gainsay what Mr. Macon had said. Cherry dissented from Mr. Macon's opinion, and, to the surprise of others, spoke lightly of that great man. The Warrentonians promptly retorted that John Randolph, in his will, had said that "Nat. Macon was the wisest man he had ever known." At that time a suit was pending in the Court of Appeals, at Richmond, contesting Mr. Randolph's will, chiefly upon the ground of insanity. Cherry, in reply to the quoted opinion of the eminent Virginian, said: "Mr. Randolph's will is contested in Richmond now, upon the ground of insanity, and I think the strongest proof of his insanity is that he said that Nat. Macon was a wise man."

Mr. Cherry was once in a public meeting at Gatesville, in the court-house, and there was some difficulty with the chairman in determining a question that was submitted to vote. The ayes and noes were called. Not satisfactory. Divide. Not satisfactory. The ayes will go to one side of the house and the noes to the other. Cherry called out to the ayes, of which he was one, to seize the noes and carry them over to their side of the house. It was a scuffling vote that was some hours in the determination. Finally, the panting ayes "appeared to have it, the ayes had it." This illustrates Cherry's pleasantry.

In 1844, Cherry was the Clay Presidential elector opposed by an able champion of Democracy, Thomas Bragg, afterward Governor. It was the battle of the giants. Cherry stood his ground and maintained his position with great ability. Bragg was a battle-axe, Cherry was a scimeter. He carried the District.

In 1846, Mr. Cherry was nominated for Congress by the Whig Convention that met in Edenton. He was nominated without opposition, and after being introduced, delivered a speech of great power and interest. We, then a young man with a fresh license, being Secretary of the Convention, reported, in brief, Mr. Cherry's speech. After writing it out from our notes, we submitted it to him, and, after his approval, sent the proceedings of the Convention with the speech reported in full, to the *Raleigh Register* for publication. The same paper which contained the proceedings of the Convention, contained the notice of his death. He died while attending North Carolina Conference the week after his nomination, at the early age of forty-three years.

"What shadows we are and what shadows we pursue."

Mr. Cherry was small in person, with a rather large head and a winning expression of face that won all hearts. Nature had not been kind to him in his personal make-up, of which he frequently jested. His face was angular, his hair coarse and stiff, and he was negligent of his dress. To be plain, he was unmistakably ugly. But he had all the virtues that we love and admire, with no counteracting vices. He was a most charming and attractive companion, and the District sustained a great loss in his untimely death.

THE MINISTERS OF GOD.

"Pointing up to Heaven,
They led the way."

THE pulpit of North Carolina has furnished saintly men who were the leaders of public thought in matters relating to godliness, and who by wise counsel and burning words have made the world the better for their living.

Among these great men no one has been more conspicuous than Rev. Thomas Atkinson, Bishop of the Diocese of North Carolina of the Protestant Episcopal Church. He was a native of Virginia, and was elected to the Episcopate of North Carolina after the apostacy of Bishop Ives. He was elected in the early fifties. It was a most fortunate selection, and God's wise guidance was manifest in it. He was a comparative stranger to the Convention that made the selection. He was elected after many ballotings, over men who had a large following and who ranked among the most distinguished theologians, and were a great force in the sacred desk. The time when he came was inauspicious. The blow given to the Church by an apostate Bishop was not yet healed. But his coming was a benediction. It soothed and cemented factions, and every one became satisfied. He was soon recognized as one of the princes of the pulpit, a godly man, without guile or selfishness, of kindly social instincts, firm without dogmatism, and learned without ostentation; imposing in person, graceful in action, effective in oratory, simple and natural in every act. His sermons were models of every eloquence; masterful in argument, forceful in logic, touching in pathos. Every subject he touched, he invested with a new and sacred interest. His sermon on "Necessity and Free Will" was the clearest and most profound exposition of that most intricate religious puzzle we ever listened to.

Turning from this brief reference to this eminent servant of God, we select Dr. Thomas H. Pritchard, the distinguished Baptist minister, as a star of brightest lustre in the firmament of the clergy.

Dr. Pritchard was a Henderson on the maternal side of his lineage, and that means strength in intellectuality, profundity in thought, taste and elegance in diction, and the most charming gifts of social intercourse. Scratch the soil in North Carolina where great men grow, wherever you will, and you will find a Henderson there. The stock is indigenous to North Carolina, and it has illustrated every department of its intellectual life. Dr. Pritchard was no exception to this unvarying rule.

We first met Thomas Pritchard when he was a student of the Baptist ministry and a private tutor in the family of Richard Felton, a wealthy planter in the county of Perquimans. We spent a week with him, and had frequent conversations with him. To us he then gave little promise of the great factor he was afterwards to become in the pulpit and councils of the Baptist Church in North Carolina. He was modest, retiring and diffident. We thought him too much so. He seemed deficient in strength of conviction, and too ready to acquiesce in suggestions on religious and other subjects before he had sufficiently examined them.

Forty years from that time, we were in attendance at a Baptist Association, sitting in the far-end of the church, near the pulpit, in which its annual session was held. Way down at the lower door of the church a portly man came in, and he was soon greeted by friends who came up and shook hands with him. His step to the end of the church, where we sat, was an ovation. We saw at once that a big man's shadow was over the crowd. His person and manner were imposing and in admirable taste. He had a kind word for this and that brother as he approached us. As he came near, the word "brother," as it came from his lungs in deep sonorous tones, fell on our ear. We scanned him closely as he came. That man must be a Henderson, thought we: we can see our old Aleck all over him. Then we looked at him through the glasses of forty years, and we could see glimmering through the darkness the modest Tom Pritchard that we had passed a week with at Richard Felton's forty years before. When he reached our place, he swung around in a seat just in advance of us.

After he had rested awhile, we rose, stood before him, and extended our hand; and he, not recognizing us, we asked if he knew us. He said not, and then said enquiringly, "Who is the brother?" We replied, "Not a brother, a first cousin, perhaps." We then gave him our name, and he said with much heartiness, "God bless me! Dr. Tom Martin and I were talking about you last week, when we went fishing."

We saw much of Dr. Pritchard afterwards, and heard his admirable addresses on education after he became President of Wake Forest College. His public speeches were models of excellence. His voice was a bugle call, his elocution as graceful and tasteful, and every sentence he uttered was the expression of a great truth.

Among the pioneers of Wesleyan Methodism no one's memory is held in higher estimation for his usefulness, his exemplary Christian character, and his efficient labors as a faithful minister of God than Louis Skidmore. He was emphatically a good man, a good and influential preacher, and his mellow voice with its sweet intonations melted hearts to tenderness and won them to the paths of a Christian life.

When a small boy, hardly in our teens, it was our good fortune, when away at school, to board with a pious Methodist family in the town of Oxford. Their house was the hospitable home of all Methodist preachers. None was more welcome than Louis Skidmore, and no one contributed more to the happiness of the household. His voice was an Eolian harp, with a bugle attachment. The old Methodist hymns of eighty years ago he had at his tongue's end. He often preached in the village church, and he would bring an audience to its feet when he uttered the sweet notes of the "Old Ship of Zion," or some other rally hymn of the olden time. He could wake a shouting revival at any time by his powers of song.

Other names of great pulpit power in North Carolina crowd upon us. Dr. Hawks was a born orator, and a man of genius without the nose of a historian. Quentin Trotman was a great master among men. President Wingate, of Wake Forest College, was a pulpit orator of superior gifts and an unequalled executive officer.

Rev. Thomas Lowe, of Halifax, whom we never met, is pronounced by competent judges a paragon of oratory: and Dr. Closs, the greatest and best of men.

UNION LEAGUE AND KU KLUX KLAN.

Gorgons, Hydras and Chimeras dire.

THE history of North Carolina is full of civil and military revolutions, social convulsions and upheavals that threatened at times her existence as an organized government; but there has been no civil and social convulsion in her history that equals in horror and atrocity the sad scenes that threatened the peace and happiness of our people in the time of reconstruction and Freedman's Bureau that followed as a sequel to the unhappy "War between the States."

After the war, with the passions and bitterness of the sanguinary conflict still burning with unabated fury, the more unrelenting elements of the North seemed to turn their swords, yet reeking with slaughter, into reaping hooks of gain, gleaners in the desolated harvest fields of a conquered enemy. The South was overrun with Northern emissaries, some animated by a feeling of sincere philanthropy, stimulated by the ardor of a fanatic crusader, and with a charitable desire to elevate a race whom they had been trained by romance and song to believe had been kept in subjugation by long oppression and torture, and who needed only a helping hand to be lifted to a plane of equality with the best Caucasian blood of the South. Some came to spy out the nakedness of a land overrun by the fortunes of war; but generally from a desire of gain and to gather up the fragments that were left of a luxury that had once adorned a land that bloomed with wealth and happiness.

They found a race, lately emancipated, happy, credulous, ignorant and easily deceived. They became their leaders, and in many cases inflamed the passions of the late slaves against their old masters. They established secret orders or lodges, which fitted the nature of the late slaves, admitted them to membership and inspired them with wicked and diabolical purposes.

The Union League was the first fruits of this invasion of the South after its desolation and sorrow of an unsuccessful four years' war. It combined various elements of our much-mixed population—philanthropists, carpet-bag adventurers, some native Union men, negroes, and others led by sheer curiosity. It soon produced legitimate fruits. Southern men of high character were objects of vengeance. Barns were burned; their owners were sometimes shot in the darkness as they ran out to extinguish the flames; negroes were urged to pillage and plunder; and there was a reign of apprehension and terror.

This condition of disorder produced its natural results. Proud, intelligent and patriotic men, crushed to earth by combinations that they were powerless to resist, determined to accomplish by artifice what they could not do by open resistance.

They knew the negro character better than the new comers, of whom they were the dupes. They knew their caution, their superstition, and their timidity.

A new protective secret organization had been started in Pulaski, Tenn., and had acquired a local celebrity, and had sought an extension in North Carolina. It was called the order of the "Ku Klux Klan." It was considered by our wisest, most fearless and patriotic leaders. A branch of the order was soon established in some of our western counties, and its ritual, regalia, masks and passwords were adopted. Its operations were by night, and its visitations and equipment struck terror into the superstitious minds of the negro race. It acted well for some time and had a salutary influence in the counties where the outlawry prevailed. But excess followed the success of the order, and these excesses were greatly exaggerated.

Governor Holden, of Raleigh, then held the office of Governor of North Carolina. Either influenced by fear of his own safety or by love of display and authority, he issued a proclamation, putting the counties in which the Ku Klux were operating under martial law and suppressing all civil law, intending to break up the order by the rule of his own autocratic will.

In the central counties he arrested some of the most
distinguished citizens of the State, imprisoned them without trial, and tortured them in the most cruel manner, to
extort confessions that might implicate others as members
of the Ku Klux order.   He called to his aid outlaws and
desperadoes from East Tennessee, invested one Kirk, from
Tennessee, who had been a buffaloe in the Confederate
war, with autocratic authority to arrest and punish as he
might please any persons that he should suspect of being
in any way connected with the Ku Klux organization.
Kirk was a willing and a ready agent of Holden.   He
imprisoned old men, gray-headed, distinguished for long
and patriotic service to the State, such men as Judges
Roane and Carr, and subjected them to inhuman treatment.

The whole State was aroused.   The Supreme Court
was appealed to to issue a writ of *habeas corpus* and have
the persons brought before the State Courts.   The writ
was issued, but Holden refused to give heed to it.   The
Chief Justice was appealed to to enforce its execution,
but he declined to enforce it.

At length Judge George W. Brooks, of Elizabeth City,
a Federal Judge of great firmness and integrity of character, finding his authority in a Federal statute, issued
a writ of *habeas corpus* for the imprisoned citizens; and
he served the State with a courageous fidelity which,
though appreciated at the time, has never yet been duly
honored by the State of North Carolina.

The Democratic Legislature of 1870, early in the session, properly passed a bill of impeachment against Governor Holden, and impeached him for high crimes and
misdemeanors for his conduct in the Ku Klux matters;
and after a long judicial examination, convicted him,
expelled him from his high office, and made him incapable
of holding office thereafter in the State.   He lived to
advanced age, a pitiable old man, an object-lesson in Carolina history of the punishment that awaits an evil-doer.

WESTERN SCENERY.

Pelion piled on Ossa.

WERE you ever among the mountains of Madison County, North Carolina? If not, go; and you will see old nature in her grand majesty, and if not pompous and proud, you will feel the littleness and humility of humanity. You will feel like a pigmy among giants and will involuntarily breathe the Scripture— "Oh, God! what is man, that Thou art mindful of him: or the son of man that Thou regardest him?"

You look around, see nature in her august majesty; you feel your own littleness and your kinship to the worm that crawleth on the earth. Look around you and wonder! You are in the "Land of the Skies," six thousand feet above sea-level, with mountains piled on mountains all around you, and tinkling rills dancing to the monotone of their melody in the valleys below; a sight lovely, picturesque and grand beyond description to the dwellers in the alluvial plains.

Put yourself in Waynesville, look around at the mountain peaks piled on mountain peaks, and cast your glance on Pigeon River below, as it goes gurgling and singing to the sea. We once stood among those scenes, and a half-tone photograph of them still lingers fresh and undimmed upon our memory. It read us a sermon in rocky mountain cliffs that we have never forgotten.

While there, we went, with an old bear hunter of the mountains for a guide, to the mountain peaks near by. His name was Wid Medford. He was guide, pilot and yarner of Lickstone Mountain. We saw the eagle in his eyrie, and saw our National bird in his domestic surroundings, with his eye like Mars commanding the sun below him. Every glance of the eye from that land that kissed the skies was an anthem and a poem. But amid all that grandeur of nature that gave us foretaste of the grandeur of that higher destiny to which we aspire, there was a grotesque piquancy in the stories related to us by our guide, of "hair-breadth escapes" by flood and field, of deadly grapple with the beasts of the forest in their homes in the mountain gorge and jungle, and other incidents of sixty-five years of a wild hunter's life of peril that brought us back to the realities of this mundane sphere.

The fluency with which Wid reeled off his stories recalled the aphorism of the "twice-told tale." Some of them we can never forget. Pardon one of them.

Wid had been wandering for some days among the mountain peaks and canyons of Lickstone in a vain search for a panther whose unaccustomed scream he had heard some nights before. While pursuing this lead, he saw, by signs well known to a mountain hunter's practiced eye, that he was near the camping grounds of several large bears. He followed the trail slowly and carefully. The signs grew more and more numerous. Here would be seen a broken limb, there the berries were lapped, and again there was a pause at a pool to take a "wallow" bath. He saw by studying the hunter's alphabet that there were three bears in the herd—an old dam and two well-grown cubs. He soon scented them, and approached them on the leeward side and saw three bears lapping chestnuts in the top of a large chestnut tree. His ammunition had been exhausted to two charges in the barrels of "Old Betsy." They lapped apart, and he could not hope to bring down three bears with two loads. He manœuvered dexterously for some time, but could never get them in range. At length he determined to secure two of them with his two loads, discharged in quick succession. "Bang! went 'Old Betsy,'" said he, "and down tumbled one. Bang! she repeated, and down came another." The third one staid up the tree, at first in wild amazement. At length he climbed down slowly. Wid secreted himself at the bottom of the tree, drew his butcher knife, and when bear number three came within reach of him he clasped him in his arms and cut his throat, and then secured him. Some one in our party, bolder than the rest, said: "Wid, you know that's a lie." To which Wid replied, with great earnestness and fervor, " 'Fore God, it's a living truth, and if the bear was here he'd tell you so."

While we remained and wandered among the wonderful scenes of the mountains, that wondrous "Land of the Skies," where the devout man may dwell in contemplation of heavenly scenes, we saw many things which yet we love to linger on. We were much pleased with a little church we saw—"Grace Church in the Mountains." It is a memorial church for a little grandchild of Bishop Atkinson, a daughter of Dr. Buell. It is built of black walnut, curled black walnut, poplar, ash and oak, and is a gem. The furniture of the church was made of black walnut and manufactured in Waynesville. It will seat about two hundred persons. One of the windows, a memorial window, was presented by the good Bishop.

We did not see, but heard of a Presbyterian church in the near vicinity of Waynesville that was built entirely of one poplar tree, and enough timber was left over of the tree to fence in the yard. The tree was ten feet across the stump. This may seem to savor of Munchausen, but we heard the fact frequently mentioned, and it was vouched for by persons of unquestioned veracity.

GENERAL J. J. PETTIGREW.

Twine a few sad cypress leaves around the brow of any land, and it becomes lovely in its consecrated coronet of sorrow.
—*Father Ryan.*

DURING his absence in Europe, Pettigrew had devoted much study to military science. The conviction upon his mind before his last visit to Europe and during his absence, was strong and decided that a bloody crisis impended over his own country, and that the muttering thunders of war which had so long threatened its peace, which several times had been averted by the patriotic and earnest efforts of those to whom the country turned with confidence in times of difficulty and listened with reliance and trust to their peaceful counsels, could be calmed no longer. While they lived, while the venerable patriots whose life-long service had been given to their country and whose patriotism and devotion to the whole and every part of it, none could question, the storm of sectional strife had been often allayed; so often, indeed, that the conviction became general of a special good providence which held the favored land in the hollow of its hand and would bear it safely on over the surging billows of domestic discord. But the trusted hands that had so long held the helm and guided the ship when tossed by the tempest of political strife were cold in death, the voices so potent to calm the angry waves of sectional commotion were hushed, and the calm and peaceful counsels, left as a legacy to their countrymen, were forgotten, or really unheeded by the maddened and reckless zealots of party, urged on by desperate partisans who, unmindful of the perils that threatened, sought the triumph of sectional success even at the price of fraternal blood and a ruined country.

With the conviction firmly impressed upon him that the slumbering fires of long years of angry contention could not be much longer suppressed, and that, studied by the ordinary manifestations of our nature and the lights furnished by the lessons of history, the theatre of contention must soon be transferred from legislative halls to tented fields, and political questions, to which the statesman-ship and patriotism of the times were unequal, must be determined by armed battalions amid the realities of war, Pettigrew began his work of preparation for the anticipated conflict of arms. While in Paris he had opportunities of military study and observation in that metropolis of war, of which he was not unmindful. He had been favorably introduced to those who had become distinguished in the art of war, and the chief purpose of his visit being well understood, he had such advantages of acquiring knowledge of the science of war and its practical details as are seldom afforded. Upon his return to Charleston, he was elected captain of a rifle company, which he organized and formed after the plan of the French Zouave model, with the efficiency of which mode of drill he had been much pleased in France. The company soon attracted much attention. Its novelty, and the spirit with which it was animated, won the commendation of the city of Charleston. It became a model military organization, and was regarded as the best of the volunteer companies in South Carolina. Nor was it a mere mimic pageant of war. It was the serious and earnest offspring of Petti-grew's conviction of the necessity of preparation. The portents were all ominous of the dreadful future, and a prudent forecast dictated preparation for coming events of serious and alarming magnitude. For this purpose the rifle company was formed. It was soon joined by other volunteer organizations, formed after the same model, and Pettigrew was elected Colonel of the First Rifle Regi-ment.

And now the time, so long deferred, had come. So long deferred that many thought a special providence guarded the destiny of the country, to bear it safely through all political perils, and avert the dire calamity of war. Deferred by the earnest exertions of patriotic hearts, by the eloquent appeals of trusted statesmen, by the sin core prayers of the faithful, by the proud memory of the past and the bright hopes of the future of our country. But it could be deferred no longer. The fiat of the Omnipotent had been uttered in the wrath of God and the decree was to be sealed with the lives of martyred heroes and patriots, and the record made eternal in the inextinguishable baptism of blood. Where the fault, or upon whose shoulders rests the burden of the great sin and its grievous sequences, this is not the occasion to enquire. Let it be buried, so far as feeble mortals may, until nations, as individuals, shall stand around the throne and at the judgment bar of the Great Eternal God, and answer for all the deeds done while in the body.

Upon the secession of South Carolina, Pettigrew immediately offered his regiment for military service. Upon the occupation of Fort Sumter by Major Anderson, Pettigrew was assigned the command of Castle Pinckney, and was afterward transferred to Morris Island, in order to prevent the reinforcement of Fort Sumter by the Government of the United States. The unexpected occupation of Fort Sumter by Major Anderson, under cover of night, precipitated events. Pettigrew was ordered by Governor Pickens to demand of Anderson the evacuation of the Fort, as its occupation was in violation of an agreement that the situation of Charleston harbor should remain unchanged and await the efforts to avert the impending troubles. The result of that demand we give in Pettigrew's own words, in a letter to Governor Pickens:

"*To F. W. Pickens, Governor, etc.*

"Sir: I have the honor to report that pursuant to the instructions of your Excellency, I proceeded this morning to Fort Sumter in company with Maj. Ellison Capers, Acting Adjutant of my Regiment.

"We were courteously received by Major Anderson, the commanding officer.

"I stated to him in the presence of all of his officers that you had been astonished at the reception of the news of

his having transferred his garrison to Fort Sumter, that
by the understanding between the State of South Carolina and the President of the United States, the property
of the United States was to be respected, and on the other
side the military posts should remain in an unchanged
condition, in a word that the question was to be considered a political, and not a military one. I enforced upon
him strongly the fact that we had punctiliously performed

"He declined acceding to my demand.

repressed every attempt to precipitate the people upon the
property of the United States, and I demanded in your
name that affairs should be restored to their previous condition.

"He replied that he was a Southern man in his feelin_s
upon the questions at issue, and had so informed the department when appointed; that he knew nothing of the
agreement mentioned; that he was the Military Commander of all the forts in the harbor and did not consider
that he had re-enforced them in merely transferring his
garrison from one to another; that he had been informed
from various sources that he would probably be attacke i
in case the report of the Commissioners was unfavorable;
that Fort Moultrie was indefensible against an ordinarily
skilful attack; that he had acted entirely upon his own responsibility.

"He declined acceding to my demand.

             "Very respectfully,

                    "J. JOHNSTON PETTIGREW."

In the interval until the bombardment and surrender
of Fort Sumter, Pettigrew was at Morris Island, perfect-
ing his regiment in drill and discipline and training them
to the rigorous hardships of military service. His command, from the nature of its organization, did not take
part in the bombardment of Fort Sumter.

Early in 1861 he received a stand of colors for his regiment, which he acknowledged in these touching words:

"The flag of the old Republic is ours no more. That
noble standard which has so often waved over victorious

fields; which has so often carried hope to the afflicted and struggling hearts of Europe; which has so often protected us in distant climes, afar from home and kindred, now threatens us with destruction. In all its former renown we participated. Southern valor bore it to its proudest triumphs, and oceans of Southern blood have watered the ground beneath it. Let us lower it with honor, and lay it reverently upon the earth."

With the fall of Sumter, all hope of reconciliation or peace was abandoned, if indeed all hope of peace had not flown before, and each section of the country confronted the other in the grim-visaged antagonism of war. The position of Adjutant-General of the State was tendered to Colonel Pettigrew by the Legislature of South Carolina. This position, requiring great administrative ability and of eminent usefulness in organizing the State forces, the acceptance of which was urged upon him in consideration of greater usefulness than when restricted to the duties of a single regiment, Pettigrew declined. He sought the active duties of the field as more congenial to his temperament, and at the request of General Beauregard he proceeded to organize a rifle regiment for service during the war, of which he was to be Colonel. The regiment was soon made up, and companies exceeding the number required had to be refused. Staff and field officers were agreed on and a junior officer dispatched to Montgomery, then the seat of the Confederate Government, to offer the regiment to the Secretary of War, and obtain authority to muster it into service. But the plan of the Confederate Secretary of War, at the time, was to receive companies, and not organize regiments, reserving to himself the organization into regiments, and the selection and appointment of field officers. This arrangement of the Secretary of War met with much opposition from the companies that composed the regiment, and their efforts to retain the selection of officers to themselves being unsuccessful, they, many of them, sought admission to other regiments, which were being formed in the State, under authority of the Department of War.

Colonel Pettigrew was thus without command, but his ardent spirit was not long at rest. The State of North Carolina, his cherished mother, shortly afterward rendered him the command of the Twelfth North Carolina Regiment, which he accepted as Colonel, and proceeded at once to Raleigh to assume the command.

During the winter of 1861-'62 he was in camp at Evansport on the Potomac. He discharged all the duties pertaining to his situation with such eminent ability and skill, and with such satisfaction to his superior officers, that entirely without his knowledge, he was recommended for promotion to the rank of Brigadier General. This appointment was tendered him by the President, but with rare modesty the appointment was declined by Colonel Pettigrew on the ground that he had not seen sufficient active service for so important a command; that he had never been under fire and had never commanded troops when in action. This rare case of modesty surprised the President, who remarked that it was the first case in which an officer had refused promotion to an office because he had not proved his fitness for the place by an actual discharge of its duties. This reluctance to assume a higher command was, however, overcome by Major General Holmes, who, upon General French (Pettigrew's brigade commander) being ordered to report to Wilmington for duty, insisted that Colonel Pettigrew should recall his refusal of promotion and succeed General French in command of the brigade. This request of General Holmes being urged with earnestness, as a patriotic duty, overruled his judgment, and he wrote to the War Department revoking his refusal. He was then at Fredericksburg.

Soon after, General Pettigrew was ordered to Yorktown and with Whiting's division, was engaged in the hotly-contested battle of the Seven Pines. In this battle he was wounded in the neck and shoulder and fell into the hands of the enemy. On the 31st of May, while the battle was raging, he was instructed to drive the enemy from a position in the woods where they were strongly posted. The attempt had been made before by a regiment of the division and had failed. The position held by the enemy was a strong one, and in making the attack the regiment was exposed to the fire of a battery of artillery on the flank. Pettigrew, leading one of his regiments, was attempting to carry the position by assault when he was wounded. An attempt was made to remove him from the field, while exhausted from the loss of blood, by a captain of one of his companies, but inquiring how the day was going, and being told it was against us, and hearing some of the officers rallying their men, he insisted that the officer and men who were assisting him, should leave him on the field and join their company. For some time he was thought to be mortally wounded, and he was mourned by his kindred and his country as one who had passed from earthly scenes. But it was afterward ascertained that he had been sent to Fort Delaware as a prisoner of war.

Upon returning from Fort Delaware, still suffering from his wounds, he took command of his brigade, near Petersburg. The necessities of the service had transferred his old regiment to another command, but he soon perfected the discipline of the new organization, and his reputation for military skill and the rare attractiveness of his personal character filled his ranks with North Carolina's most sterling sons.

With his brigade filled and disciplined anew, he joined the army of the Potomac, under Lee, and entered upon the Pennsylvania campaign. When the Confederate Army entered Pennsylvania, the orders of General Lee were most positive in regard to the conduct of the troops. Whatever might be their sense of wrong, he ordered that no acts of retaliation should be allowed. This order, so consonant with his own sentiments, was carried out by General Pettigrew with the most careful and rigid enforcement of discipline, nor did he alone maintain the most perfect discipline in his own immediate command, but he was also prominent in bringing to the notice of his division commander any lapse in the discipline enjoined by General

Lee, and which Pettigrew regarded as essential to the preservation of the army.

Gettysburg and its sanguinary slaughter came. In the first day's fight Pettigrew and his brave command were in the thickest of the fight and bore their proud banners pressing the retreating foe. His more than decimated troops bore witness, with the testimony of blood, to their gallantry and daring. Pettigrew's personal bravery and coolness were everywhere conspicuous. "Look, boys," said a young lieutenant, while shot and shell were singing the carnival of death. "Look, boys; did you ever see a nobler man. Hurrah for General Pettigrew!" "I never realized before," said Capt. Jo. Davis, of Franklin, "I never realized before, how much one man was worth. His presence and cheering command nerves the arms of thousands."

On the second day, Pettigrew was held in reserve, but victory still followed the Confederate banners.

On the third day, Pettigrew was placed in charge of Heth's division, and in that fatal and gallant charge on Cemetery Hill, he was in a line on the left of Picket's command. His was not a supporting column. Both were repulsed by superior numbers, occupying a strong and impregnable position. Pettigrew was painfully wounded, and Burgwyn, Marshall, McCrea and Iredell—all North Carolina's dead jewels—wrote with their blood the dying declaration, that North Carolina had followed the Confederate banners to the farthest point that Lee had planted them. On the first day of July Pettigrew's brigade went into the fight with 3,000 as gallant men as ever answered the bugle-call to battle. On the morning of the 4th it numbered but 835.

The Confederate army fell back upon Hagerstown and the Potomac, crossing the river at Williamsport and Falling Waters. After a night's march, the troops were resting on the morning of the 14th of July, near the bridge, at Falling Waters. General Pettigrew, with other officers, was walking to the left of the division, when their attention was attracted by a small body of cavalry issuing from the woods near by. The small number caused them to be mistaken for Confederates. There was an irregular skirmish, a scattering fire, and General Pettigrew was mortally wounded. He was removed with the army, was taken to the house of Mr. Boyd, near Winchester, Va., where, on the 17th of July, his noble spirit, with all of its rich endowments and splendid culture passed peacefully away to its bounteous Creator.

THOMAS S. ASHE.

See what grace was seated on his brow.
—*Hamlet.*

THOMAS S. ASHE graduated at the University of North Carolina in the class of 1832, several members of which afterward became men of rank in the country. Thomas L. Clingman was the best scholar in the class, and graduated with its highest honor, distinguished for his genius, his ability, his awkwardness, and his endurance as a bandy-player. He spoke the "Latin Salutatory" speech at graduation, which, at that period, was the speech of highest honor. J. H. Parker, of Tarboro, spoke the "Valedictory," second in honor, and Thomas S. Ashe the third speech. The other members of the class who became distinguished were Jas. C. Dobbin, Secretary of the Navy under President Pierce, and R. H. Smith, of Halifax, always prominent as an able and public-spirited citizen in North Carolina. Thomas W. Harris was the handsomest member of the class, and Tom Ashe the best looking and most commanding. James C. Dobbin was the most popular man in the class. Tom Ashe commanded the most respect, Clingman was the most wondered at, and Dick Smith was the most beloved.

Throughout their respective careers in life the characteristics these men developed at college seemed to adhere to them.

Clingman in public life was a very strong man. He was

chairman of the Committee on Foreign Relations in the House of Representatives, and greatly prided himself on some of his speeches on foreign affairs and on his insight into world-wide politics. But he still found time to study philosophy and science, and he measured mountains, and explained in minute detail the track through the heavens of a great meteor, whose course he traced from Alabama over into Kentucky, calculating to a nicety how high it was above the surface of the earth. And he was likewise a great authority on water-spouts.

When the war came on, he was animated by a great ambition to attain military renown. In battle he was cool, collected and philosophical; and in personal bravery no soldier excelled him. To crown his work, he, after peace, collected his principal writings and speeches and published a book of them--setting a pace for other Carolinians who have been too remiss in matters of authorship.

Tom Ashe, in many respects, was just the opposite of Clingman. Clingman was a pushing politician; Ashe was of a modest, retiring nature; but withal as manly a man as was ever born on our soil. He was hardly known outside of his judicial district as a lawyer, but when put on the Supreme Court Bench, his opinions were recognized by the profession as models of rare excellence.

Without solicitation, he was elected Confederate States Senator; and, indeed, whatever public honors came to him, they came because of the respect his course in life inspired.

We recall a little incident in regard to him:

In 1868, by military order, the negroes were to vote upon the question of adopting the proposed Constitution. The Conservatives, who were opposed to all these proceedings, met in Convention at Raleigh. Governor Graham addressed them in a speech of great power, urging that the white people should make a party to themselves. At the same election, a governor and other officers provided for in that Constitution were to be voted for. If the Constitution were rejected by the people, the officers elected would not be installed.

14

Vance was nominated by the Conservatives, and Holden by the Radicals. It looked like it was to be the same old contest of 1864 over again. But Vance, after thinking over it, declined. The executive committee then tendered the nomination to Judge Merrimon; he, too, declined. Other names were brought forward—but all the politicians declined. The executive committee was thus confronted by a serious situation. Finally, Colonel Bob Cowan said that he could name a man who would not decline to lead North Carolinians in any struggle for their rights and happiness—no matter if it was a forlorn hope. "Name the man," the others said. "It is Tom Ashe. He will not decline to be the leader of our people. I pledge myself to that." And so Colonel Cowan was commissioned to see Tom Ashe about it. And Bob Cowan was justified. Ashe came out and made a memorable canvass, with no expectation of any personal advantage; for if the Conservatives defeated the Constitution, the election of the officers was a nullity; and if the Radicals succeeded in carrying the Constitution, they would also certainly elect his opponent, Holden, Governor.

Well, that was a campaign in which ebony shins and "forty acres and a mule" played a leading part. If the venerated George Washington had been our candidate, the sable cohorts would have downed him. The darkeys wouldn't have known the Constitution from an elephant had they met a travelling circus in the road, and they were inflamed to the sizzling point against the whites. Truly, those were days of humiliation and mortification to the flesh. But we had the spirit to endure—and lofty souls like Tom Ashe led us along until after awhile we came out of the wilderness into the promised land.

UNIVERSITY REMINISCENCES.

"The old, old tale of long ago "

The University of North Carolina nearly seventy years ago was in many respects unlike the University of to day. Probably the discipline was more rigid, and the great law of obedience was more strictly enforced. The students were then boys, and boys need watching. Now we suspect, they are "young gentlemen," and their own sweet will is more recognized. Then some of the boys wore homespun and home-made square-tail coats, and well fitting tailor-made store clothes were not common. The bon-ton wore Litchford's best, made to order by the fashionable tailor of the little town of Raleigh, and reserved for Commencement occasions. The square-tail coat boys, who brought their goose quills for pens and their dip-candles from home, were the best students. And when a boy had the self-sacrifice and manhood to defy the proud boy's contumely and save an honest penny by taking his frugal meal of molasses and corn-bread cold from a tin plate in his room, that boy cast before him the shadow of a coming man. Poor, dear old Murray! next-door neighbor to us, Old South Building, west end corner. Looking down through the long and darkening vista of the corridors of time we can see him now. Working, working, studying, delving, earnest, never tiring day and night, early and late, living hard and working hard. Always the same dear old Murray, with his dip-candle at night and his tin plate at meal times. He struggled on with it all, poor and uncomplaining. But when bewildered in a mathematical labyrinth, old Murray was a staff to lean on and find rest. What was his lot in the chances and changes of life we have never known. But there was a man in him then. And it is a comfort to us now, and proof that we were not wholly bad, that we sometimes brought him from "Miss Nancy's" on the hill the first and second joint of a chicken leg, to cheer his scanty fare. Dear old Murray!

Do our boys remember Dave Barum and George Horton? How unlike in appearance, in tastes, in pursuits; how diverse in distinction; and yet how sharp and bitter and jealous was their rivalry. Both lineal descendants of Ham. One of the guinea, the other of the bacon type. One a sturdy, short, stout, strong-handed and stout-hearted faithful college servant, a great favorite with the boys, always ready to serve them, of few words, but his words were sense, tending day by day the young sprouts of literature, but without one spark of literature within him. This was Dave. The other, George Horton, was a forest-born poet, who learned his letters while turning his plow at the end of the furrow, and framed his verses while driving his team.

On Saturday evening he came up to college from the country with his week's poetical work in manuscript which was ordered by the boys on the Saturday before. When he came he was a lion and attracted all the light from Dave. His average budget of lyrics was about a dozen in number. They were mostly in the love line, and addressed to the girl at home. We usually invested a quarter a week, and generally to the tune of the girl we left behind us. But once we taxed George's genius with a grave text. We gave him for his muse, *"Gar nux erkelai"* (we believe it's Greek), and explained to him, with learned emphasis, that it meant in English -"For the night cometh in which no man can work." He was equal to the task, and brought us a learned poem on "industry," in which occurred the oft-repeated couplet:

> " For the yoke of industry is wealth,
> And the yoke of industry is health."

DEATH OF DR. MITCHELL.

Such graves as his are pilgrims' shrines.
Shrines to no code nor creed confined—
The Delphian vales, the Palestines,
The Mecca of the mind.
                              —*On Burns.*

THERE is perhaps no tragedy in the private walks of
life in North Carolina that equals the death of Dr. Elisha
Mitchell, the Professor of Geology in the University of
North Carolina, for its mournful and dramatic incidents.

He was a native of Litchfield, Connecticut, a graduate
of Yale College, a class-mate of George E. Badger, and
was appointed to a Professorship in the University of
North Carolina upon the recommendation of Professor
Olmstead, of Yale. He came to North Carolina in the
early part of the last century, and passed his life at the
University of the State until his sad departure.

He was a great favorite at the University, he won
the affection of the students by his learning, his varied
attainments, his quaint and quiet humor, and his amiable
eccentricities. He was a unique representative of the
University faculty, and was a connecting link between
austerity and freedom in college intercourse.

A great lover of nature, he would sometimes head a
select party of students and in freedom and abandon
would court nature in her sylvan solitudes. They were
occasions of enjoyment, and while ostensibly a scientific,
geological and botanical exploration, it was in fact a social
festival in which preceptor and pupil unbent, and, waiving
the formalities of dignity, had a good time.

With all his ease and geniality, there was an air of
pensive thoughtfulness about him that seemed akin to
melancholy or a silent communing with the inner depths
of his soul, as if some dark cloud lowered over the horizon
of his life as a portent of evil to come. His walk at
times was slow, meditative and abstracted, and he seemed
to be absorbed in his own companionship; and then he

would recover his consciousness and give vent to some
quaint expression that would wreath his face in smiles.

We once heard him say to Judge Duncan Cameron,
while Thomas L. Clingman was delivering his senior
speech on the rostrum in Gerrard Hall: "Judge, that boy
has got a mind as big as my arm," at the same time stretch-
ing out his muscular arm to its full length.

We once heard Dr. Mitchell and Rev. W. M. Green
(afterwards Bishop Green) discussing the subject of the
Immortality of the Soul. The good Bishop, with instinctive
kindness, was contending for the universality of the immortality of all animals; and he illustrated his position
by the life of the weary stage-coach wheel-horse. "He,"
said the good Bishop, "is one of God's creatures; chained
to a wheel with a burden behind it, and lashed through
life by a merciless driver. It has always seemed to me
that such a fate should have its compensations in green
fields and shady pastures, to find happiness in an immortal life." "That is all well," said the erudite doctor
of laws and letters, "but when you come to an oyster it
don't apply."

In 1857, after the Commencement of the University in
June, Dr. Mitchell felt the old impulse of his geological
tastes, and determined to gratify a long-cherished wish
to explore the mountain peaks of Western North Carolina,
and taking with him the implements of his favorite science,
he set out, unattended by his staff of explorers, to commune
with science in that Wonderland of Nature—the "Land of
the Skies" the invalid's hope and the pilgrim's shrine.

He went. It was his last journey to the undiscovered
country; went alone into the vast solitudes of the Black
Mountains of Western Carolina. He had for some days
explored the lower mountains of the range, staying at
night with some of his plain friends in their humble cabins among the mountains.

On the 27th of June he ascended its peaks. It was a
perilous and an arduous journey, but he was in robust
health, on the high plateau of middle life, ardent, enthu-

THE GLEN IN BOSS

siastic, and hopeful of discovering in North Carolina the highest mountain peak east of the Rockies. He did not return to his friends at night, but it excited no alarm, because he was brave and adventurous in his scientific pursuits, and it was naturally supposed that he was lured on in his researches in the laboratory of nature.

Time wore on and he did not return. There was suspicion, then fear, then, with some, came assurance that something of evil had befallen the great and good scientist. Alarm came on, and searching parties were formed to solve the mystery. Their search was vain. No tidings of the missing came.

At length an old mountain bear hunter, long familiarly known as "Big Tom Wilson," who was trapping by night in the gorges of the Black Mountains, discovered what he supposed to be a human body. He staid by it until the morning sun lighted up the mountain hollows, and there, to his horror, he saw the lifeless body of the good man he had known in life, lying half hidden in a pool of water.

He looked around to see how harm had come to the body. All along the mountain steeps he saw broken limbs and other evidences of a struggle to arrest disaster. To his practiced eye the sad story of the tragedy was written in object-lessons along the mountain sides. He had lost his foothold and had taken the fatal plunge to death into the gorge below. A sad plunge into the unknown; but could any death be more fitting to the great Carolinian whom it befell?

Loving friends bore his body to the highest mountain peak of the Black Mountains, 6,717 feet above tide-water, the highest mountain peak east of the Rockies, which now bears the honored name of Mt. Mitchell.

AMONG THE CAROLINA WRITERS.

Suit the action to the word,
The word to the action.
—*Hamlet.*

NORTH CAROLINA has not been prolific in writers of
her majestic history. But she has some bright stars
that shine in the firmament and give lustre to the
name of their nativity, that we would not willingly let
die. He who stands at the gateway of our history was
consecrated by the companionship of Shakespeare, Bacon
and Ben Johnson, and left his mark upon the lettered glory
of the Elizabethan period of English history. During
the twelve years of his dreary imprisonment under the
charge of treason, after the death of his patron Queen,
his pen was his comfort and his companion, and while there
he wrote a "History of the World," on whose stage he had
been so potent an actor. That name was Sir Walter
Raleigh—statesman, historian, poet, warrior. As a writer,
he was followed by Hackluyt, the distinguished scientist
who was sent over by Raleigh with Amadas and Barlowe
to write an account of their discoveries in the land of the
setting sun. Hackluyt's style is of the antique. His work
is now a rare gem of early American literature, and was
written of and on Roanoke Island. These are the early
pioneers of literature associated with the name and early
history of North Carolina.

Next to these, though not in close proximity, come
our historians—Lawson, Williamson, Martin, Wheeler,
Hawks. Of these, Wheeler is the most useful; inaccurate
in some instances, but full of filial loyalty to the State.
Williamson was a "canny Scot," and his history was a
financial venture written for a Philadelphia publisher
upon a contract at a price per page, and its pages are a
dark thread running through a wide blank margin.

Martin was well equipped as a historian, but left the
State for a judicial position in Louisiana, and his histor-

ical materials, which were ample, were lost or destroyed at sea in their transit to New Orleans.

Dr. F. L. Hawks followed Martin as the historian of his native State. Great things were expected of him. It was a natural genius, of literary tastes and inclines, of elegant accomplishments, of profound learning, but he had not the historic nose.

Following Hawks, came Jo. Sewell Jones, an erratic genius, gifted in a certain way, enthusiastic, sensational. His work should have been entitled the Romance of North Carolina History.

Before Jones there were fragmentary works that added much to our historical collection—Caruthers, Foote, General Graham's sketches of Revolutionary history, and other literary labors with which we are not sufficiently familiar to speak definitely of their merits and demerits.

The elder James Iredell, the Associate Justice of the Supreme Court of the United States, was the recognized best writer of our Revolutionary times. He did not write a continuous history of the State, but as a letter-writer, in which he chronicled contemporary events, he was incomparable. Griffith McRee, of Wilmington, rendered the State a great service when, at the suggestion of James C. Johnston, of Hays, near Edenton, he prepared a Life of Judge Iredell, and left the State his debtor in gratitude.

James Iredell, Jr., inherited the literary tastes of his distinguished father, and if his life had been given to literary pursuits instead of the law, its jealous rival, he would have reached an equally high, if not higher, distinction on the round of ambition's ladder. His Address at the University of North Carolina at the Commencement of 1834 was a masterpiece of literary excellence, but it was too short for so grave an occasion.

Floating down the tide of our history to a later period we come to Dr. William Hooper, of the University, confessedly the finest writer of his period. A web of sorrow was woven in his mental constitution, but wit and humor bubbled up through its interstices whenever he touched pen to paper. His Address at the University in 1834, upon the defects of primary education in North Carolina, was inimitable in humor, and convulsed a large and cultured audience as we have never seen before or since. His address at a later period. "Fifty Years Ago," was but a step behind it in moving men to merriment.

The press has played its part in our prose literature. The blood of the Hales of Fayetteville runs in editorial channels. The elder Edward J. Hale, the veteran editor of the *Fayetteville Observer*, was for forty years identified with the press of North Carolina, and long exercised through the *Fayetteville Observer* an influence for good that is yet felt in the State. When the war of the States was in progress, he continued the publication of the *Observer* until Sherman and his bummers came to Fayetteville and desolated the town. After the war, Mr. Hale removed to New York and established himself, with his son, as a publisher of books. The change of scene produced no change of heart with him, and while he lived in New York, the old love of his nativity seemed to glow with a warmer and more intense flame. He was greatly beloved in his old home, and travellers from North Carolina generally regarded Edward J. Hale as an interesting object of their Southern tour. After a brief illness, he passed away, leaving the odor of a sweet and saintly memory which, we trust, will be long cherished among us in North Carolina.

Weston R. Gales, of the old *Raleigh Register,* was a greatly gifted man, and handled a gifted pen. He was a charming social companion, an unsurpassed post-prandial orator, and but for convivial excess would have been a model man. The line of heredity shows plainly, too, in the Gales blood. Father, son, brother and grandson, all handled pens mightier than the sword.

Col. W. L. Saunders was probably the best writer the State has ever produced. In force, clearness, directness, in power of illustration and in unflinching tenacity he was without a parallel. If there was any defect, it was in the humor that gives sparkle to composition.

Gaston, as a penman, was as pure and pellucid as Addison. Badger's force was marred by his infinite drollery. His sense of ridicule was so dominant, even on the gravest subjects, that it impaired his sincerity.

Gen. J. J. Pettigrew was distinguished as a writer as well as a military commander. Had he lived out his natural life, no Carolinian would have lived, greater than he. The two Camerons, John W. and John D., were both gifted penmen. George Davis, our gifted school-boy friend, was a gifted man, and the law, though it gave us a good lawyer, deprived us of a prince of letters.

Engelhard, Price and Fulton, Holden, the Camerons, the old *Asheville Citizen* and Joe Turner's *Raleigh Sentinel* shine in the array of able writers.

Others we would gladly mention. They multiply as time rolls on, but they are on this side the line of historic chronicles, and we deal with the books that are made up, balanced and closed.

THE BOMBARDMENT.

Stand not upon the order of your going.
              —*Macbeth.*

PERHAPS the most memorable day in the annals of Elizabeth City was the day of the bombardment, early in February, 1862, after the fall of Roanoke Island. After the fight and Confederate defeat at Hatteras, the year before, the sound and river towns of the Albemarle section were in a condition of perpetual trepidation in fear of the invasion of the Federal troops who had taken possession of Hatteras, and the apprehension of injury was conjured into a thousand fancies of outrage and destruction of life and property. But Burnside, who was in command at Hatteras, was in no hurry to push his advantage, and the next step for him was to capture Roanoke Island, which was occupied by various troops, under the command of Col. Henry M. Shaw.

Roanoke Island was attacked and captured early in February, and the people of Elizabeth City were first to hear the sad news. There seemed to be a sort of mental telegraphy between Roanoke Island and that town, and the news of Roanoke and its fall was soon followed by the news that the Federal gunboats were preparing for a hostile visit to the water towns in North Carolina. We, as nearest to the strategic point, were in a state of tremulous business. On the streets the enquiry every day from man to man was, "Are they coming? When are they coming? Will they shell the town? Shall we fight, or what shall we do?" Some said fight. Col. S. D. Starke, highest in command, ordered out the militia and threw up breastworks at Cobb's Point for the defence of our harbor. Many thought it best to set fire to our houses and retreat by the light, as the Russians had successfully done at Moscow when invaded by Napoleon. Colonel Starke approved it. Others did it when the time came.

We were living on Pasquotank River in the country,

nine miles from town, but were in town every day to keep up with current events. Returning from town one day, we heard when in town that the Yankees were getting their gunboats ready to come to town. The news so greatly excited the town, and the people were not to disturbed what to do when they came. We got home late, communicated the startling news to our disturbed household, and retired. About midnight a messenger from Elizabeth City roused us from sleep and delivered a message from Rev. E. M. Forbes, Rector of Christ Church, saying that a statement had reached town that the Yankee gunboats were preparing to leave Roanoke Island for Elizabeth City, and requesting that we would send up wagons to remove his books and valuables to our home in the country for safety. We hurried Isaac off immediately with a farm wagon, a three-mule-cart with driver, and little Peter with a single box wagon. We rose early next morning, in fact we didn't go to sleep any more that night. While at breakfast, a servant ran into the room from upstairs, saying with great alarm that the river was full of steamboats going up towards town, like a wedge, that there was more'n forty of 'em. We ran upstairs, looked out of an upper window, and there they were, moving like a phalanx, to disturb our peace and happiness. When we went down, Isaac had returned with the debris of Mr. Forbes' goods, wares and chattels. Great drops of bead sweat were rolling down his ebony cheeks, and his emotions overcame his utterance. To our enquiry where Mr. Forbes was, he said, "Mr. Forbes was flusterated." "I an' he was a talkin', you know, Master Richard, when he was a pilin in his books and pictures and sich, a big 'bung' flew over our heads, un he said to me, said he, 'Isaac,' and I returned 'Yeth, thir,'; and again he said to me, said he, 'Isaac, you better get away quick as you can.' I said again, 'Yeth, thir, Mr. Forbes, sir, I will, for it looks like judgment,' and then I jumped on my seat and 'Old Buck' (Old Buck was gamy and the off-horse) let out like Satan was atter him. When I came to the Cobb's Point road de bungs was a flyin' all round, and Buck and Bill, who allers minded me when I sot behin' 'em, didn't ker no more for me den a born-bline tom kitten." "Where's Mr. Forbes?" "Dunno. When I seed him he was lookin' like he was gwine to run." "What did he say?" "Well, Master Richard, he was sayin' some words he hadn't ought to sed. 'Peared to me like cuss words."

"Well, Isaac, where's Mr. Forbes' things?" "Lord o' massy, Master Richard, I tell you how dat is. Dey's scattered all along the road from here to 'Lizabeth."

Finishing our hasty breakfast, we mounted our horse and set out for town, and our eyes opened on a sight we hope never to see again. All the people of the town were on the road, most of them were afooot, shoe-tops deep in mud and slush, muddy, bedraggled, unhappy, wretched. They were looking for an asylum of safety among country friends. We met scores of our town friends, forlorn and miserable. We asked for others, and they told us the town was on fire and was deserted, and that a naval engagement was raging in the harbor; that two Confederates were killed and three Yankees. We soon met General Heningsen on the road, flying before an unseen enemy, from the fort at Cobb's Point, and "minding not the order of his going." We met some ladies afoot, unhappy, looking for an asylum. We met the Piemonts in "Little Billy's" three-mule cart, looking for our house. They told us of the distress. That it was a dead town. That it was dead as a graveyard, that all had left, some never to return. We asked after our friends. They said that some had set fire to their houses and made tracks for Currituck, that others had done the same, and that the whole town was then on fire, to spite the Yankees; that the Elliots had started on foot for Oxford, that the Martins were in a buggy, flying for Oxford, that Rev. E. M. Forbes was staying in town to meet the Yankees when they landed on the wharf, surrender them the town and ask protection; that Mr. Forbes, when they left, was putting on his ecclesiastical vestments, in order that they might respect his sacred office.

It was a grand, gloomy and peculiar time, such as this town had never seen before, has never seen since, and we trust may never see again.

GOVERNOR WILLIAM A. GRAHAM.

And like the down that rides upon the breeze.
His form was grace and every action ease.
—*Anon.*

If we were called on to designate the most distinguished and influential Governor of North Carolina in its long roll of Chief Magistrates in all its history up to the "war between the States," we should answer without hesitation, William A. Graham. His life had not fallen on the trying times that confronted Governor Vance, but, had it been his lot, he would have met them with the same heroic and unflinching spirit that distinguished our great War Governor. But, unlike him, he would not have found grains of merriment in every pound of sorrow, for Governor Graham was wrapped by nature in an environment of dignity that shrouded mirth and repelled familiarity. There has been no man, perhaps, in North Carolina that has been endowed with such graces of manner and address that marked him as a great master among men. He was grave and dignified without austerity, easy without familiarity, and he always had a courtliness of personal bearing that commanded every one's respect and offended no one's self love.

Mr. Graham's life forms a conspicuous feature in the drama of North Carolina's history while he lived. With its political history he was identified from the early outset of his life.

He entered life with the prestige of ancestral distinc-

15

tion, descended from that Scotch-Irish race which has
illustrated our annals, he added new honors to its illustrious lineage.

Soon after his entrance upon the legal profession he was
elected to the Legislature from the county of Orange. He
made his mark in that body soon after he became a member, and retained a prominent position in the councils of
the State ever afterwards, and added National honors to
his subsequent career.

In the Harrison Presidential storm of 1840, Mr. Graham bore a conspicuous part in the Whig phalanx of can-
vassers, and the subsequent Legislature had to elect two
United States Senators for North Carolina, in the place of
Senator Strange, who had resigned, and Senator Mangum,
whose term had expired. Mr. Graham was elected to fill
the unexpired term of Senator Strange, and Senator Mangum to succeed himself. It was a high compliment to
Mr. Graham, considering his age and his residence in the
same county with Senator Mangum. In this exalted position Senator Graham soon gave evidence that the State
had acted wisely in selecting him as Senator to supply
the place of Senator Strange. He took part in the leading
subjects of debate, was always heard with attention and
interest, and his speeches were commended by the ablest
statesmen throughout the country.

In 1844 he was nominated as the Whig candidate for
Governor of North Carolina, which nomination he was
reluctant to accept, but he was urged to accept it by his
political friends of the Whig Party, and finally accepted
it. His opponent of the Democratic Party, Mike Hoke,
of Lincoln County, was a foeman every way worthy of his
steel. Young, accomplished, well educated, eminently
magnetic, the Democrats of that day confidently calculated
on his success. Of a warmer temperament than Graham,
more gifted as an orator, not less gifted in personal attractiveness, they were well matched in the canvass. But
before the canvass was ended Hoke was beckoned away by
the pale messenger, and Graham was elected by a large

majority   He served as Governor for two terms with signal usefulness and satisfaction to the people of the State. He left the office of Governor with a National reputation that gave him the appointment of Secretary of the Navy in President Fillmore's Cabinet, the duties of which office were discharged with an administrative ability that crowned the administration of the Department with great éclat. He established intercourse with Japan which opened its ports to the world, and placed that gem of the Orient into the family of nations. Under the auspices of the Navy Department the region of the Amazon River, in South America, was successfully explored, and a new market was opened to our commerce.

Subsequently, he was nominated for the Vice-Presidency with General Scott, and it was confidently expected that, with General Scott's military reputation and Governor Graham's reputation as a statesman, the election would be a Whig triumph; but it fought its last battle, and was folded up among the treasures of our history.

Governor Graham's great strain was the part he first bore in our fratricidal war. His constitution was calm, conservative and deliberate, and he was naturally a Union man in the early stages of our sanguinary civil war. He was less impulsive than the people whom he had served so long and faithfully, and as long as he could he clung to the Union with which he was identified; but when the tocsin of war was sounded and an invasion of his native State was threatened, he returned to his normal position, joined the councils of the Confederacy, and sent his five sons to defend his home.

THE MOUNTAIN GRANDEUR OF WESTERN CAROLINA.

I'll to the mountains. I will not think the thoughts
Nor breathe the breath of other men.

—*Festus.*

THE most beautiful scenery in America, if not in the world, is to be found in Western Carolina. There by the workings of nature's laws, mountains have been piled on mountains, and between the ranges are lovely valleys watered by picturesque streams. In the Alps the craggy mountain tops are bare, but in blest Carolina, the verdure extends to the very pinnacle of the loftiest ranges. It is a region that fosters individuality, and trains the inhabitants to boldness and enterprise. Children are born among the wonders of nature, and by their daily experience they are taught self-reliance and attain rare powers of physical endurance. In the seclusion of their mountain homes, they develop the attributes of a sterling manhood, and among them are found many families richly endowed with intellectual gifts and bearing the stamp of marked superiority.

As two of a type we recall Samuel P. Carson and Zebulon B. Vance, names that are closely associated because of a most unhappy affair.

Dr. Robert Vance, the uncle of him whom our people so much loved as their great War Governor, was a man of fine characteristics. Like his distinguished nephew, he had boldness, and strength of character, determination and zeal. He was a student of public affairs and was well informed in all branches of knowledge. He represented the Buncombe District in Congress three-quarters of a century ago. An aspirant for his seat was young Sam. Carson, who had served a session or two in the Legislature, and was unusually gifted as an eloquent orator. During the canvass, Dr. Vance charged that Carson's father had been disloyal during the Revolution. Carson denied the charge, but Vance would not retract. And so Carson proposed to have it out with him after the election. The celebrated Davy Crockett was a friend of Carson and undertook to train him in the use of the pistol; and Davy was reputed to be as sure a shot as any man in America. When the election was over Carson challenged Dr. Vance and they fought a duel at Saluda Gap on the South Carolina line, Davy Crockett being present. Vance fell mortally wounded. Carson had been chosen at the election and he continued in Congress some ten years. At Washington he was regarded as one of the readiest debaters in Congress, and he stood high up in the esteem and confidence of Andrew Jackson, who was then President. And at home the people delighted in honoring him, for his splendid powers of oratory made him the idol of the mountaineers. His last public service was in the Convention of 1835. He then moved to Texas, and a few years later died, after a long period of ill-health.

Among all the great men the West has given to Carolina, perhaps none were superior to Carson except Zeb. Vance, the nephew of the man he slew in mortal combat. Zeb. Vance is too well known for us to dwell at length on his great capacity and surpassing excellence as an orator. We will only say that when he was in the zenith of his powers, he swayed men with a force that has never been excelled among our peple. Truly the West has been as prolific of great men as she is notable for the number of her mountain peaks; and the mothers who could rear such men and give them to the State, must have been as remarkable as the valleys in which they lived are noteworthy for their loveliness.

FLORA McDONALD.

On man
He tried His 'prentice han',
And then He made the lasses O.
            —*Burns.*

THERE IS only one woman who has been identified with North Carolina history that has been mentioned in two hemispheres. Flora McDonald, a Scotch lassie, when a sweet, bright girl in the island of South Uist in the Highlands of Scotland, where she was born and reared, sheltered and concealed Charles Edward, known in English History as the Pretender, in her womanly apparel, after the disastrous battle of Culloden, in 1745, with courageous defiance of danger and at the peril of her own safety.

Edward became a fugitive after the battle of Culloden and was closely pursued by his enemies. The power of the Highland "lairds," who were his adherents, was destroyed by their defeat at Culloden, and Charles Edward sought concealment in the mountains of Rosshire, escaping capture by the generous self-sacrifice of Mackenzie. He found a temporary shelter in the mountain fastnesses of the island of South Uist. He was in hiding with Laird McDonald. He was in imminent danger of immediate capture. The wife of the laird on whose domain he was in hiding was in deep sympathy with Prince Edward and proposed several projects for his escape. Finally she suggested that they should disguise him in female attire and pass him off as a travelling waiting-maid. But it was difficult to find any one who would assume the dangerous place of his mistress. Two had declined. Flora McDonald, the young and beautiful daughter of a petty laird on the island, had a stepfather who was an adherent of the government. She was approached by the good woman who knew the peril of the Prince. She asked Flora if she would undertake the escape of Prince Edward as her waiting-maid. With the womanly in-

stinct of sympathy for the distressed, she accepted the
perilous task. The Prince was concealed in a rocky wild
in the mountain. Thither Flora was taken by a trusted
officer of the Prince's forces. They found him alone,
broiling a small fish on the coals for his solitary repast.
At first he was startled, supposing them to be his enemies,
and made ready to defend his life. He soon saw they
were his friends. He readily accepted their plans for
his escape. Preparations were made for leaving the island. Flora secured a passport from her stepfather, who
was a British officer, for herself and her companions, including a stout Irish woman, whom she called Betsey
Burke.

Soon after, the travelling party set out from Uist in an
open boat for the Isle of Skye. A violent storm arose.
All were alarmed for their safety. The heroic girl encouraged the oarsmen with words of cheer. Betty Burke
(the Pretender) sang Highland songs and recited wild
legends to encourage them. As they approached the Isle
of Skye a band of soldiers drawn up on the shore fired
on them, and as the balls were whistling near them they
changed their course and landed at another point on the
island. Concealing the Prince in a hollow rock on the
beach, Flora repaired to the Chieftain's headquarters.
The Laird was absent, but Flora saw his wife and appealed, not in vain, to the generous enthusiasm of woman.
The heart responded to the appeal of humanity, and she
gave orders for the fugitive's safe departure. He was
conducted to a safe retreat and embarked for the Isle of
Rearsay, where he found friends.

At parting with Flora, Charles Edward, the unhappy
fugitive that she had so bravely protected, kissed her hand
and said, "Gentle, faithful maiden, I hope we shall yet
meet in the Palace Royal." But they never met again.

After Charles Edward had escaped to France, the indignation of the officers of the crown fell upon those who had
aided him in his flight. Flora was arrested with others,
and imprisoned in the Tower of London, to be tried for

her life. While in prison, the beauty and bravery of the girl, who, without religious or political motive, had suffered so much for the cause of distressed royalty, deeply interested the English nobility. By their influence and exertions she was finally released. Presents were showered upon her after her release. She received gold ornaments and coin, which she brought with her when she emigrated to Carolina. She was presented to George the Second, King of England. When he asked her how she dared render assistance to the enemy of his crown, she answered: "It was no more than I would have done for your Majesty, had you been in a like situation." She was returned to Scotland under the escort of Malcolm McLeod, a fellow prisoner, with great show and equipage.

Four years after, she married Allan McDonald, a Scottish Laird, who in 1775, emigrated to North Carolina with his family and some friends and settled at Cross Creek, now Fayetteville, where a large number of distressed Scottish families sought refuge from the civil disturbances in the British Empire.

But they soon found disturbances and war in their adopted home, where commotion was rampant. The contest between the British Government and its American colonies was then imminent, and it soon burst into flame. The Highlanders, who fled from Scotland for peace and quiet, sympathized with the Government that they had so lately been in arms against. They were summoned by the Colonial Governor to support the royal cause. They responded to the call. General Donald McDonald, a kinsman of Flora and the most influential man among them, erected his standard at Cross Creek, and on the first of February, 1776, sent out his proclamation, calling on all his true and loyal countrymen to join him. The husband of Flora and most of the Highlanders joined the royal ranks. Flora gave her influence to the cause her husband and kinsmen had espoused and animated her countrymen in arms. They met the Patriots at the early "Battle of Moore's Creek Bridge," and found another Culloden.

After the battle General Donald McDonald, who had been commissioned as General of the royal forces in North Carolina, was taken prisoner while sitting on a stump near his tent. Allen McDonald, the husband of Flora, was also taken prisoner, and they with some twenty others were sent prisoners to Halifax.

Allen and his family, after this disastrous experience, and release, as a prisoner, determined to return to their old home in the Highlands. On their return voyage in a British sloop of war, they encountered a French ship of war and an engagement ensued. In the action Flora, who was in the thick of the fight, encouraging the men, was wounded. The enemy was beaten off and the heroine was landed safely on her native soil.

Her eventful life closed March 5th, 1790. More than three thousand persons followed her remains to the cemetery Kilmuir, in the Isle of Skye. According to her wish, her shroud was made of the sheets in which Prince Edward had slept the night he was her guest at Kingsbury.

THE BLACK FLAG.

(SCENES OF FRATERNAL STRIFE.)

Eighteen hundred and sixty-three was the dark year in the history of the Civil War, in this town and the adjacent section of North Carolina. It was the dark and bloody district. Human life was not more valued or more secure than a raccoon's. The battlefields of Northern Virginia were havens of rest and happiness to it. We have heard of black flags in war, in which human beings became incarnate devils and laid aside all the instincts of humanity. We never saw a black flag but once. The man who carried it we suspected was an Ishmaelite, and that his hand was uplifted against every other man. Its pictorial emblems were a skeleton, cross-bones, and sockets whence eyes once looked out. He showed it to us and told us it meant war to the invaders without quarter and without mercy. He had another, and we were told that he showed it to the other side. Buffaloes, spies, tale-bearers, non-combatant buffaloes were everywhere. The worst features of human nature were developd in a rich soil and danger was all around you. We have heard of "marching through Georgia" and its horrors of bummers and pillage and rapine. But this was marching into Elizabeth City and staying there. It is a common reference to the sad days of the reconstruction period from 1866 to 1870 as full of outrage, oppression and hardship, but they were halcyon days for Elizabeth City, compared with the bloody black flag days of 1863.

Roanoke Island was in the hands of the Federal troops and it was a safe retreat for negroes, and a paradise of Union men, spies and Northern sympathizers. No whisper of a true Southern man, but it was reported at headquarters at Roanoke Island in less time than twenty-four hours. Your nearest neighbor was often your truest end cruelest enemy.

Our little children (the largest were away) had a toy

Confederate flag about as big as your hand, and in childish sport they nailed it to the outside gate. It was not there two hours, when it was taken down from motives of prudence. Next day a raiding party of negroes and white men came to the house from the river landing, and in an imperative manner demanded a search of the house for Confederate flags. Trunks were rudely burst open and rifled. A little flag, the childrens' plaything, was found. They bore it off in triumph, and it was doubtless exhibited at headquarters on Roanoke Island as a trophy of victory. Raids of whites and negroes were of weekly occurrence, and oftener. We carried our lives in our hands. In Perquimans, Tom Newby, a quiet, estimable and inoffensive citizen, a cultured gentleman, was called to his door at night by a raiding party from Roanoke Island and cruelly shot and killed without a word of warning. Our guerilla protectors shot and killed Black Sanders from the bushes, in retaliation, and the cruel war without military organization went on. The Sanders Federal gang shot and killed Ad. White, an innocent man found with a gun on his shoulder. The guerillas under Elliott and Sanderlin shot and killed Cox at Trunk Bridges and a child that he held before him as a shield. Buffaloes and their allies were rampant. Pete Burgess, of Camden, a noted buffaloe, with a gang of buffaloes, shot and killed McPherson in or near his own house before the eyes of his weeping wife and children. Later, Wild, the one-armed commander of the negro troops who disgraced his epaulettes and blue coat, arrested Daniel Bright, a soldier of Hinton's regiment at home on furlough, and hung him without accusation or trial at the "River Bridge," now "Hinton's Corner." A raiding party of Hinton's regiment, arrested a buffalo, hung him, suspended his body from a limb and placed a placard on his breast stating that he was hung in retaliation for the murder of Daniel Bright.

That surely was a time of horrors, a war without truce or the pomp and pageantry of military array. It was an internecine war in which all the ties of neighborhood, brotherhood and civilization were rudely sundered. The charge at Ballaklava in which no question of the reason why, no action but to do or die, was in the minds of those heroes on the march to death, pales before the glare of such warfare. Pettigrew's bloody charge at the heights of Gettysburg is child's play in comparison with it. In General Sherman's classic phraseology, "war is hell." What, pray, would he have called such a war as we had here in old times in this town. It was war without its pomp and pageantry, without the amenities and chivalry of organized warfare, without a recognized code and rules of civilized war, without the "paths of glory" leading to the grave. It was one long, weary, suspicious, frightful watch, surprise and reality. For months we never went to our front door without unconsciously turning our sleepless eyes to the river shore in search of a foeman, who was a wolf in his lair, ready to spring upon us from covert.

During the whole of this long, black night of terrors there was but one fight in the open, between our Ranger protectors and the Federal cavalry raiders. It was in the upper part of Pasquotank, near the fatal spot where Daniel Bright was murdered. It was popularly called the battle of "Tuttle's Run," not so called from any local association, but from the rapid "run" made from the field by Jack Tuttle, a member of the company who had never before heard the siz of a rifle ball. One struck Jack's gun and gave him a sudden attack of St. Vitus' and he "got up and dusted," the boys cheering as he ran. It was the battle in which our boys behaved like veterans in the open field, in which the Federal cavalry were driven back, and in which the brave captain Tom Tamplin was wounded and was borne from the field in the arms of his loving comrades.

REMNANTS OF LO.

Oh, a wonderful stream is the river of Time
As it runs through the realm of tears.
— *Taylor*.

IN JACKSON and Swain counties is a reservation where a remnant of the Cherokee Indians still dwell, and we believe it is the home of more of the aboriginal Red men than can elsewhere be found east of the Mississippi. The Cherokees were Southern Indians and traditional accounts say they originally had their hunting grounds in the region of which Charlotte is now the centre. It was somewhere about the year 1600, some fifty years before North Carolina was settled, that a powerful tribe came down from Canada and fought three consecutive days with the Cherokees, great slaughter being inflicted on both sides. Then they took a breathing spell; and finally it was agreed between them that the Cherokees should move to the mountains and allow their adversaries to have the lands. And so the Catawbas became settled in North Carolina.

The Cherokees were in the early days described as being less savage than most of their race, and they gave the whites no great trouble, until the French, who claimed the back country, induced them to become hostile to the English. However, they had their wars with the colonists who year by year pressed harder and harder on their hunting grounds; but they continued to hold their land in the mountains. As they were not citizens, and as their government was tribal, the whites regarded them as a foreign nation, although they lived here in their own country. And so treaties were made with the tribes as with foreign nations. By our treaty with the Cherokees a large territory in the mountains was set apart as their property, and no white man could lawfully buy an acre of it. But the whites wanted it, and so they interfered, and at length they induced some of the chiefs to ask the government to give them other lands across the Mississippi for their hunting grounds; and eventually this was done, but the tribe repudiated the contract.

However, about 1837 General Winfield Scott was sent with some troops and forcibly moved the Cherokees from our State, and the Creeks from Georgia, and carried them across the Mississippi to new hunting grounds in the Indian Territory. But some of the Cherokees took to the woods and escaped, and after a while a new treaty was made by which a large part of their reservation in our mountains became the property of the State, and was opened to white settlers.

The land retained by the Indians lies in Jackson and Swain counties, and there the Indians have lived unmolested for fifty years, increasing in numbers and becoming more and more civilized. They now dress like white people, and cultivate the land. They have schools, and are taught to speak English. It is pleasant to think that at least a remnant of the aborigines still survive in their old homes, and that within the beautiful mountains of North Carolina they have a retreat where they can enjoy the blessings of peace and security while having some of the advantages of civilization.

One of these Cherokees has achieved fame that will perpetuate his name for centuries. He constructed an alphabet of fifty signs that represented the sounds of his Indian language, and three-quarters of a century ago his alphabet was used in printing a paper and books for his people. His name was Sequoia, and the story of his performance became known to a great Italian scientist who was travelling in this country. Years later when General Bidwell, who a few years since was the Prohibition candidate for the Presidency, discovered the giant redwood trees in California, the scientist at Washington proposed to call them Washingtonienses; the British called them Wellingtonia; but the Italian scientist called them Sequoia, in honor of the Cherokee; and this name was adopted. So those big trees, which are 4,000 years old, and which are the wonder of the world, will hand down the name of a Cherokee Indian to the remotest ages.

A DREAD TIME.

"A time that tried men's souls."

WE HAVE sometimes, yea often, regretted that we did not shoulder our rifle during the times that tried men's souls and bodies, in the bloody era in our history from 1861 to 1865, and that age and domestic exigency kept us away from the field of conflict.

But we have frequently thought, that we, who remained at home in the Albemarle section of North Carolina, were in more danger and trouble than the honored soldier that responded to the first bugle call to arms and left home and all its endearments to face a world in arms against his home. Up to the fall of our forts at Hatteras, we were undisturbed by a hostile presence. Our troubles were such as we imagined. It was considered an asylum for those who from stress of circumstances or other cause were not in the camp or on the battlefield, which was their normal place.

But when Hatteras fell, the scene was wholly changed. Our Illiad of woes then began. Squads of soldiers came up occasionally. Some of them were inoffensive, especially the early visitors. They seemed uneasy, but looked around with searching eyes, as if to take in the situation for some ulterior purpose.

In 1863 a small body of Federal troops were sent to occupy Elizabeth City. They were under the command of two brothers, named Sanders. One of them, having black hair, was familiarly known as "Black Sanders." The other having light hair was known as "White Sanders." Our local guerilla company had their eyes upon them and were secretly keeping informed of all their movements. One night Black Sanders, with some "buffalo" friends, attended a negro dance party near town. Some of our guerilla friends, knowing the street they would come back to town, secreted themselves at the west corner of Main street, opposite the Albemarle House then the Leigh House). Sanders was mortally wounded. He fled to their headquarters at the Grandy House on Shepard street and died soon after reaching town.

It was a hot time in town the next day. The Federal camp on Shepard street was wrought up to intense excitement and the atmosphere was lurid with threats of vengeance. The pall of death and secrecy that hung over the dreadful tragedy was well established, but no trace of the actors could be found.

The Federal soldiers of the camp were out scouring the country to find some clew to the tragedy, but their search was unavailing.

At length they fell in with Ad. White, somewhere in town, with a gun on his shoulder. They took him prisoner. There was no evidence of his guilt. He disclaimed all knowledge of the circumstance of the shooting. He was a citizen of Perquimans, and a visitor to Elizabeth City. He was obstinate, unyielding, and an intense Confederate of the stalwart type. He made no confessions. They wanted a victim, and Ad. White was found with a gun on his shoulder. He was condemned, sentenced to be shot, and the sentence was executed the same day. He was a brave and obstinate man and died without fear, a martyr to his convictions and his patriotism.

The man in the guerilla camp who fired the fatal shot that sent "Black Sanders" without shrift to his dread account, has never been known with certainty. He was probably killed by a volley.

It was supposed by many at the time that he was killed by Arthur Butt, a man of many intellectual gifts, but more eccentricities and of infinite jest.

He was the life of the social circle, a man of ardent temperament and Southern sympathies. He was a country schoolmaster and a good elocutionist.

During the bloody times a newspaper was a rare sight, and sometimes we got a Confederate paper published on dirty brown paper, and sometimes, though rarely, we came in possession of a Northern paper. When we got one it was the attraction of the town, and Arthur mounted a goods box and read the war news to an attentive crowd of eager listeners.

Poor Arthur! peace and blessings on his memory. How oft he sat an audience on a roar. How oft he roused the drooping spirits and brought cheerful happiness out of the depths of despair.

After the death of Ad. White there was intense excitement throughout this vicinity. Some clamored for retaliation, but we were disheartened, broken in spirit, trodden under foot by raids, and we do not know that there were any retaliatory steps.

16

THE KING OF BIRDS AND THE BRAVEST
OF BEASTS.

For an island twelve miles long and two wide, and in-habited by some seven hundred people, Roanoke Island has been as loud a spot as any of the same number of square inches on the globe. It has been full of sensations from the jump; and from the birth-day of Virginia Dare in 1585, to the bully fight of recent date, in which birds, beast and woman bore a hand, a period near unto three hundred years, it has seldom been without an eye-opener in the shape of a sensation. It has been the scene of bloody fights between hostile Indian tribes, and between civilized armies in hostile array. Savage and civilized relics of remote ages and modern convulsions are hidden beneath, or wave-washed upon the surface of its golden sands. Indian forts, and cairns, and tumuli attest its hoary history. Abel's pet dog that sings in church meetings; and the canary that praises itself in parrot English, attest the attainments of its beasts and birds, in polite accomplishments. Lewis Mann's sixty alligators, hatched and reared in a potato-house, attest the fecundity of its soil —or the fecundity of Lewis' imagination. Two miles from the shore, at the point at the gateway to Oregon, lie luscious bivalves. Wild fowl of every name feed upon its grasses. Its men are the best specimens of stalwart and athletic manhood; its women of feminine loveliness.

But to our tale.

At Roanoke Island, a soaring eagle, towering in his pride of might, turned his proud eye from gazing at the sun, upon the quiet yard of Walter Dough. A flock of fat geese that did the tender sward grass, invited his eye and tempted his taste. The glance was father to the thought and instantly performed. The feathers flew the geese squawked, and there was a sensation in that farm yard and there was a dog there, too. A goose is put down as a fool, but it is a clear error. A goose is a particular smart fellow.

And so was this one the eagle struck.   As soon as the eagle struck, the goose ran under the house, which was some two feet above ground, with the eagle fastened to her back, and the rest of the flock in hot pursuit.   And there the fight grew fast and furious.   Forty biting and flopping geese on one side, and the king of birds on the other.   Although outnumbered, the eagle maintained the fight and clung to his victim.

But soon another enemy presented himself.   An enemy more terrible than an army of geese— a bull-terrier dog— little, but full of fight.   It wasn't fair; and the dog had no natural, belligerent rights in a combat between birds; but he came with a bound, and the eagle had no time to settle questions of military ethics; so he threw himself on his back (eagle fashion) to do his best in this hard fight between tooth and toenail.   The dog made a lunge at the eagle's breast, and the eagle stuck his claws deep into the dog's fore-shoulder.

The blow was simultaneous on either side.   Both blows told.   But a terrier never, and an eagle hardly ever, says die.   The only witnesses of the dread combat were the geese, who now stood off and looked on, and Miss Martha Brothers, who was singing to her spinning jenny, in the house alone, when the fight began; and who in the end was to be the conquering hero, crowned with the laurels of victory.   The battle raged.   Teeth gnashed.   Claws staved. Eyes flamed.   But eagles, like men, contend against odds when fighting against two, and so this eagle's great heart sank within him, and turning tail upon his foe he sought safety in flight.   But his retreat was slow and full of difficulty, for the bull terrier pressed closely upon him, raging behind him.   He reached the yard fence.   With one desperate remove again he made it.   He reached the top most round.   He beat his flight for a moment and fought no further away. There upon the post he stood triumphed.   It was in vain that Miss Martha Brothers, the conquering hero of the day, came to the field and seized the palm of victory.   Seizing a rail with one full sweep she came down with terrific upon eagle's head, and left him prostrate, struggling in the agonies of death; the victim of a combination too powerful to be resisted. Alas poor eagle! He measured nine feet between the tips of his outstretched wings.

GEN. JAMES MARTIN.

While a foreign troop was landed in my country, I never would lay down my arms, never! never! never!

—*Lord Chatham.*

JAMES GREEN MARTIN was born on Main street in Elizabeth City, N. C., on the 14th of February, 1819. From the Academy in Elizabeth City, he continued his education at the Episcopal school in Raleigh, until the year 1835, when, upon the recommendation of Hon. Wm. B. Shepard, representative in Congress from the First District, he was appointed to a cadetship at West Point. After the four years course at that institution, he was graduated, No. 14, in the class of which Generals Sherman and Thomas were members, and was assigned to the Artillery. He was first assigned to duty on the Maine frontier, when the boundary dispute threatened conflict with Canada.

He went to the Mexican war under the command of General Worth, and was with him at the capture of Monterey. He was afterward transferred to General Scott's command, and was with him in all the fights in his advance on the city of Mexico, up to and including the battle of Churubusco, where he lost his right arm. After the Mexican war he was transferred from the line to the staff.

When the war between the States was declared, he was at Fort Reilly, and when North Carolina, by her act of secession, resumed her paramount authority. Major Martin, recognizing his allegiance to his State, his home and his kindred, returned and offered his sword to North Carolina. He was made Adjutant-General, with the rank of Major-General, and commenced at once the organization

of that splendid body of troops that in the Confederate
Government was the right arm of the service. This work
done, he went into the field as a Brigadier-General in the
Confederate Army. In the proposed attack on New Bern,
by General Hill, he was ordered with his brigade to Shep-
ardsville, to cut off communication between Morehead City
and New Bern. He attacked and took the forts at Shep-
ardsville, capturing a good many Federal prisoners and
destroying Federal property. The attack on New Bern
was abandoned and our troops in retreat, when the news
reached General Martin. He moved away to avoid an
attack from New Bern and reached Wilmington, with all
his prisoners. In 1864, his Brigade was ordered to report
to General Beauregard, at Petersburg, and was engaged
in the fight at Bermuda Hundreds where General Butler
was "bottled up." Thence he joined General Lee, with
his brigade, at Richmond, and was at the second battle of
Cold Harbor, thence back to Petersburg, and engaged in
many of the fights at that place. From Petersburg, General Martin was sent by General Lee to Asheville to take
command of the western part of the State of North Carolina, where he was when General Johnston surrendered.

After the close of the war General Martin studied and
obtained license to practice law, in which professional business he was engaged to the time of his death.

In the private relations of life General Martin was
blameless and exemplary. He was an earnest and devout
member of the Protestant Episcopal Church, an earnest
worker in its religious enterprises, and an influential member of its diocesan and general councils. Doubtless, ere
this, he has entered upon that new condition of life where
a beneficent Creator bestows the higher rewards of a well-
spent life.

CHARLES R. KINNEY.

"A pebble in our path oft turns the current of our life."

ABOUT the year 1820 there came from Norwich, Conn., to Norfolk, Virginia, on his way to Mobile, Alabama, to repair his broken fortunes, Charles R. Kinney, a young man about twenty-six years of age, destined, in after years, to fill a place in the affections and influence and antagonisms of the bar in the Edenton District and also, in our judgment, to occupy the foremost rank in ability and legal attainments and in large practice among the members of a bar distinguished for learning and ability. There happened in Norfolk at the same time, a gentleman from Camden County, N. C., Miles Gregory, a wealthy farmer, who was stopping at the same hotel with the young stranger, and happening to get into conversation with him, found he was in search of employment. The conversation resulted in making an engagement with Mr. Kinney to come to Camden and teach the children of Mr. Gregory, in his family. He came out to Camden through the Dismal Swamp Canal in a canal boat, according to the custom of the period, and becoming a member of the family he took charge of Mr. Gregory's children, and taught them for two or three years. While he was at this business, in that county, in the vicinity of Elizabeth City, he occasionally came over to the town where he formed the acquaintance of Jno. L. Bailey, a practicing lawyer on the circuit. The acquaintance ripened into an intimate friendship, which continued, without abatement, through life. Mr. Bailey, afterward Judge Bailey, was a kind man, sympathized with the struggling, and soon became acquainted with the condition of young Kinney, a poor man, ardent, ambitious, educated, with refined and noble instincts, and every inch a man. The result of the friendship was the entrance of Kinney as a law student of Bailey. He had left in Norwich a wife and infant child, entirely dependent upon

him, and he continued his labors as a schoolmaster in the
family of Mr. Gregory, while pursuing his law studies under the tuition of Mr. Bailey. He made proficiency in
his legal studies, and obtained his admission to the bar in
regular course. After obtaining his license at the bar, he
discontinued his employment with Mr. Gregory and removed to Elizabeth City to enter upon the business of his
life, and to make it his home until he died. His attainments in his profession, his superior natural gifts, and his
impulsive and chivalrous nature soon made him conspicuous in his new home, and made him friends and foes. To
his friends he was most faithful, sympathizing, affectionate, making himself part and parcel of all their joys and
sorrows; to his foes he was dauntless, unyielding, firm, and
bold as a tiger with fresh blood upon his teeth; but his
heart was tender as a child's, and melted at the offer of
kindness from his bitterest foe.

Mr. Kinney did not get into practice rapidly. In
infancy he fell from his nurse's arms, and his back was
injured by the fall. This deformed him in the back below
the shoulders, and lowered his stature from about six feet
to about five feet, nine inches, but it did not impair his
activity or gracefulness. He was unrivalled in feats of
activity and horsemanship. He was a member of the
cavalry company in town, and none of the members of the
company were superior to him in feats of daring rough
riding. This deformity, and perhaps some traits of independent character, had caused him to incur the prejudice
of some of the young men of the town who proposed to be
the regulators of society and to make everything conform
to their ideas of taste and propriety. Kinney was unwil-
ling to accept their dictatorship, and thought and acted for
himself, independently of their social influence. This
wore on until it amounted to positive and active hostility,
leading to crimination and recrimination, newspaper and
pamphlet controversy and to street encounters, and finally
to challenges to mortal combat. Kinney defied them on
every field. He was opposed to duelling from principle.

He so proclaimed it, and his known opinions may have made it their chosen mode of redress. He was taunted with his nativity, with his lineage, of which they knew nothing. He was goaded to madness. In one of his newspaper controversies, in reply to the allusion to his lineage, in a burst of feeling he said:

"My father yet lives, old and venerable. He never had the honor of sending or accepting a challenge. His courage ran in a different channel. Ere he had reached the threshold of manhood he bared his bosom to the battle's rage in the eventful struggle which separated the American colonies from British dependence."

He accepted the challenge, and it was no fault of his that it was bloodless.

On the general circuit of the Edenton District, Mr. Kinney had so small an appearance that for a long time he was little known or considered. At Currituck where, in later years, his opinion was law, and he had an appearance on one side of every important case on the docket, it was five years that he went to the Court an unsolicited, briefless barrister, and at the expiration of that time a mere accident gave him an appearance.

In the county of Currituck, in 1828, an atrocious murder of an old man was committed, and from suspicious circumstances public sentiment settled upon John Chittem and his wife. They were arrested and confined in the common jail, and the body of the murdered man was found in an old well. Chittem was a wealthy man, and employed all the bar to defend him, except Mr. Kinney, thinking he was not worth employing. Tredell was prosecuting attorney for the State. Before the case came on for trial, during the Spring Term, Judge Lowry, who was presiding, died on the circuit, and Mr. Iredell was appointed by the Governor to fill his place. This created a vacancy in the office of Solicitor. When Currituck Court came on, Mr. Kinney was the only lawyer unemployed, and the Judge *ex necessitate* had to appoint him to prosecute. When the case was called, from some cause, probaably from the recent appointment of the Solicitor and his want of time to examine the case, it was continued to the next term of the Court. There was a formidable array of counsel for the defense, headed by Isaac Lamb, then a leading attorney in that part of the District. Kinney, as acting Solicitor, was alone in the prosecution. The testimony was entirely circumstantial. Chittem had married the young widow of the murdered old man soon after his death. Other circumstances, many, pointed to the foul work of the old man's taking off. Kinney had ample time, and had made thorough preparation. His speech was written out, but not committed to memory. We have seen it in manuscript. It was the closing speech, but before its close the case was decided. It summed up the testimony with terrible effect, and when, at the close of the artistic presentation of all the circumstances in phalanx, he pointed his long arm and index finger at Chittem, and with his deep, sonorous tones, said: "As Nathan said unto David, thou art the man." The bosom of the prisoner heaved a sigh, and Isaac Lamb's foot moved to and fro, his customary signal of mental giving away. Chittem was convicted and executed near Currituck Court House.

We have heard Mr. Kinney say that that speech was worth a thousand dollars to him in an hour after he left the court-room. He was always after employed in all the leading cases on the docket.

He rose about that time to be the leader on the circuit. From Currituck to Tyrrell and Hertford he was the acknowledged leader, *primus inter pares*. His practice was large and his income probably the largest from law practice in the District. But he never valued money and cared not about it; accumulation, squandering large sums upon agricultural experiments, of which he was very fond. We often said the reason he did not accumulate money was that he knew not the difference between six cents and six and a quarter.

We have often mentally enquired what were Mr. Kinney's infirmities, for as the sparks fly upward, it is the common penalty of life. He had fewer than most men. He was impetuous, quick, but his heart was as large as humanity. As he truly said in a memorial address upon the death of the lamented W. W. Cherry, if he could he "would have wiped all tears from all eyes." In his professional practice, perhaps, his fault was that he was not sufficiently aroused to the minor matters of the law. In a matter which involved large property, or in a matter in which a poor client was greatly wronged, all the energies of his nature were fully aroused and all his great ability was put forth, and upon such occasions we have never seen him equalled. At other times he was a sleeping lion. At such times, to use the vulgar but significant phrase, he was apt to "go off half-cocked." This perhaps was the fault of his professional life.

His voice was soft, variable and full of sympathy, capable of expressing the deepest emotions of horror, disgust and denunciation. When a boy we happened in the court-house when he was defending a client where the defendant's brother was a witness for the State, upon a charge of larceny. The denunciations of the witness as a "base betrayer of his brother's blood," and his irate manner, still thrill us.

About 1844 his health began to decline, and he was often compelled to be absent from his courts. In 1845 he went to the Virginia Springs and his health was much restored. He was greatly encouraged. At Gates Court he was in fine spirits, and the accounts he gave of the men he met during the summer were exceedingly interesting. We went up with him to the court, and he remarked if he could go every year to the Greenbriar Springs he could live to three-quarters of a century. From Gates Court he returned to Elizabeth City with fine prospects of health and happiness. The next week was Chowan Court, at Edenton. We went up in our sulkies. (We hope the kind reader will pardon the egotism of this last brief narrative.) On Wednesday of the week Mr. Kinney was engaged in the trial of the Mesmer-Norcom case, a case of intense interest, in which a whole community was torn and terribly excited with angry passions. He entered upon the trial with his customary zeal and fearlessness. We went into the court-house while the trial was progressing, after having been absent a short while. We missed Mr. Kinney, and some one told us he had a slight hemorrhage in the excitement of the trial. We went out in search of him, found him in the office of Dr. Norcom, on Queen street, silent, wan and greatly depressed. He enquired when we were going down, said he would go immediately, and requested us to join him on the road. We hurried off to overtake him. As we passed through the town of Hertford, Mr. Jones came out from Dr. Johnson's office and motioned us to stop. Mr. Kinney, he said, was in the office in a dying condition. We hurried to the hotel and returned to the office. As we entered the ante-room, Mr. Jones, in silence, pointed to a bowl filled with blood. We went into the ad-joining room where lay our dying friend. He turned to us his dying eyes in recognition and gave us his hand. He died with his hand in ours, and with the last words, feebly uttered, "I know my fate. I'm not alarmed. My wife and children, that's all," passed away without a struggle, at the age of fifty-three years.

MRS. RACHEL CALDWELL.

" Woman's wit is wiser than man's wisdom."

Dr. David Caldwell is a conspicuous figure in the annals of North Carolina. He was the pioneer of education in North Carolina. He antedates both Murphey and Wiley, and established a school in Guilford County before the war of the Revolution, that gave education to many prominent professional men and clergymen of the Presbyterian Church, of which he was a distinguished minister.

His wife was his "helpmeet indeed." He was an ardent patriot and Whig during the troublous times of the Revolution, and was an object of hatred to the Tories who lived in his neighborhood, and his wife often rendered him and the patriots assistance in times of peril that made her greatly beloved by her countrymen during and after the war.

Several cases are mentioned of her readiness in dangerous emergencies. Upon one occasion, Dr. Caldwell, who had been in hiding in the woods to escape capture, returned stealthily to his house, and while there his house was suddenly surrounded by armed men who seized him before he could escape, designing to carry him to the British camp. He was put under a guard of one or two men, while the others searched the house for plunder. When they were nearly ready to depart, the plunder being piled in the middle of the room, the prisoner beside it with his guard, Mrs. Caldwell, who was in an adjoining room, came in, stepped behind Dr. Caldwell, leaned over his shoulder, and whispered to him as if intending the question for his ear alone, asking if it was not time for Gillespie and his men to be there. One of the soldiers near by caught the words, and knowing Gillespie was a brave and dangerous Patriot partisan, demanded with apparent alarm what was meant by the whispered words. Mrs. Caldwell replied that she was merely speaking to her brother. The party was panic stricken. Hurried questions were exchanged among them, and they soon hurriedly fled, abandoning their prisoner and the plunder. This simple manœuvre of a thoughtful woman produced consternation among the enemy, and relieved her husband and her property. That whisper drove them away.

In the fall of 1780 a stranger, weary with long travel, stopped at the house of Dr. Caldwell and asked for supper and a night's lodging. He said that he had stopped there because Dr. Caldwell was a clergyman, and he knew that he was a friend of his country. He said he was the bearer of dispatches from General Washington to General Greene of an important character. Mrs. Caldwell told him of his danger, that she was alone and her husband was an object of peculiar hatred to the Tories, and it was uncertain when an attack would be made on the house. Should they hear that a messenger from Washington was in the house and had important papers, he would be robbed before morning; that he should have something to eat immediately, but advised him to seek a safer place of shelter for the night. Soon hoarse voices were heard outside, crying "Surround the house," and a body of Tories rushed in. Just before they entered the house, Mrs. Caldwell bade the stranger follow her, and she led him out by a private door. A large locust tree stood outside. Pointing to it, she directed him to climb up in its thick and thorny branches and conceal himself. The night was intensely dark. She directed him to conceal himself until they commenced to plunder the house. He could then descend on the other side and make his escape. The house was pillaged, but the express messenger escaped.

Dr. Caldwell and his brother Alexander had plantations nearby. One evening when Alexander was absent from home, two British soldiers, marauding in the neighborhood, came to Alexander's house, and after plundering it, ordered his wife to get supper for him. She hurried a messenger over to her brother-in-law to advise her. He sent word to treat them kindly and get supper for them.

but she must observe where they placed their guns and set the table at the other end of the house. He promised to come over at once, conceal himself in a haystack near by, and she was to inform him as soon as the men had set down to supper. The directions were followed. While the men were sitting at supper, Dr. Caldwell quietly entered the adjoining room in which their guns had been deposited, took up one of the guns and stepping to the door of the room where they were enjoying their supper, presented the weapon and informed them they were his prisoners, and that their lives would be the forfeit if they attempted to escape. They surrendered immediately. Dr. Caldwell marched them before him to his own house, kept them till morning, and then making them take an oath of parole on the Holy Bible, he released them. The pledge was faithfully kept.

Dr. Caldwell lived until after the war, continuing his labors as a teacher and preacher. He died in 1824, in the hundredth year of his age.

Z. B. Vance

HE LOVED EVERYTHING IN THE STATE.

"Alas! we ne'er shall see his like again."

Z. B. VANCE is the most unique character that has ever lived in North Carolina history. In our Pantheon of great characters he stands apart. His was an all-round, well-balanced, even-poised, symmetrical, lovable character. To say that it was without fault, would be to belie our common nature. But the faults of his lovely make-up were like sun spots, scarcely visible to the naked eye. Looking down the long vista of great names and comparing them with Vance, we find Gaston his superior as an intellectual prodigy, a profound statesman, a laborious student, an accomplished scholar, an able lawyer. Badger was his superior as an acute dialectician, and in the versatility of his attainments. As a professional anecdotist, but differing in kind, Ham Jones was his equal, if not his superior. Jack Stanley, of New Bern, was his superior in caustic, sharp and cruel repartee. Bartlett Yancey, of Caswell, was his superior in withering and fierce invective. William A. Graham was his superior in style and courtliness; W. W. Cherry, of Bertie, in ready wit and copious phraseology.

But in his cornucopia of varied and numerous gifts, Zeb Vance was the superior of them all. He was "our own Zeb." He was "our great tribune." He was "our great War Governor." He was our loved leader in the times that tried men's souls. He gave one of his eyes to his loved State, and then congratulated himself that thereafter he would have one nevertheless to her service. His head, his heart, his strength, his manhood, his love were given to North Carolina with an ardency of devotion that none other of her sons had given. In all the grand tributes of manhood he was the equal of most and the superior of all.

He was Gaston without his austere dignity, Badger without his frivolity, Ham Jones without his insanity, of habits: Jack Stanley without his asperity; Bartlett Yancey without his tempestuous impetuosity; Graham without his frigid imperturbability; Cherry without his diminutive personality.

Turning from this glance at his comparative intellectual anatomy, the enquiry arises, What made our great Tribune the loved and honored character that he was, so loved and admired when living and so mourned when dead?

Why? Why is it that he is the Confucius of North Carolina mythology? Mainly, it was his simple, childlike faith and love for North Carolina. Everything in North Carolina was lovely in his eyes except its tincture of Republicanism. We can never forget his denunciation of that stench in his nostrils when he climaxed his phillipic by an expansive snort from his great nasal organ, and then, after a short rest, uttered the word—skunk. It was nasal oratory that "Horatius might have envied and Cicero not despised." There was no demagogery in Vance's love for North Carolina, no pretense, no ostentation.

In the many times we have hung delighted on his lips, we can recall but one in which he gave vent to his State love before a popular audience. After telling, with tones and simplicity that moved all hearts, how he loved the dear old State, he said he was like an old North Carolina negro who came before a committee of the Senate, to testify as to the exodus of the negroes to Kansas. He said the old man looked old and weary, poor and foot-sore. The old man described to the Senators the beauties of Kansas, its roads and fields and fine buildings. He was making his way back to North Carolina. Senator Vance asked him why he came back to North Carolina, if Kansas was so beautiful. He answered: "Well, I tell you, Marse Senator, things had a onwelcome look out thar, and Caliny's old fields and crooked fences was home." Vance loved North Carolina with an unfeigned love. He loved its young men, its old men, its old women, and loved all the children.

We can not forget an incident at New Bern, at an annual

The Vance Monument,
At the Capitol Grounds, Raleigh.

17

fair. Vance was sitting in a reception-room, and his old friends were calling and shaking hands with him. We were sitting near him, and for an hour we were interested and amused by their cordial greetings.

A tall, bony and awkward fellow came in, reached out his hand, Vance grabbed it, and they shook and shook and shook, and I thought at one time they would long right there before me. It was "How do, Bob," and "How du, Colonel," on 'll my nerves trembled and we didn't know whether we were on our head or on our heels. In their reminiscences there was an allusion to Goose Creek, which seemed to tickle them both mightily, but which we did not understand. After Bob left, Vance explained it to us.

On the retreat from New Bern, they were stopped at Goose Creek, and they had to construct a raft to get the regiment across. Bob concluded he could ford the creek, and divesting himself of his clothing placed them in a bundle and gave them to a comrade to bring over to him when they came over on the raft.

Bob pitched in, got across and waved his hand in sign of safety. At length his comrades came over on the raft, but Bob's clothes could not be found. When the roll was called Bob was there, *puris a 'artibus*, with his musket on his naked shoulder. He marched that way for several miles before he could cover his nakedness.

This analysis, already too long, must close. Great as was our loved Governor, rounded as was his character, versatile as were his gifts, God had much to do with his greatness. He drew before him such opportunities as had never before been offered to any Carolinian. He was God's chosen vessel for them, and he was equal to the opportunity. He took them up and rode into fame on a chariot of fire, and came out unscorched. He was a co-laborer with God in utilizing the opportunity for this rare workmanship.

THE BUREAU RULE IN 1866.

"Honey, ef you feelin' prime
Never min' de sky;
Long ways ter de summer time,
But bright days by en by."

WE HOLD these truths to be self-evident. There are but two leading principles upon which government can be successfully administered: One is the principle of love and the other is the principle of fear. A government administered upon either of these principles as its dominant feature may be a success and a strong government. The one based upon fear is that typified by the language of the centurion—*go* and *come*. Generally, but not necessarily, its chief motive power is the will of one man. Sometimes that one will may be aided by the concurrent and subservient will of a council or congress, but the one will is the dominant motive power of the government, exerted either directly or indirectly. A government, or an administration of government of this kind may be a strong government; it often is; it may be a power upon the earth, command respect abroad and promote the material prosperity of the country at home; but it dwarfs the governed, it lowers them in the scale of creation, and consults neither their opinion nor their happiness; it is a despotism, or leads directly thereto, and if not already a recognized despotism, it rapidly and surely becomes so. Of this class of government the *recognized* representatives are Russia and Turkey, both autocratic governments in which the governed are

"Like dumb, driven cattle."

This government in its origin was the offspring of compromise and good-will, formed by the mutual surrender of individual interests to the general welfare. But for that generous surrender of separate interests in order to promote the general welfare, this government would never have had an existence. But for that spirit of compromise and kindness, North Carolina would never have entered into the compact of government. She stood off for a long time before she entered into a closer political compact with her sister States, and even when she did enter into that compact and surrender certain of her rights, reserving to herself those she did not specially surrender, it was done against the advice of some of her ablest and purest sons, and against the earnest protest of Governor Samuel Johnston, of Edenton, who, when a defeated candidate before the people, in opposition to the adoption of the Constitution, went to Halifax while the Convention was in session and "lobby'd" against it.

One pleasant evening in the sixties, sitting on the verandah inhaling the odors of lilacs and laburnums, feeling quite at ease much as Cæsar felt the "eve he overcame the Nervii" there presented himself a worthless negro that we had sent off from the farm shortly before for - well we won't say. His air was pompous, self-possessed and somewhat threatening. He bore in his hand a paper addressed to us. We examined critically the written summons, in order, with the little knowledge we had of the science of reading character from handwriting, to determine what manner of man he was before whom we were to appear. We could learn, from this examination, but two things about him. Unquestionably he was not a lawyer; and as unquestionably he was not a *speller*.

Armed with this learning, and

"A little learning 'aint' a dangerous thing."

although Pope, the poet, says it is, we proceeded on Wednesday morning, as a law-abiding man, to make our preparation to respond to the awful summons.

We drew from its long, low rest a towering old "beaver" of the vintage of 1858, which had seen no service during the clash and clangor of a four years' war. An old suit of seedy black, once the tegument of a *gentleman* alas! now "none so poor to do him reverence" a suit which had not suffered capture during the war, was produced and donned. An old bandana of antique size and cut, which, in other days, had seen other service, was thrown gracefully around our war-attenuated neck. The coat was cut from the model of the swallow's tail; the pants were large and baggy, and the bandana cumbrous and heavy, but the beaver was the redeeming feature a towering black beaver, though old and venerable, can, somehow, defy criticism and even ridicule.

Thus far fixed, we came out, and it almost opened the fountain of our eyes that the little children didn't know "their father dear."

We presented ourselves at the open door of the temple of jus— no wickedness, and with one of those graceful sweeps of the right hand, while the right foot was getting into position, with which we were once wont to "charm all hearts," we made what the French call *un profond reverence* a low bow

Sam Boler was there ahead of us, at his ease and quite at home. The Bureau was in position. We made a quick and rapid survey of his physiognomy. Eyes small, set close together; cunning, rat type. Jaws large, spreading firmness. Then, hurriedly as we could, we threw our phrenological eyes around his head to see if we could find any hope there -perceptive organs small, no sense; secretiveness large, do anything mean and keep it to himself. Oh! what a great big lump just over the top of his ear, large, very large; acquisitiveness large; money--he's money on the brain. The fellow'll *steal.* Our first thought was to address ourself to that organ, but we had no bribe money, in fact, none at all, and we gave that up.

Having made this rapid survey, we handed in our summons, listened to Bureau's statement of the case, and proceeded to make the opening speech. Sam Boler replied— we *rejoined*—Boler *surrejoined,* and then we *butted.* We come with a *rebutter* and he paid us back with a *surrebutter.*

During the whole of this trial of strength between Sam and us, Bureau sat mute and unmoved, with eyes fixed on the combatants, save once. Once we put on, as best we could, a confidential *old*, *I*, expression and made a pass at his organ of acquisitiveness by saying "we were fully able to pay all costs and expenses, *incidental* and other which might arise out of this trial," and then Bureau smiled—smiled a ghastly smile.

The battle over, we awaited the decision which was to determine the rations for ten children and three adults. Bureau cracked his finger joints, looked wise, and simultaneously with his last crack, gave his decision, which to us was like a rifle cracked at our breast: Sam Boler had won the day.

Then it was we, *par ties*. We took our old beaver in our left hand—we reared, we pitched, we charged, we beat in our old beaver, we represented that "race tied to a gate post," we talked about the monumental principles of eternal justice, and the inalienable rights of man. Bureau opened his mouth once and said, "I've heard that talk before." We left the court room like Macbeth's ghosts, without "minding the order of our going."

We went outside and blowed... and then went back to the door and when I put my head in the door, Boler had changed his place. He and Bureau were sitting "cheek by jowl." Bureau had a pencil in his hand, and I think they were doing a sum in *division*.

As I was withdrawing my head I threw an unamiable glance at Sam Boler; and, "holy father!" would you believe it, he had his right hand thumb stuck on to the end of his nose, and his left hand thumb hitched into his right hand little finger and waggling his fingers just like a "poomp handle," and looking right at us.

THE CAPTURE OF THE MAPLE LEAF.

"Strike—for your altars and your fires!
Strike for the green graves of your sires,
God! and your native land!"

WE have sought information of the Maple Leaf from many sources. We obtained much information from Mr. Joseph Wilson, one of our oldest and most esteemed citizens, who fed the Confederate captors of the Maple Leaf in the swamps of Currituck when they were pursued by Federal cavalry: from Mrs. Henrietta Walker, a resident of Currituck County, a venerable and veritable book of chronicles of the war, whose husband, now dead, carried the captors across Currituck Sound, and took care of them in the Currituck swamps, and more recently from a communication by Ed. McHarney, who, when a boy of 17, with his brother and a companion, conveyed some of the Confederate captors in their boat to Yeopim Creek in Perquimans County, and thence piloted them across Chowan river into the Confederate lines.

A few days ago we were were looking over the contents of a recent publication "*The Camp Fires of the Confederacy*"—when we came across an article headed "Capture of the Maple Leaf," written by Captain A. E. Asbury, of Higginsville, Missouri, who seems to have been one of the captors of the Maple Leaf. He says that he with twenty five other Confederates were confined by Ben. Butler in Fort Norfolk, in a small room, on half-rations, half cooked and under great suffering. There were 26 of them in a room 12 by 30 which was used as cook-room, closet, hospital, bed-room and exercise. While panting there in this "Dark Hole of Calcutta" there came a Federal Government transport ship the "Maple Leaf"—bound for Fort Delaware with 75 Confederate officers, prisoners of war. Captain Asbury, with his 25 half-starved comrades, was put on board the transport for the same fort on the 13th day of June, 1863. Among the prisoners were Col. A. K. Witt, of an Arkansas Regiment, and Lieutenant Semmes. They were cordially received by the prisoners, and at once passed out to sea by Fortress Monroe. The one hundred Confederate prisoners were guarded by about twenty United States soldiers. The prisoners were allowed free intercourse, being unarmed. They plotted to seize the vessel at the tap of the great bell at twilight. At the signal agreed on, every man, from his station, pounced upon his man, armed and unarmed, and a desperate struggle for supremacy ensued, man to man, arm to arm, breast to breast. "Freedom or death" was the slogan. The Federal guard was overpowered, and their arms taken. The Confederates armed themselves with the guns, sabers and pistols of the guards. Two Confederate officers broke into the cabin where was the commander and commanded him to surrender. He drew his sword to defend himself. The Confederates warned him of the danger of resistance as the boat was in their possession. He gave up his sword. It was the work of about three minutes, and the Maple Leaf was under Confederate command. No life had been taken and no gun had been fired. The gray uniform supplanted the blue. Colonel Witt took command. A council was held and it was determined to empty and burn the vessel. But later, on account of the sick and disabled Confederates on board, it was determined to head her for the nearest beach. The Federal officers were parolled and sworn to proceed to Fort Delaware and give no notice of the capture. They also agreed to take care of the Confederate sick on board. A few Confederates stood guard over the Federal officers until the last Confederate was landed on the beach of the Currituck coast, near the Virginia and Carolina line, having taken with them all the arms and ammunition. Then with a yell and salute they surrendered the Maple Leaf. She headed for Fort Delaware, but soon turned back for Fortress Monroe, and before the next day the Federal Cavalry were scouring the Currituck swamps in search of the captors of the Maple Leaf.

HUMORS OF THE MAPLE LEAF.

Why should a man whose blood is warm within
Sit like his grandsire, cut in alabaster?

—Hamlet.

It is said that there is a silver lining to all the dark and dismal clouds of life. We think it was Rochefocault (its spelt somewhat that way), the French epigrammaist, who said that in the greatest misfortunes of our friends there was always something to comfort us. It is so in the Currituck episode of the "Maple Leaf." Since we struck this neglected "pocket" in the mine of Confederate war history, we find that every old man has some bit of reminiscence of this brilliant achievement in the annals of the war. But we are the first that put it in the custody of cold, unsmiling type. And we were first drawn to it as a feather in the Albemarle's cap of war.

The High Sheriff of Camden County was a "Swamp Fox" when the captors of the Maple Leaf were scouting about in hiding in the swamps of Currituck and Camden. Most of his time he was hunting a buffalo bull known as Pete Burgess. While our "Swamp Fox" was scouring the Camden swamps, he fell in with the Maple Leaf Confederate captors, and was introduced to Captain Semms who was commanding a squad of the captors. Captain Semms taught the Sheriff some new tricks in guerilla warfare. He trained him in the back-step drill. This was to deceive the enemy by walking backward into a swamp, so it looked like walking out of it. The Sheriff dodged Pete that way, when not pursuing him.

Milt. Snowden, then a boy, now one of our oldest and most esteemed citizens, toted victuals to the Maple Leaf Confederates in the swamps of Currituck when they were dodging the Yankee cavalry. He thinks now, as he thought then, that the Yankee cavalry did not really want to find the Confederate officers, because they would have had bloody work when they found them.

Old man Abe Baum, of Currituck, with his long goosinging-gun "Old Betsy," took one of the yankee cavalry a prisoner during the Maple Leaf affair. He took him in the evening, disarmed him at the point of "Old Betsy," kept him all night, slept with the Yankee in his arms for security all night, and next day took him across into the Confederate lines by a grapevine route, delivered him into the hands of the Confederate authorities and returned next day to pick up another Yankee by the aid of Betsy.

Dr. McIntosh was an old Doctor of Medicine, then living in Currituck. He lived near the public road. He was a good doctor, used to the technicalities of the learned profession, and called little things by big names. For instance, one old fashion abdominal ache he would call "abdominal epigastritis," or something like. Long habit had given him a linguistic vocabulary that was astounding, and he used it in his ordinary conversation. He was standing at his gate looking both ways for the Yankee cavalry. They came up on his back, without his hearing them, as he was quite deaf. "Seen any of them dam Rebels, ole man?" "No," said the Doctor. "Which is the way to Moyock?" said they. "Well," said the Doctor, "... pursue your circumambient way, and when you get ... to the ... bifurcate ... take the ... rectangular ... and perhaps you'll find it."

WILLIAM S. ASHE.

What a piece of work is man! how infinite in faculty: in form and moving how express and admirable.

—*Hamlet.*

WHEN William S. Ashe died the discriminating editor of the *Wilmington Journal* wrote: "Taking him all in all, we shall seldom look upon his like again: nor can this community and the State at large soon cease to mourn the loss of the noble, generous, big-hearted gentleman, the ardent patriot and the useful citizen."

And certainly no man was ever more sincerely mourned by the people of the southeastern counties than "Bill Ashe," as the people called him, for no other was so beloved in the homes of the humble as well as in the mansions of the rich.

After the war, the venerable General Holmes said he lamented Mr. Ashe's death the more because had he lived he could have done so much more than any other man to lead the people of that section to an acceptance of the hard condition of defeat and disaster and to bear the ills that had overtaken them with resolution and fortitude.

Springing from his stock, he naturally concerned himself about public matters and moved on a high plane of action. As soon as he had received his license to practice law, just twenty-one, his party friends manifested their interest in him by electing him County Solicitor in four different counties; but he soon found a professional life was too exacting for his social nature. He preferred rice planting, and the deer hunt. But he read much, thought more, and was a profound student of political questions.

He sometimes represented New Hanover County in the Assembly, and in 1848 was elected to Congress and to the State Senate at the same election. Although a strong party man he was a progressive statesman, and favored all measures that tended to the advancement of the State or the people.

At a time when others shrank from such a great meas
ure, he drew and introduced the bill to charter the North
Carolina Railroad, appropriating two millions of dollars
for that work.

Taking his seat in Congress he at once became a mem
ber of influence, and indeed few men knew so well how to
manage other men.

Wishing to improve the Cape Fear River, he introduced
a bill making an appropriation for that purpose. His
party was in the majority in the House, but they were all
opposed on principle to such appropriations. He pre
vailed on most of them to leave the Chamber and let the
Whigs pass his bill. But when the vote was taken there
was not a quorum; so he had to call in some more Demo
crats to vote against the bill to get a quorum for its
passage.

His habit throughout his life was to retire at 9 o'clock,
and to rise at 4.

He attended to his correspondence and arranged the details of his business for the day before breakfast. While
others were taking their naps he was hard at work. He
thus had a large part of the day at his own disposal, and
had ample time to indulge in courtesies and pleasant intercourse so agreeable to him and so necessary if one proposes
to wield a personal influence.

Few men ingratiated themselves more than he into the
hearty good-will of his associates whether of his party
faith, or otherwise. Even such Abolitionists as Gerret
Smith had a warm spot in their hearts for him. He de
tested duplicity. Once when Dr. Shaw was being opposed for Congress by Hon. W. N. H. Smith, Ashe went
to see President Buchanan and told him that there was a
report that he (Buchanan) had written a certain letter
about Kansas-Nebraska affairs that was damaging Dr.
Shaw, and if he could deny that, Dr. Shaw could be
elected. The President told him to deny it. It turned
out that Mr. Buchanan had written a letter similar to that
alleged; and Mr. Ashe after that always refused to go

into Mr. Buchanan's presence. He therefore did not attend at Chapel Hill when Old Buck and Jake Thompson and all the other Democratic brethren were there.

After six years in Congress, he became President of the Wilmington and Weldon Railroad, and under his administration that road became prosperous and paid good dividends.

In its interests he went to England and made a very advantageous arrangement in regard to its bonded debt. He addressed himself particularly to relieving travel of its tedium, and he built up a large Florida travel. He also established regular steamboat connection between his road at Wilmington and New York; and when the North Carolina Railroad was finished, he arranged with Colonel Fisher, its President, to run through trains from Charlotte to Wilmington. Thus in 1858 he gave practical effect to the measure he had introduced ten years before to haul the freights of Western Carolina to the sea and send them to the world from a North Carolina port.

In railroad circles he took rank as the best railroad president at the South; and when the war broke out President Davis asked him to take charge of all Government transportation from east of the Mississippi to Virginia. This service, requiring such high administrative talent, he rendered for a year with signal ability; but as his great desire was to be in the field, in the summer of 1862 the President authorized him to raise a legion of infantry, artillery and cavalry, to be commanded by himself. But he soon met an untimely death by an accident. He with some others had started some salt-works at Wrightsville Sound. Returning from them one evening in September, 1862, he received information that one of his sons—with Jackson's corps—had been taken prisoner. The other was also in Lee's army in Maryland. Much concerned, he procured a hand-car to hasten home—some fifteen miles distant. On the way, after dark, a train without a headlight ran into the hand-car, and so wounded him that he expired after three days of suffering.

THE CHARGE AT GETTYSBURG.

"O. fiction, where is thy blush."

If written history be a fable, as Napoleon, the great maker of history, said; if Thermopylæ, one of history's great landmarks in the mists of time be but a fable born in a poet's fancy to illustrate his dream of self-sacrificing heroism; if Gettysburg, yet fresh in living memory, be but a fictitious narrative to build up local reputation and give to one what is the property of another and to blow the bubble reputation away from the cannon's mouth, then the muse of history must change her garb of solemn black and be arrayed as a wanton, reckless of truth.

The earliest recorded historical reminiscence of the great battle of Gettysburg by a Southern writer is the narrative of Esten Cooke, author of "Surry of Eagle's Nest," in his Life of Gen. R. E. Lee. Mr. Cooke is a dramatic writer, fluent and florescent, but his style is that of a novelist rather than a historian. He soars on eagles' wings with gorgeous plumage. History wears the solemn garb of truth, which is its polestar.

Cooke follows a chronicler of the war who is notoriously untrue, and who cut his cloth to suit the Virginia measurement the notorious Pollard of the *Richmond Enquirer.*

Colonel Walter Taylor follows Cooke, and this array of partial historians has given such plausibility to error that truth is much puzzled in their pursuit.

But truth is a mighty combatant and will ultimately triumph over error in an open field and a fair fight.

Pickett was a grand man, and needs not the tawdry tinsel of fiction to gild the immortal wreath of glory that crowns his gallant brow, and would scorn the attempt to snatch a leaf from the heroes who fought by his side and suffered more than he in that fatal charge. Pickett did all that man could do in that bloody charge. And so did the heroic Pettigrew. Pettigrew suffered more because his was the laboring oar in the assignment of duty. Pickett commanded fresh troops. Pettigrew commanded troops that had borne the brunt of the second day's fight. Pettigrew was himself wounded on that second day. In the lengthening line of battle Pickett's position was half a mile nearer the Federal fortifications on Cemetery Ridge than Pettigrew's, and he was there because his troops were fresh, and had he succeeded in his charge the victory would have been won. But as it was, he was beaten before Pettigrew reached his point of attack, and when Pettigrew had stormed the Federal breastworks and was driving the artillery from their guns, Pickett had surrendered some of his regiments and was compelled to retreat in disorder. Could Pickett have held his ground over the Federal breastworks for a half hour longer, Pettigrew would have won the day, and Gettysburg would have still been one of the great pivotal battles of the world, and an adjustment of fraternal strife would have been made in thirty days.

But as it was, Pickett's failure was in fact the beginning of the end. His retreat left Pettigrew's flank exposed to the fire of troops flushed with victory, and he was compelled to follow the example of Pickett when victory was smiling on him, with a loss of officers and men unparallelled in human warfare.

This is our plain tale of Gettysburg, and the early chroniclers of its dramatic history have invested it with a halo of fiction that truth must ultimately dispel.

MRS. WILLIE JONES.

"God shares the gifts of head and heart.
And crowns blest woman with a hero's part."

WILLIE JONES. of Halifax, was a conspicuous Whig Patriot of the Revolution. He was a prominent member of all the Conventions of North Carolina during the Revolutionary period, and in all the debates of those Conventions he was the great tribune of the people and watched their interests.

His wife was a woman of great refinement, vivacity and beauty, an active advocate of the Patriot cause, and on all proper occasions asserted her convictions.

The society of Halifax was the most cultured in the Colony and distinguished for its wealth and influence. It was also a political centre. Its leading citizens were gentlemen of eminence in social, civil and professional life. Although political feeling ran high there was a pleasant social intercourse between all shades of political opinion, and sometimes it extended to the officers of the British army who were in occupancy of the town, or were there on parol.

The family of Willie Jones were society people, his daughters were pretty and attractive, and the asperities of war were softened by the amenities of social festivity. This was peculiarly the case in the society of Halifax. Some of the officers in the British army had lived in Halifax prior to the war, had espoused the Royal cause, were popular in their old home, and still, to some extent, maintained their old relations with their old townspeople. This had the effect to narrow the bloody chasm and introduce a more tolerant social feeling than in some other parts of the Colony.

In this way the adherents of royalty and the Patriots were occasionally brought in social contact. On one of these occasions, at the hospitable home of Willie Jones the celebrated British officer Tarleton and Mrs. Jones were

18

in pleasant conversation relating to the war, and in the course of conversation it fell into a strain of playful badinage.

Col. William Washington was a Whig Patriot that Mrs. Jones greatly admired and she spoke of him in conversation with Tarleton in high terms. Tarleton had received a sabre wound from Colonel Washington, in his arm, when he was on the retreat from the battle of the Cowpens in South Carolina, and he was disabled from it at that time. He said, in conversation with Mrs. Jones that he would like to see Colonel Washington, that he had heard-him spoken of as a little diminutive fellow. Mrs. Jones replied quickly: "You might have seen him, Colonel, if you had looked over your shoulder at the battle of the Cowpens." Tarleton bore the retort with calm politeness and silence. When the conversation was resumed, it turned again upon Colonel Washington. Tarleton said sneeringly that Colonel Washington was an ignorant fellow and could not write his name. Mrs. Jones replied, at once· "Colonel Washington can at least make his mark, as your arm shows." Tarleton withdrew.

Mrs. Willie Jones was the daughter of Colonel Montfort, and was a fit companion of her illustrious husband. It was our good fortune, when a boy to know well and be under the kind care of two of the daughters of Mrs. Jones

Mrs. Joseph B. Littlejohn, of Oxford, and Mrs. Burton, wife of Governor Hutchins G. Burton, of Raleigh. Both of them were models of every womanly virtue—pious, kind, gentle, sympathizing

We once heard that Willie Jones, the Revolutionary Patriot and statesman, became imbecile in his old age, and that his mental weakness was shown in his anxiety to do no harm to any human creature. When he walked out on the ground he always swept before him with a broom lest he might step upon an ant. We have never seen it confirmed.

Feminine heroism is a conspicuous thread running through all war, especially those waged in defence of home

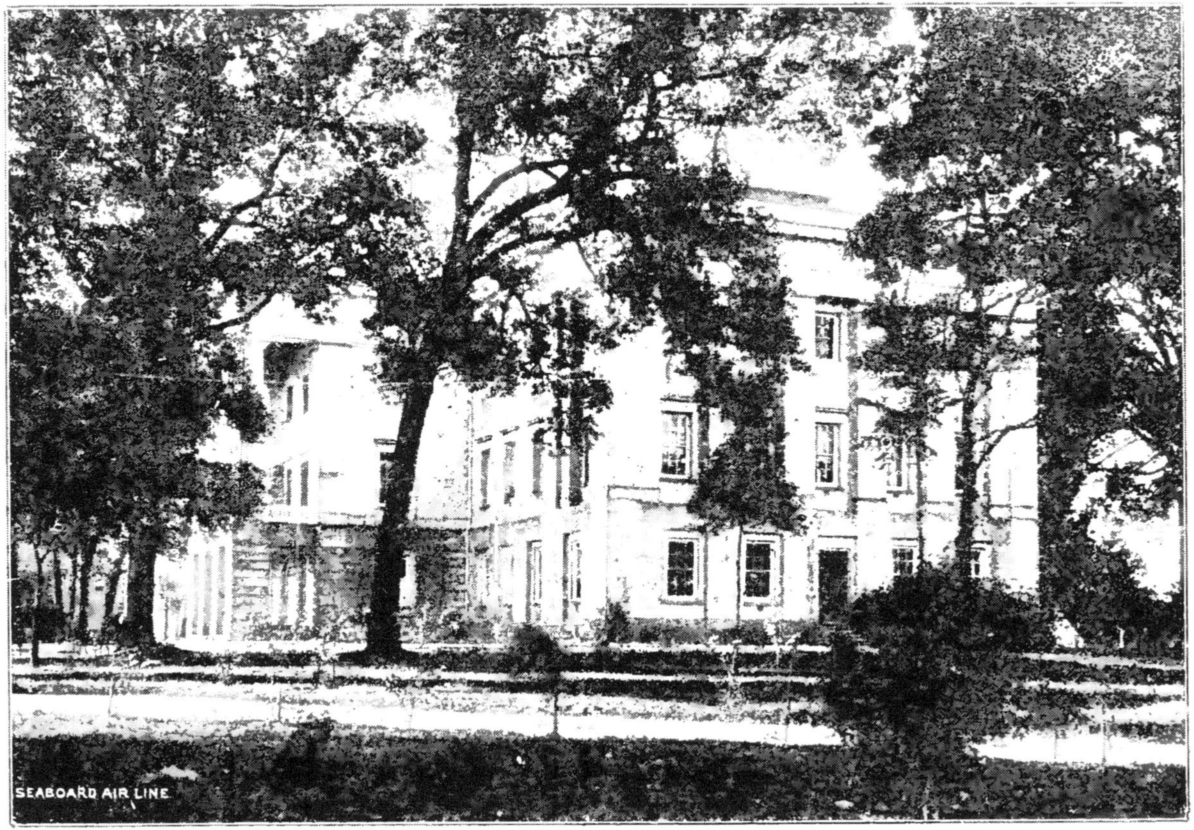
SEABOARD AIR LINE

and country. They were conspicuous in our war of Independence, and in the war of 1861-1865, North Carolina's daughters made sacrifices and underwent suffering
in defence of their homes that entitle them to the admiration and everlasting gratitude of their countrymen.

RALEIGH.

O Raleigh! noble namesake of a man of fairest fame.
—*Miss Curtis.*

As a GENERAL rule great events, great nations, great
men have been the fruitage of great tribulations. They
have been nurtured to greatness by the discipline of
adversity. It is the ordering of a wise but mysterious
Providence that sturdy loins should be girded and strengthened by opposition. According to this theory of the workings of Divine Providence, Raleigh, in the cycles of time is
destined to be a great city, the busy centre of active trade,
the moulder of public sentiment, the seat of empire, of letters, learning and art and the home of the greatest and
best of men.

When, in the early history of North Carolina it became necessary to establish a permanent seat of government for the State, a legislature of the people, sitting in
Tarboro, requested the people to instruct their delegates
to "fix on the place for the unalterable seat of government." At a convention in Fayetteville in 1789 an attempt was made to carry into effect the plan of locating
the seat of government, but it was lost by one vote. It
produced rivalry between the leading towns in the State.
The western counties favored Fayetteville, and Edenton,
New Bern and Wilmington had a following. Edenton
had been the seat of government, New Bern had succeeded
Edenton by diplomacy, and sessions of the Assembly had
been held in Wilmington and Fayetteville. Among these

contending aspirants the business of the State was an am-
bulatory government and the papers of the government
were moved about, sometimes in one place and then to another, at great trouble, expense and loss.   The State was
miserably divided by contending factions and divergent
centers of trade.

Finally, driven by necessity, the Assembly, after angry
contentions, appointed a committee to select a permanent
seat of government.   The committee regarded the matter
geographically, and discarding the relative advantages of
trade they determined to consider the public convenience
and to select the seat of government with reference to its
central location and accessibility.

After much log-rolling the site was selected in Wake
County.   At that period the advantages of navigation
were a prime object of consideration and the selection of
a place on a navigable stream was greatly desired. Strange
as it now seems, the site of the seat of government
was selected on Isaac Hunter's farm in Wake County,
mainly because it was near Neuse River; the seat of government would be a port of entry and ships laden with foreign goods could be landed at her wharves and "jack tars"
could be seen swaggering on her streets.   This idea capti-
vated the sound counties on Albemarle and Pamlico and
secured the present site of Raleigh as the permanent seat,
by a very small majority.   Stranger, perhaps, is the fact
that Hamilton Fulton, a distinguished Scotch engineer in
the employment of the State, some years after, gave it as
his opinion that Raleigh could be connected directly with
the ocean by a system of locks and dams.

In the selection of the capital of the State, the town of
Fayetteville felt most aggrieved.   It had a growing trade
with many of the western counties of the State.   It was at
the head of navigation of the Cape Fear River.   Many of
the most distinguished citizens of the western part of the
State favored Fayetteville and protested in public meetings
against the selection of another place.   Fayetteville was
probably the most progressive town in the State and it had

received bounties from the General Assembly at various times. It was evidently at that time the pet of the State

The next step after the selection of a site was the inauguration of the new capital.

Nine Commissioners, representing the nine judicial districts of the State, were appointed to inaugurate the State capital and $20,000 appropriated by the General Assembly to build a "State House" to accommodate the public business of the State. This was in March, 1792. The Commissioners laid off the future city of Raleigh. It was a town of "magnificent distances," of unsightly bramble bush and briars, of hills and morasses, of grand old oaks, with no inhabitants and an "onwelcome look" to new comers (to recall an anecdote of Governor Vance). The Assembly soon made the State officers come to Raleigh to live, but for some time the Governors evaded the law and wouldn't come and stay in the woods. But as it grew and grew and its social status improved, the Governor came, and then some prominent men from other parts of the State and their families, and the town of Neuse began to hold up its head with the leading towns of the State.

But the unexpected oftenest happens and misfortunes oft are blessings in disguise.

On the 21st of June, 1831, soon after breakfast, the citizens of Raleigh were startled by the cry of "Fire!" Smoke was seen issuing from the top of the "State House." It was soon found that the roof of the building was on fire. There was no fire department and the efforts to extinguish the flames were unavailing. There was great destruction of public property. The statue of Washington which adorned the rotunda of the capitol, the *chef d' oeuvre* of Canova, was crushed by the falling timbers and was in ruins, the archives of the government were, many of them, destroyed and Raleigh was in mourning.

Misfortunes, it is said, come in clusters. 'Twas so with Raleigh. The capitol building was destroyed. A new State House had to be built. If not rebuilt in Raleigh that town, now taking on the habiliments of eminent respectability, would lose its heritage.

Fayetteville was ambitious; had a distinguished and influential body of citizens; was still the great mart of trade from western North Carolina; was identified with it by commercial and social relations, and the antagonist sectional feeling between the eastern and western sections of the State had grown in strength since its origin in the selection of Raleigh as the seat of government forty years before. So this was Fayetteville's opportunity.

The General Assembly was to meet in the ensuing winter, and it was known that the rebuilding of the State Capitol would be the most prominent question for legislative consideration.

Fayetteville, at an early day, had put in nomination as its borough representative Louis D. Henry, its most distinguished citizen. Raleigh, seeing the object of this dangerous step, and fearing a combination of western North Carolina with Fayetteville to accomplish the removal of the capital to Fayetteville, looked over the State to find a member of the Assembly who could meet Henry in debate. They put themselves in communication with William Gaston. There was a vacancy in the borough representation from New Bern, by the death of the lately-elected member, and they induced Mr. Gaston to be a candidate for the place. He was elected just before the meeting of the Assembly by one vote. His arrival in Raleigh was announced by the firing of cannon. He took his seat and the "appropriation bill" for the rebuilding of the capitol was introduced at an early date. It was introduced in the House of Commons by Wm. H. Haywood, the young member from Wake County. Gaston and Henry were the acknowledged champions of Raleigh and Fayetteville. Both of them made able speeches to a full house and a crowded gallery. Gaston spoke first. Henry replied and Gaston rejoined. The interest was intense. We had the good fortune to be present as a boy. Gaston's second speech was the finest effort that the parliamentary history of North Carolina affords. It saved the fate of Raleigh and gave it its subsequent proud career as the permanent capital of the State.

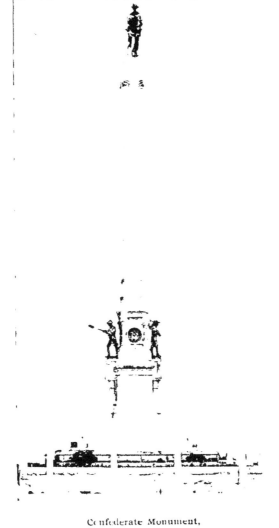

Confederate Monument,
On Capitol Square, Raleigh.

AMONG CURRITUCK DUCKS AND DUCKERS.

Quack! Quack! Quack!

WE NOW regard ourself as better posted in all the learning of shooting and wild fowl than any man in North Carolina not a "native" ducker and "to the manor born." We know all about geese and swan, and can tell, to a nicety, the difference between a "Black Duck" and a "Wigeon," between a "Wigeon" and a "Sprig Tail," between a "Sprig Tail" and a "Teal," between a "Teal" and a "Peter," between a "Peter" and a "Mallard," between a "Mallard" and a "Red Head," and between a "Red Head" and a "Canvass Back," that head of the family, joy of the gourmand and duck of ducks. Red heads and canvass backs are the aristocracy of the family. They closely resemble in appearance and in taste, but the canvass back feeds on the water celery, bears a higher market price and a better name, and "names are things" among ducks as among men. All the others are known as "common ducks." The present season has been a ducker's paradise, and the 9th of December was the climax of his happiness. The weather opened early and has been of unprecedented severity, and game, consequently, has been more abundant than for many years. Sport and profit have gone hand in hand. Dunton and Walker, of Vanslyck's Landing, are probably the best shots and have done the most profitable shooting in the "goose honk country" of Currituck Sound. They are young men, with the healthy, hearty, alert bearing that close contact with nature in her rough wildness always gives. Wiley and Alma Midyett, who shoot together, had killed and sold $600 worth of wild fowl up to last week of the present season. Josephus Banm, who lives at the headquarters of "Currituck Shooting Club," killed on the 9th of December, 120 ducks, 30 geese and 3 swan. This is the best day's shooting of the season. Josephus is a veteran among the three-score-, but solid as a boat hook, and has probably sent more duck:

to their long account than any man among the living. On the same day, John Dimond, of New York, a member of "Currituck Shooting Club," killed 107 ducks and 3 geese. On the same day, Newton Dexter, of Providence, Rhode Island, bagged 26 swan, 25 geese and over 50 ducks, with a 10-bore gun. On the same day, Stratton Berrety, of Rhode Island, a member of "Currituck Shooting Club," and who ranks A No. 1 in the club, killed 80 ducks besides other game. This is all tall shooting, but it's true as it's tall. The sportsmen, both native and foreign, are well provided with all the appliances for success, and "Stool Ducks" and "Batteries" and "Breech-Loaders" and "Blinds" form part of their equipments. Those who shoot from "batteries" are most successful. They shoot in pairs. One lays in the battery, flat of his back, with his "stools" around him, and as the wild fowl hover over the stools he rises and fires into them. His partner lays off to windward in a boat, and picks up the dead game floating on the water. The battery fellow, on his back, has the hard berth, but we suppose they "turn and turn about."

Formerly Currituck Sound had only a local habitation and a name for its game fowl, but the opening and use of the Albemarle and Chesapeake Canal has introduced it to the outside world and made it a favorite resort of amateur sportsmen, and nearly every locality has now its "Club." Many notabilities from abroad, members of the various clubs, are familiar names to the native sportsman. Judge Tuff, from near Boston, President of "Monkey Island Club," is favorably and kindly spoken of. Gordon Bennet who has recently been shooting at larger game, is a member of "Light House Club." He did not make a name as a shot, in Currituck, but there lingers a memory of his lavish use of money. Emory, of New York, Stratton Berrety, of Long Island, and Jack Dimond, all we believe, members of "Currituck Shooting Club," are considered the best shots from abroad. Lawrence Jerome, of New York, a member, we think, of "Crow Island Club," is accorded the place of the humorist and funny man of the club, a position so jealous that no other distinction is ever attained by its occupant. Captain Palmer, of Boston, is often mentioned by the natives as a green old veteran of 75 years, whose migrations to Currituck Sound were as regular as the fowl, and who for many years has come like a goose and goes when they go. He loves the sport, they say, and shows a boy's enthusiasm in its enjoyment.

We must not, however, further display our learning in the intricate and mysterious profundities of duckology: how they come, when they come, whence they come, the differing notes of a duck's "quack," each after his kind, the different meaning of each intonation of a goose's "honk," and the long-drawn, rattling, crackling note of the deep-throated swan.

BATTLE OF SAWYER'S LANE.

"The foe himself recoiled aghast,
When, striking where he strongest lay,
We swooped his flanks throughout the fray,
And braving full their murderous rain,
We won the day at Sawyer's Lane."

The BATTLE near South Mills, in Camden County,
N. C., was fought on the 19th of April, 1862, and was a
signal victory for the Confederates. The Federal forces
were commanded by General Reno and Colonel Hawkins.
They came up from Roanoke Island, which was captured
on the 8th of February, and landed at Chantilly, on lower
Pasquotank River, on the night of the 17th of April.
Their landing at Chantilly spread throughout the county,
and very soon their destination for the village of South
Mills in upper Camden became known.

On the morning of the 18th they commenced their
march through Camden County. There were no Confederate troops in the county, as the active fighting men were
with the army in Virginia. The Federal army under
General Reno was left to make their march to South Mills
unmolested.

A Georgia regiment commanded by Colonel Wright had
their headquarters at South Mills, but when the news
came of the invasion of the Federal troops they were scattered over the country from Elizabeth City to South Mills
watching the movements of the enemy. who held possession of Elizabeth City by gunboats after the bombardment on the 8th of February. Colonel Wright collected
them as fast as he could, and Colonel Ferebee, who was
at home, called out the Camden militia, and they deter
mined to make a stand at Sawyer's Lane and make preparations for an engagement.

Meanwhile, General Reno was marching leisurely from
Chantilly to South Mills, arresting some of the most conspicuous citizens who were in sympathy with their homes,
and establishing intimacy and confidence with the buffaloes who made their headquarters at "Old Trap."

They committed some depredations and used the torch to some extent.

An incident is mentioned in connection with the march through Camden which illustrates the celebrated Masonic tie. The order had been given to fire the house of a man who was obnoxious on account of his Southern sympathy. He was allowed to remove his property from the house, and in taking out the property he was observed to attach value to an apron which he was taking out. The Federal officer enquired of him what it was. He replied that it was a Masonic apron which belonged to him as a member of the Masonic Lodge. The officer was a Mason, and he ordered the house to be spared and the property not to be disturbed.

When they reached Sawyer's Lane on the morning of the 19th, Colonel Wright, with about 500 of his regiment and some of the Camden militia, were in line on the west side of the Lane. A large ditch intervened. Colonel Wright ordered it to be filled with old rails and brush and fired so as to be an obstruction to the Federal forces. The smoke of the burning brush prevented their approach and obstructed the steadiness of their fire. Notwithstanding this obstruction, a deadly rifle engagement was kept up during the day. Towards evening there was an arrival of Confederate troops on the opposite side of the canal. When they came near they broke out in a hideous yell that so frightened and demoralized the Federal troops that they were struck with panic and commenced to fall back. This increased the disorder, and soon the whole Southern army was in retreat in great disorder. It was a second "Bull Run" before they reached Chantilly, where they had landed two days before.

The old citizens of Camden give graphic accounts of the wild retreat of the Federal troops on their return from Sawyer's Lane to Chantilly in contrast to their march from Chantilly to the battlefield. The march through Camden County was orderly and with the pomp of assured victory. The return was ... to make the his most" retreat. The road was strewn with abandoned haversacks, muskets and canteens, and when the Federal soldiers stopped at the houses by the wayside to beg a hasty bite of something, they looked famished and haggard; and while they swallowed their half-chewed food they kept one eye on the watch westward, whence they were fleeing. They would sometimes eagerly ask if the "Rebels" were coming, and how much farther it was to Chantilly.

In the engagement at Sawyer's Lane the Confederate loss was three killed and several wounded. The Federal loss was between sixty and seventy. Twenty-three bodies were removed from one pit in which they were buried and another pit contained more bodies.

The result of the fight was a complete rout, although it is claimed by Federal reports that it was a retreat in good order. They took some prisoners with them to Chantilly, and all the prisoners describe the retreat as a rout and a panic.

The success of the battle was due to the strategy of Col. A. M. Wright, of the Third Georgia Regiment, and its final disaster and panic was due to a vigorous Rebel yell from the throats of new recruits.

COL. WILLIAM L. SAUNDERS.

Full many a flow'r is born to blush unseen
—*Gray*.

No MAN who has lived in North Carolina has rendered more faithful service or been inspired by a more ardent patriotism than Col. William L. Saunders. He was a loving son of the State in every fibre and tissue of his constitution. He has left a record of his service both with pen and sword. He gave his blood to North Carolina in the defence of his home when it was invaded in the civil strife which crimsoned her sacred soil with fraternal blood; and when peace came and spread her blessed wings over a land that was made desolate by the loss of her sons and her treasures, Colonel Saunders, in impaired health, laid down his sword and took up his pen, and the work of his pen was of more signal benefit to his State than all her marshalled battalions on the tented field.

No man can read "Saunders' Colonial Records and Prefatory Notes" without rising from its perusal a better informed man in the annals of his country, and every North Carolinian will feel prouder of his heritage of glory. It is worth all the histories of the State that have ever been penned by its most illustrious sons. The "Prefatory Notes" are a marvel of lucid historical style, accuracy and ability, written in a plain and unostentatious narrative.

Governor Jarvis once told us that "Bill Saunders" was the wisest man in North Carolina, and could give you the most sensible opinion upon any subject you might put to him of any man he had ever known, especially if you gave him time to whistle some snatches of an old familiar tune; and Governor Jarvis is a shrewd observer of men. The State of North Carolina is under a debt of gratitude to William Lawrence Saunders that it can never fully repay. His monument should stand by that of Zebulon B

19

Vance in the Capitol grounds at Raleigh, as a lesson of virtue, heroism and devotion to our grand old mother State.

William L. Saunders was born in Raleigh about the year 1838. His parents were Rev. Joseph H. Saunders and his wife Laura Baker Saunders, both, the specimens of intellectual and moral manhood. His mother was a gem of womanhood, kind, affectionate and true to every relation of life. His maternal grandfather was Dr Simmons J. Baker, a gentleman of the old school, a worthy representative of the best Halifax blood, and the last man in North Carolina that wore an old-time gentleman's cue. The father of Colonel Saunders was a devout Christian minister of the Protestant Episcopal Church. He was of sturdy intellectual mould and his fondness for antiquarian lore was as conspicuous in him as in his more distinguished son.

Raleigh was the home of Colonel Saunders for the greater part of his life. He entered the Confederate service when the State joined its seceding sisters. He soon rose to the command of a regiment, and his bravery was conspicuous in the war, to its end.

After the war he settled in Wilmington. In the troublous times of the reconstruction period he was prominent in every act for the protection of the people of the State. There were some irregular acts of retaliation to counteract the oppressive conduct of the "Union Leagues," and he was suspected of complicity in those acts, was arrested and arraigned for trial before a Congressional investigating committee. He was subjected to a rigid examination on the witness stand by that committee He shrank not before that severe ordeal. When he was examined as to his complicity, and that of his friends, he answered never a word to betray them or criminate himself. To every ingenious device to extort a confession from him, he was dumb. In the face of great peril he maintained an obstinate silence, and he finally triumphed over his enemies. Saunders was a nut they could not crack.

WINSTON-SALEM.

" Like two twin cherries hanging on a parent stem."

Tobacco is so potent a factor in the history of plants, it has had so much to do with the commerce of modern civilization, it has been the builder of such great towns, and it is so identified with the early history of North Carolina, having been first introduced to the English-speaking race, and probably to the world, from Roanoke Island, and having been first introduced to polite society in the Court circles of London as a social accomplishment by that grand sentinel at the gateway of our history, Sir Walter Raleigh—that it has a just claim to recognition in any work relating to North Carolina annals.

Amadas and Barlowe, on their return to England from their explorations in America in 1584, brought to Sir Walter, as a memorial of their voyage, from the island in America where they landed, specimens of sun-cured tobacco, which the aboriginal race that they had found, used upon ceremonial and social occasions as symbols of peace and friendship. They smoked tobacco in their calumets of peace, when the arrow and battle-axe were laid aside.

A little incident is mentioned of Sir Walter, that after he had received the tobacco and pipe from Amadas, he went into the august presence of Queen Bess smoking his huge calumet, and it does not appear that he said—"Is smoke offensive to your Majesty?" As the smoke rolled in volumes from his mouth and nostrils, the Queen became alarmed for her favorite courtier, and seizing a bucket of water, dashed it over him to extinguish the fire that was burning within him.

In Winston-Salem two centuries clasp hands. Salem is an old Moravian town, gray with age, laurel-crowned with its achievements, conscious of its dignity, and marching slowly on with measured steps in its career of improvement, altogether unmindful of its sturdy young brother who has sprung up in a night by its side, and is

making giant strides beside it with its coat off and its
sleeves rolled up, and heavy bead-drops on its earnest brow.
It bears no moss on its proud and lofty crown, but instead,
it has a pipe in its mouth and the aromatic tobacco juice
stains its once spotless shirt front.

Thus, in juxtaposition, separated only by a narrow
street, these two representatives of the present and the
past generations are almost one in location, but are widely
separated in manners, habits, customs and individuality
Its line of separation is as distinct as the channel of the
Gulf Stream. They are under separate organizations of
government. One has an eye turned askance at the unripe
tobacco plant that grows so lustily by its side, without the
social crown of ancestral dignity, and the other an eye of
pity at the decrepit old grandsire that totters on its staff
and can not keep step with the surging tide in the march
of life. But there is no clash of contending factions between them. No angry surge of rivalry disturbs their
harmony, but each keeps on the tenor of its way, one by
bounds like a giant to run its course, the other with the
dignity and slowness so becoming to nobility that is conscious of its lofty pedestal and disdains to enter the lists
with a stripling in shirt-sleeves and short pants.

But each of these twin towns is great in its way. Be
fore Winston was born, or had cleared the briars out of
the way for its first rude settlement, Salem was an old
and progressive town, with its schools and churches and
factories, and with its refined and devout colony of steady
Moravians who had left their homes in Saxony, and found
among the mountains of North Carolina a place of safety,
where they could worship God according to the dictate
of their own conscience. They found this asylum a'
Bethabara, in Western North Carolina, six miles north
of the present town of Salem. This was about the year
1760. There they pitched their tents. They were holy
men of God. They had with them their ministers in
holy things, who preserved their sacred tenets. Here they
buried their dead, with their uniform memorial tablets.

Here they worshipped God, first in temples not built with hands, later in sanctuaries consecrated to His service. Regarding education as the handmaid of religion, they next established a school for girls, which, under the guidance of Divine Providence, has been a gushing fountain of blessing to generations. Venerable in age, it is the *Alma Mater* of a long line of distinguished graduates, who turn to it in love, veneration and gratitude.

Quiet as Salem is, it is not asleep. The hum of industry is heard on every hand, in cotton, woollen, flour, iron and water-works. It is lighted by electricity, has no saloons, and is sustained by a prosperous agricultural back-country. It is a model of propriety, morality and virtue.

Winston is the great centre of the tobacco industry of the United States, and claims to be the most progressive town in North Carolina. It is a creature of yesterday but it has its factories of various kinds, its big men, its public enterprises, its associations of every kind, its electric lights, its water works, its institutions of learning and education, and its grand public spirit and pride of place. It lives in an atmosphere of tobacco. Everybody smokes, everybody chews, and tobacco is the talk of the town. It has its tobacco factories, its tobacco warehouses, and its tobacco "breaks."

We were once in Winston, and attended a "tobacco break". It was a new revelation to us. Immense crowds were in attendance; the auctioneer was stript to the belt and ready for the fray. It was a new, wild scene to us. We had been at corn shuckings, corn hillings, oyster roasts, camp meetings, revival meetings, and all sorts of convivial gatherings, but never before had we seen such a scene. Little piles of gold-leaf tobacco were everywhere on the floor and everybody was feeling and smelling of them. The auctioneer was going rapidly from place to place, a large crowd following him and eagerly bidding. We were passing about with the madding crowd, accompanied by our friend and press-brother, John D. Cameron, a citizen of Asheville, a lover of tobacco and familiar with all the ways of the tobacco trade. He was smelling and feeling, and we, to be in fashion, were feeling and smelling. He was descanting to us of the value of a certain brand, feeling as he talked. We reached out our gloved hand to manipulate the soft leaf.

You have probably, when a boy, put a live coal of fire on the back of a big tomato worm to enjoy his squirms and wriggles in the death agony. Cameron was like that worm. With an exclamation of horror, he drew around us a crowd of spectators to see a man who had the hardihood to handle a leaf of tobacco with a gloved hand! And they gazed at us as they would at a cannibal savage from Timbuctoo. We loved old Cameron then, and treasure his memory now, but we always thought he never thought so well of us after committing the unpardonable sin of handling a tobacco leaf with a kid-gloved hand!

THE INVASION OF THE CARPET-BAGGER.

The Goths overran Rome.

To many persons it may be an incomprehensible mystery how the State of North Carolina, with more than a million of people within its bounds, many of them distinguished by eminent statesmanship, ability and patriotism, by great sagacity, forecast and influence over opinions, and a strong hold upon the affections and confidence of the people—how the State of North Carolina thus fortified, and with the ballot in her hands, could have been successfully invaded by a horde of hungry carpet-baggers, who, in combination with her unnatural sons, subjugated her to their power, and despoiled and humiliated her. It is not only a political but a philosophic and historical question. Many would now suppose that the question itself would have roused the fury of the people, that the double odium of the disgraceful alliance would have consigned the guilty parties in the parricidal compact to an eternal political and social infamy from which there could be no resurrection, and that one universal shout of execration "louder than the loud ocean" would have risen from mountain top to ocean shore, and driven the miscreant howling from the land. But those who think so have forgotten the history of the times or the manifestations of the human mind under peculiar circumstances. There is a stupor which sometimes precedes battle. There is a stupor which often succeeds defeat. There is a stupor which generally attends despair. Such was our condition. Rather we were in the stupor most conducive to this combination. The black pall of mourning brooded and hung over the State; the funeral pall for those to whom we were wont to turn in our hour of doubting and distress, and to whom we never turned in vain. We here too utterly overthrown by the united power of the world and we seemed, for the time, almost annihilated and almost crushed out from the pale of earthly sympathy and recognition. Despair, which maketh the heart sick, was upon us. That despair, twin sister of desperation, was within our bosom. The "slough of despond" was upon us. North Carolina, riven by the thunderbolt of war, stood like Rachel weeping for her children and would not be comforted because they were not. She turned in her despair to her Fishers, her Stokes, her Penders, her Pettigrews, her Branches, her Andersons and her Shaws. They were all dead. Turning from the dead to the living, she called to her Grahams, her Outlaws, her Braggs, her Barringers, her Moores, her Ransoms, her Clingmans, her Ashes, her Warrens, her Carters, her Martins, her Gilliams and her Speeds. They were powerless. Then, writhing in the frenzied agony of a moment's desperate determination, she turned to her Holdens, her Pools, her Caldwells, her Pearsons, her Dicks, her Settles and her Sam. Phillips, and lo! they had joined the carpet bagging vulture birds and were driving their beaks into her bowels. Then it was, that, uttering a cry of despair that pierced the heavens, she veiled her face in shame and fell like Cæsar at the base of Pompey's statue, for lo! shame! she had called in her agony unto her *recreant sons.*

JAMES C. DOBBIN.

He was a gentleman on whom I built an absolute trust.
            —*Macbeth*.

A NORTH CAROLINA book would be imperfect without a reference to the character and career of James C. Dobbin, of Fayetteville. He was the friend of our youth, and as a boy he was an example of every manly and gentle characteristic, and won to him, as no other did, the admiration and love of his companions. His smile was a benediction, his laugh was a murmuring ripple that never overflowed its banks into the semblance of loud laughter and sincerity was graven on every lineament of his face. If he had had no other qualities than those that belonged to his gentle and kindly nature, he would have been a signal success in life. But his head was a dome of thought. It was like an inverted pyramid, and would have made a phrenologist leap for joy.

We once heard old Dr. Caldwell, the distinguished President of the University, say that he had no children and that he did not regret it, but if he had such a son as Dobbin he would rejoice. And he was not a man who dealt in compliments.

James C. Dobbin graduated at the University in 1832, in the famous class that was led by Clingman and Tom Ashe. He stood in the front rank at graduation, but as a lovable man he was easily first.

After leaving the University he returned to his home in Fayetteville, and entered upon the study of that profession "ancient as magistracy, noble as virtue, necessary as justice"; but his charming personality, his positive convictions of public policy, and his intellectual gifts made him an available candidate for public office. He was a Democrat, and his party friends, when he was a young man, put him in nomination for the General Assembly from the county of Cumberland.

He was elected. He soon acquired an influential po-

sition in the Legislature, and was an active participant in
its important debates. He grew in influence and popularity.

A sad incident will illustrate his influence in the General
Assembly after a service of some years. His wife, to
whom he was tenderly attached, was an invalid, and accompanied him to Raleigh during a session of the Assembly.
It was during the session, in the early fifties, when
the subject of making an appropriation to establish
an asylum for the insane was under consideration.
It met with much opposition. It was urged by
a philanthropist—a Miss Dix, of New York, a
sister of General Dix, Senator from New York in the Senate of the United States—who, it was said, had been herself a victim of insanity. Miss Dix had urged the matter
upon the Legislature with the zeal of a Christian and a
philanthropist, and the blessed woman was giving it up
in despair.

She had nursed Mrs. Dobbin in her extreme illness.
She had enlisted her sympathies in the cause of the "unfortunate step-sons of nature" bereft of reason. She had
induced the dying wife to use her influence with her distinguished husband in promoting the bill for the insane.
Mrs. Dobbin grew worse, and as her eyes turned for the
last time to him whom she loved most on earth, her dying
words were a supplication that he would give his support
to the bill for the comfort of the insane.

She passed away, and good angels bore her to the mansions of the blessed. He consigned her, "dust to dust,"
mourned her in his sad bereavement, and after some days,
bowed with grief over his loss, took his seat in the Hall
of the Assembly. After some time, he rose in his seat,
and with the sad scenes of his domestic bereavement
swelling his heart and choking his utterance, he called
up the bill to establish an asylum for the insane. He
addressed the Assembly in a lengthened speech, full of
feeling and reminiscence that melted the audience to
tears, and the bill was passed, we think, unanimously,
and now that institution for the comfort of the "unfor-

tunate step-sons of nature," as they were once called by
a distinguished statesman, is cherished in North Carolina as the blessed fruit of the dying prayer of a noble
woman.

James Dobbin afterwards rose to higher distinction.
He acquired a national reputation, became a leader in
the councils of the Democratic party, and during the administration of President Pierce, was the distinguished popular Secretary of the Navy. He was appointed to that
important position in the Cabinet of President Pierce
without his personal acquaintance and without solicitation — it was a merited honor.

In the Democratic National Convention that nominated
Franklin Pierce, of New Hampshire, for the Presidency,
it was the opportune and emphatic speech of Mr. Dobbin
that first put him in nomination and secured his selection
to the highest post of honor among men.

As Secretary of the Navy Mr. Dobbin rendered signal
service to the country. Under his administration the
Naval Academy at Annapolis, then in its infancy, was
fostered until it reached a high state of efficiency. He
introduced into the navy the "retired list," retiring on
good pay the oldest officers, and giving young and active
officers merited promotion, and thus added to the efficiency
of the naval service. He also had built those splendid
naval vessels, the Merrimac, Niagara and Roanoke, the
finest vessels then in the world. Under his administration, also, shells were introduced into the armament of
naval vessels. Altogether, the navy and the naval service
made more progress under this North Carolinian than
under the administration of any other Secretary in the
history of the country.

Mr. Dobbin died early, in the meridian of his intellectual powers, with the love and admiration of his countrymen, and with a glorious future prospect. North Carolina mourned him as a loving son who had brought honor
to her, and when the roll of honor is called of her great
sons departed, the name of James C. Dobbin will ever
be recalled with love and admiration.

THE NEW CENTURY.

Time in advance behind him hides his wings:
Behold him when passed by!
What then is seen but his broad pinions,
Swifter than the winds!

—*Young.*

TURNING from the past we enter upon the new century of our country, of which few of us shall see the end. We enter upon it amid the throes of a political convulsion fraught with danger, of which none can forecast the future. But the Great Dispenser who holds the destiny of nations as of individuals in the hollow of His hand, and who always ultimately evokes good from evil, will accomplish His own purpose in His own time, and will reaffirm the historic lesson, that the progress of the race is the great purpose of God. Man is the agent and colaborer with God; not an agent that gropeth blindly, or a creature driven by relentless necessity or impelled by involuntary impulse, but an active, intelligent, conscious agent, reaping whereof he soweth and gathering the fruits of his wisdom or his folly. Looking over the century of our country now filed in the archives of time and labeled for eternity, we find strange and wonderful developments and alarming retrocessions in the ebb and flow of human progress. Taking our own Albemarle country as an index of the whole, we recognize its material progress in reducing the forest to the dominion of the plow, in opening and improving the highways of commerce, in its improved agriculture, in its improved mechanic arts, a progress none the worse for having been slow and steady. But in some other respects we must lament the contrast of the beginning and close of the century. Education, that great lever in the development of humanity, has obviously declined. Early in the century, at its beginning indeed, schools of high grade, incorporated academies, were established in Edenton, then the metropolitan town of the Albemarle country, and other towns had flourishing academies of high character. More interest was felt and shown in the great work, and consequently there was a better and more controlling element of public sentiment in the earlier than in the later period of the century. In the early period, the Albemarle was the controlling section of the State. It led in public spirit, in State enterprise and policy, in influence in the public councils and in the use of public prominence and position which it furnished to the State and general government. It gave a Supreme Court Judge to Washington's administration. It furnished Judges and Governors and Speakers of the Legislature to the State Government. The latter period of th century saw the sceptre of Judah depart from the Albemarle country. Well armed with the prestige of our sires, we have suffered their mantle to fall on other shoulders. Albemarle shaped the policy of the State in the struggle for independence. The reveille drums of the revolution were sounded within her borders, and the voices of her sons were potent in the field and council hall. All this is now changed, and it is incumbent upon those now coming to the front in this beginning of our new century, to see to it that the Albemarle country, by a general system of education, by enlightened culture, by improved agriculture, by selecting for political and official position the best, most reliable and ablest men, shall recover her rightful place.